GPU-Accelerated Research in Quant Finance

Using CUDA to Speed Up Backtests and Analytics

Thomas V. Trex

Published by NobleTrex Press

For permissions and other inquiries, write to:
P.O. Box 3132, Framingham, MA 01701, USA

Contents

Introduction

Quantitative finance lives at the intersection of models, markets and machines. In recent years, general-purpose graphics processing units (GPUs) have transformed from gaming hardware into indispensable scientific co-processors, capable of sustaining trillions of arithmetic operations per second. This textbook embraces that reality for a specific purpose: to help practitioners design, validate and deploy research pipelines, backtests and analytics that are not merely faster, but demonstrably sound. Speed is only an asset when it preserves truth. Our aim is to show you how to earn both.

The promise of GPU acceleration in finance is compelling. Monte Carlo engines that once took hours can complete in minutes; factor regressions across thousands of securities become interactive; portfolio optimizers scale from tens to thousands of constraints; option pricers push beyond textbook models to richer dynamics. Yet the pitfalls are equally real: numerical drift from mixed precision, hidden look-ahead bias magnified by throughput, stochastic nondeterminism from parallel random streams, and "benchmark theater" that reports spectacular speedups against weak CPU baselines. This book is organized to turn that minefield into a map.

We begin by fortifying the mathematical and market foundations that GPU acceleration cannot replace. The opening chapter, Quantitative Finance Foundations for GPU Acceleration, revisits probability, linear algebra, numerical analysis, time-series models, optimization, and the vocabulary of microstructure, risk and performance. These topics are not filler; they determine whether a kernel's output has economic meaning, whether a decomposition is well-conditioned, whether a discretization error swamps a speedup. You will learn to articulate the invariants your accelerated code must respect before you write a single thread.

Next, Research & Backtesting Methodology establishes a rigorous workflow: clear hypotheses, audit-ready notebooks, temporal cross-validation (purged folds, embargoes, walk-forward windows), and the careful modeling of slippage, latency and corporate actions. We emphasize fair comparisons between CPU and GPU results by aligning data splits, seeding strategies and performance metrics. You will see how event-driven backtest engines can be designed to feed GPUs naturally, without contorting the economic logic of a strategy.

With this scaffolding in place, GPU Architecture & CUDA Fundamentals develops a mental model of the hardware: streaming multiprocessors, warps, the memory hierarchy and the SIMT execution model. We introduce kernels and grids, synchronization, coalesced access, shared memory tiling, streams and events for concurrency, and the numerics of floating-point precision and determinism. Randomness on a GPU is a first-class citizen, so we include parallel random number generation, seeding schemes and statistical testing that withstand scrutiny.

We then ascend from primitives to patterns in GPU Programming Patterns, Libraries & Numerical Methods. You will learn to express financial workloads using map/reduce/scan/stencil building blocks; to lean on tuned libraries such as cuBLAS, cuSPARSE and cuFFT; and to prototype quickly with Python ecosystems like CuPy, Numba and RAPIDS. Chapters on Monte Carlo, PDE and FFT solvers, and GPU-accelerated optimization translate these abstractions into the engines that power pricing, risk and portfolio analytics.

The heart of the book, Accelerated Financial Models & Analytics, applies these tools to end-to-end models: derivatives and risk simulation, cross-sectional factor research, constrained portfolio construction, option pricing via finite differences and spectral methods, portfolio risk aggregation for Value at Risk and Expected Shortfall, and the integration of deep and reinforcement learning with backtests that enforce stability and risk controls. Each application foregrounds correctness, then performance.

Engineering discipline turns prototypes into production. Performance Engineering, Scaling & Production Deployment teaches roofline analysis, profiling with modern tools, kernel optimization and mixed precision with explicit error budgets, multi-GPU and distributed execution with communication collectives, and data engineering that keeps features on-device. We close the loop with validation, reproducibility and governance: property-based testing, numerical reconciliation against CPU baselines, deterministic builds, containerized environments, CI/CD, cost visibility and compliance.

Finally, Case Studies & Reusable Templates provide complete, auditable exemplars: a GPU Monte Carlo VaR pipeline, a hybrid CPU-GPU event-driven backtester, a reusable CUDA finance toolkit with Python bindings, benchmarking protocols for neutral baselines, and experiment tracking integrated with model-risk governance. These chapters are intended to be copied, adapted and extended.

This book assumes comfort with Python and basic numerical computing; C++ and CUDA familiarity is helpful but not mandatory. Each chapter pairs conceptual explanations with annotated code, profiling traces and checklists of failure modes. Read linearly for a full curriculum, or jump to the patterns and case studies to accelerate a specific project. Above all, insist on three habits: specify assumptions, measure honestly, and reconcile results. When you do, GPUs become more than accelerators; they become instruments of clarity, letting you ask deeper questions of markets-and answer them in time to matter.

Chapter 1

Quantitative Finance Foundations for GPU Acceleration

Before you worry about kernels, warps and shared memory, you need to know exactly what you're accelerating. This chapter sharpens the quantitative lens behind GPU-powered research: how we model uncertainty in markets, represent portfolios as matrices, approximate continuous-time dynamics on discrete hardware, and translate microstructure noise into risk-adjusted performance. By the end, you'll see how core quant finance concepts map naturally onto the parallel patterns that GPUs exploit-so the CUDA code you write later is numerically sound, financially meaningful, and worth making faster.

1.1 Probability & Statistics Essentials

GPU acceleration is valuable only if the numbers we speed up are meaningful. Before we launch thousands of threads to simulate paths or backtest strategies, we need a clear framework for thinking about uncertainty, randomness, and statistical evidence. This section builds that framework.

The goal is not to turn you into a pure theorist. Instead, we will connect probability and statistics directly to the practical questions you will face when designing GPU-accelerated research:

- How should I model returns and risks across many assets or scenarios?
- Which distributions are reasonable, and what goes wrong when I pick the wrong one?
- When a backtest run on the GPU looks good, is it truly a signal or just noise?
- How do I interpret the output of millions of Monte Carlo paths?

We start with the building blocks of probability, move to the distributions that commonly describe financial data, highlight the role of moments such as mean and variance, and then show how to estimate and test trading signals in a way that scales naturally to GPU workloads.

Random Variables and Probability in a Quant Context

At the heart of quantitative finance is the idea that many key quantities are not fixed numbers but *random variables*. A future daily return on a stock, the payoff of an option at expiry, or the slippage on a large order are all examples. We never know their exact values in advance, but we can describe their possible values and how likely each is.

Conceptually, you can think in three layers:

- **Outcome space:** This is the set of all things that might happen. For a one-day horizon, each possible market scenario is one outcome.
- **Random variables:** These are functions that assign a numerical value to each outcome, such as the portfolio return or P&L under that outcome.

- **Probabilities:** These are weights that tell you how plausible each outcome is. Together they define the "distribution" of the random variable.

When you run a Monte Carlo simulation on a GPU, you are really doing two things:

- You choose a probabilistic model that says how returns behave.
- You use large numbers of simulated outcomes to approximate what that model implies for risk and performance.

If the underlying probabilistic model is unrealistic, even a perfectly implemented GPU simulation will produce misleading conclusions. That is why we start by understanding common distributions and their properties.

Key Distributions in Quant Finance

Many distributions arise in finance. We briefly review the most important ones and why they matter.

Normal (Gaussian) Distribution

The normal distribution is characterized by two parameters: a mean, which controls the central location, and a variance, which controls the spread. In an idealized world where returns are small, independent, and driven by many tiny shocks, the central limit theorem suggests that aggregated returns might be close to normal.

The normal distribution is attractive because it is mathematically convenient:

- Sums of normal variables are again normal.
- Portfolio returns, under a linear model with normal asset returns, remain normal.

- Many classical formulas, including the simplest versions of value-at-risk and mean–variance portfolio theory, assume normality.

On a GPU, normal returns are often used as the default building block for Monte Carlo: normal shocks are fed into diffusion models or correlated factor structures. However, real-world returns often show fatter tails and asymmetry than the normal distribution allows.

Student-t and Other Heavy-Tailed Distributions

Heavy-tailed distributions give more probability to extreme outcomes than the normal distribution. The Student-t distribution is a common example. It has a parameter that controls how heavy the tails are. With many degrees of freedom it looks almost normal; with few degrees of freedom it has very thick tails.

In finance, heavy tails capture the empirical fact that crashes and large moves occur more often than a normal model would predict. This matters greatly for risk management and option pricing:

- A normal model might severely underestimate the probability of large losses.
- A heavy-tailed model leads to more realistic stress scenarios and wider risk estimates.

When you simulate millions of paths on a GPU using a heavy-tailed distribution, you will see more extreme P&L outcomes than in a normal simulation. The difference is not a numerical artifact; it is a modeling choice with direct implications for capital allocation and risk limits.

Lognormal Distribution

While returns are often modeled as normal, prices are naturally positive. If the continuously compounded return over a period is normal, then the price at the end of the period is lognormal. A lognormal variable is one whose logarithm is normally distributed.

This is important for modeling asset prices in diffusion models such as geometric Brownian motion. In a Monte Carlo implementation, you might generate normally distributed returns and then exponentiate them to get lognormal prices. The GPU-friendly part is still the generation of the normal draws, but it is the lognormal distribution that ensures prices stay positive.

Bernoulli, Binomial, and Poisson Distributions

Some quantities are discrete:

- **Bernoulli:** A single yes/no event, such as whether a limit order gets filled in a given microsecond.
- **Binomial:** The count of successes in a fixed number of trials, such as how many days in a month a signal was profitable.
- **Poisson:** The number of events in a time interval when events occur independently at a certain average rate, such as the arrival of trades or messages in a limit order book.

These distributions become important when modeling order flow, execution risk, or the number of signal triggers. On a GPU, you may need to generate large arrays of such discrete random variables to simulate fills, cancellations, or trade arrivals across many instruments and time buckets.

Moments: Mean, Variance, Skewness, Kurtosis

To summarize a distribution, it is often useful to look at its moments. Moments are numerical characteristics that describe different aspects of the distribution's shape.

Mean: Expected Return

The mean of a return distribution is the average return you expect over many realizations. For a trading strategy, the mean daily return multiplied by the number of trading days gives a first approximation to the expected annual return.

In Monte Carlo, the sample mean over many simulated paths is an estimator of this expected return. If you use a GPU to simulate millions of paths, the sample mean can be computed very accurately, but it still depends on the underlying model being appropriate.

Variance and Standard Deviation: Risk

Variance measures how spread out returns are around the mean. The square root of the variance, the standard deviation, is often used as a measure of volatility or risk. In practice:

- Higher variance means more uncertainty around the expected return.
- Portfolio construction often tries to balance expected return against variance.

In a Monte Carlo engine, the variance of simulated P&L outcomes is a key input to risk metrics. On GPUs, computing variances and standard deviations across many assets or scenarios is an embarrassingly parallel task: each thread can handle one asset or one path, and results are then aggregated.

Skewness: Asymmetry of Returns

Skewness captures whether a distribution has a longer tail on one side than the other.

- Negative skewness indicates frequent small gains with occasional large losses.
- Positive skewness indicates frequent small losses with occasional large gains.

Many option-based strategies have strongly negative skew: they collect small premiums but are exposed to rare but severe losses. For risk management, it is crucial to know not only the variance but also the skewness. While variance treats upside and downside symmetrically, skewness emphasizes the direction of extreme events.

Kurtosis: Tail Heaviness

Kurtosis measures how heavy the tails of a distribution are relative to a normal distribution. High kurtosis indicates that extreme events are more probable than under a normal model, even if the variance is the same.

Empirical financial returns often show excess kurtosis. This means:

- Models that assume normality underestimate tail risk.
- Monte Carlo engines using normal shocks will under-sample extreme losses.

Using heavy-tailed distributions like the Student-t in your GPU simulations raises the kurtosis to better match reality, leading to more conservative and realistic risk assessments.

Why Distributional Assumptions Matter for GPU Simulations

Two models can have the same mean and variance but very different skewness and kurtosis. In other words, they look similar if you only consider average return and volatility, but they behave very differently in the tails.

This is precisely where distributional assumptions become critical. GPU acceleration makes it easy to run massive numbers of scenarios, but all those scenarios are still drawn from the distribution you choose. A normal-based engine might produce a visually smooth, well-behaved P&L distribution that underestimates extreme risks. A heavy-tailed engine might show more frequent crashes, forcing you to confront realistic downside scenarios.

The comparison between normal and heavy-tailed return distributions is therefore not a dry academic point; it is central to how you should set up your accelerated research.

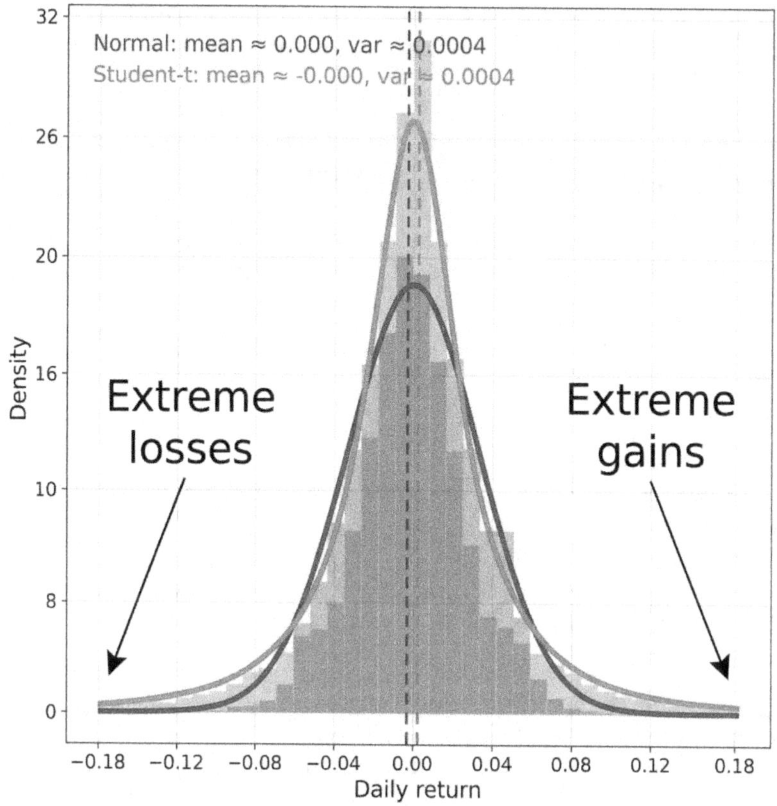

These side-by-side plots illustrate a crucial point: even with nearly identical means and variances, the heavy-tailed distribution places much more mass in the far left and right tails. When you run large-scale Monte Carlo on a GPU, this difference determines how often you see extreme gains or losses.

Sampling, Law of Large Numbers, and the Central Limit Theorem

GPU acceleration shines when you need to repeat simple operations many times. Monte Carlo simulation and resampling methods are perfect examples. To understand what you gain from simulating many paths, you need two key principles: the law of large numbers and the central limit theorem.

Sampling and the Law of Large Numbers

Imagine repeatedly sampling daily returns from a fixed distribution. The sample mean is the average of the observed returns. The law of large numbers states that as the number of independent samples grows, the sample mean tends to move closer to the true mean of the distribution.

In practice:

- With a small number of samples, the sample mean can be very noisy.
- With many samples, the sample mean stabilizes and becomes a reliable estimator.

A GPU allows you to dramatically increase the number of simulated scenarios in a fixed wall-clock time. This directly reduces the sampling variability of your estimates of means, variances, and other statistics, assuming your model is correct and the samples are independent.

Central Limit Theorem and Monte Carlo Error

The central limit theorem goes a step further. It states that, under fairly general conditions, the distribution of the sample mean becomes approximately normal as the number of samples increases, regardless of the original distribution, provided the variance is finite.

The important implication for Monte Carlo is that the error in your estimated quantity shrinks at a rate related to the inverse square root of the number of samples. Doubling the number of paths reduces the standard error by about a factor of the square root of two.

For GPU workloads, this tells you that:

- There are diminishing returns to increasing the number of paths. Each additional block of paths improves accuracy by a smaller amount.
- Nevertheless, being able to go from tens of thousands to millions of paths using a GPU can be the difference between a rough estimate and one that is tight enough for risk management or trading decisions.

Parameter Estimation: Fitting Distributions to Data

It is not enough to pick a family of distributions; you must also choose the parameters that best match observed data. This is where parameter estimation comes in. Three common approaches are especially relevant.

Sample Moments

The most basic approach is to compute sample moments:

- The sample mean as an estimator of expected return.
- The sample variance as an estimator of volatility.
- Sample skewness and kurtosis as estimators of asymmetry and tail heaviness.

These are straightforward to compute and parallelize: each GPU thread can process a subset of data, and reductions combine partial results.

Method of Moments

The method of moments extends this idea. You select a few theoretical moments of your chosen distribution and set them equal to the corresponding sample moments, then solve for the parameters.

For example, for a Student-t distribution, you might match the sample variance and kurtosis to infer plausible degrees of freedom and scale. On a GPU, you can do this matching not just for one asset but for thousands of assets in parallel, each with its own data history.

Maximum Likelihood Estimation

Maximum likelihood estimation chooses the parameters that make the observed data as probable as possible under the model. You write down the likelihood of the data as a function of the parameters and then find the parameter values that maximize it.

This often leads to numerical optimization problems. For each candidate parameter set, you must evaluate the likelihood, which involves many repeated operations across data points. This is naturally parallelizable:

- Individual likelihood contributions for each observation can be computed in parallel.
- For a cross-section of instruments, you can estimate parameters for each instrument separately in a batched GPU workload.

Maximum likelihood often yields efficient estimators with good statistical properties, but it depends heavily on the correctness of the distributional assumptions.

Confidence Intervals and Hypothesis Testing for Trading Signals

Once you have estimated parameters or observed a performance metric in a backtest, you must decide whether there is real evidence of a signal or just random noise. Confidence intervals and hypothesis tests provide a disciplined way to make that judgment.

Confidence Intervals

A confidence interval for a parameter, such as the mean return of a strategy, is a range of values that is consistent with the data at a given confidence level. For example, you might compute a range for the mean daily return such that, under repeated sampling, intervals constructed in this way would contain the true mean a high percentage of the time.

For GPU-accelerated research, you may construct confidence intervals from:

- Analytical formulas, when the sampling distribution is known or approximately normal.
- Resampling methods such as the bootstrap, where you repeatedly resample your data and recompute the statistic, using the GPU to parallelize the resampling.

If the confidence interval for a strategy's mean return includes zero, the data do not strongly support the presence of a positive edge, even if the point estimate is positive.

Hypothesis Tests and t-Statistics

A hypothesis test starts with a null hypothesis, such as "the true mean return of this strategy is zero." You then compute a test statistic that measures how far the observed data deviate from what the null predicts. A t-statistic is a common choice, formed by taking the estimated mean and dividing by an estimate of its standard error.

The larger the magnitude of the t-statistic, the more evidence you have against the null. You compare this statistic to critical values or compute a p-value, which is the probability, under the null hypothesis, of seeing a test statistic at least as extreme as the one you observed.

On a GPU, you can go beyond a single test:

- Evaluate t-statistics for thousands of candidate strategies in parallel.

- Use simulations to understand the distribution of t-statistics under realistic null models, including heavy tails and volatility clustering.

Multiple Testing and Data Mining

When you test many strategies or many parameter variations, some will look good by pure chance. This is especially dangerous in a GPU setting, because the ability to test huge numbers of ideas quickly makes it easy to overfit.

To keep your backtests statistically defensible:

- Adjust your expectations: among many tests, even a small p-value can occur by luck.
- Use validation on out-of-sample data or under alternative simulation scenarios.
- Consider techniques that control the overall rate of false discoveries, rather than treating each test in isolation.

The key idea is that the more you search, the more cautious you must be in interpreting apparent edges.

From Statistical Foundations to GPU-Accelerated Backtests

By now, a few themes should be clear:

- **Uncertainty is modeled through distributions.** Choices like normal versus heavy-tailed distributions influence how often extreme events occur in your simulations.
- **Moments summarize risk and return.** Mean, variance, skewness, and kurtosis describe not just typical outcomes, but also asymmetry and tail risk.

- **Sampling theory justifies Monte Carlo.** The law of large numbers and central limit theorem explain why increasing the number of simulated paths on a GPU improves the reliability of estimates.
- **Estimation and testing keep you honest.** Fitting distribution parameters, constructing confidence intervals, and running hypothesis tests help distinguish genuine signals from noise, even when you exploit massive computational power.

These probabilistic and statistical foundations are what make GPU acceleration truly valuable. Without them, faster computation merely accelerates the production of misleading results. With them, you can harness GPUs to explore high-dimensional models, complex risk scenarios, and vast universes of signals while maintaining a disciplined view of uncertainty and evidence.

1.2 Linear Algebra & Matrix Computations

In the previous section we treated returns and P&L as random variables with distributions. We saw how expectations, variances, and correlations describe risk and uncertainty. We now take the next step: we organize those quantities into vectors and matrices so that portfolio construction, factor modeling, and risk calculation become structured linear algebra problems.

This shift in viewpoint is crucial for GPU acceleration. Modern GPUs are exceptionally good at performing the basic operations of linear algebra on large arrays: adding vectors, multiplying matrices, and solving systems of linear equations. When you recognize that a risk engine or factor model is essentially a sequence of matrix operations, you can map it directly onto highly parallel GPU routines, often by calling optimized libraries rather than writing complex kernels by hand.

Our goals in this section are:

- To connect familiar portfolio and risk concepts to vectors and matrices.

- To show how factor models, covariances, and exposures are naturally expressed through matrix multiplication and related operations.
- To prepare you conceptually for batched and blocked computations, which are the patterns GPU libraries exploit for speed.

We will move gradually, starting with vectors and matrices, then building up to covariance matrices, factor models, and decompositions such as eigenvalue and Cholesky, all with a focus on their financial meaning and their GPU-friendly structure.

From Individual Assets to Vectors

Consider a simple portfolio of several assets. For each asset you may know:

- A weight or position, such as the fraction of capital invested.
- An expected return.
- A realized or simulated return for a given day or scenario.

Instead of thinking about each asset separately, we collect these values into vectors.

- A *position vector* contains one entry per asset, indicating how much of each asset you hold.
- A *return vector* contains one entry per asset, giving the return of each asset in a given period or scenario.

When you compute the portfolio return as a weighted average of asset returns, you are taking the dot product of the position vector with the return vector. This is a basic linear algebra operation: multiply corresponding entries and sum them.

On a GPU, you rarely compute a single dot product. Instead, you often compute many such products in parallel: across multiple portfolios, time steps, or simulated scenarios. This pattern is exactly what linear algebra libraries optimize.

Matrices for Time and Cross-Section

As soon as you consider more than one time point or more than one portfolio, you move from vectors to matrices.

Returns as a Matrix

Suppose you have returns for many assets over many days. You can arrange the data as a matrix:

- Each row corresponds to a time point, such as a trading day.
- Each column corresponds to an asset.

Now, operations that were once applied asset by asset or day by day become matrix operations. For example:

- Computing the cumulative return path of each asset turns into repeated operations by columns.
- Computing the cross-sectional mean return at each time is a vector operation on each row.

On GPUs, performing the same operation across many rows or columns is natural: each thread block can handle a subset of rows, columns, or both.

Portfolios as a Matrix

When you consider multiple portfolios simultaneously, you can arrange their positions as a matrix too:

- Each column is a portfolio.
- Each row corresponds to an asset.

The return of all portfolios on a given day can then be computed by multiplying the asset return vector by the position matrix. Conceptually, this is the same as computing many dot products at once.

This is the first hint that portfolio analytics are just structured matrix multiplications: asset returns times portfolio weights produce portfolio returns.

Covariance Matrices and Portfolio Risk

In the probability section we discussed variance as a measure of risk for a single random variable. For a collection of assets, we also need to understand how returns move together. This is captured by covariance.

Covariance Between Two Assets

Covariance measures how two asset returns tend to vary together:

- A positive covariance indicates that the returns tend to move in the same direction.
- A negative covariance indicates that they tend to move in opposite directions.

When constructing portfolios, you care not only about each asset's individual risk, but also about how their risks interact. Assets with low or negative covariance can reduce overall portfolio volatility when combined.

The Covariance Matrix

For many assets, we collect all pairwise covariances into a covariance matrix:

- Each entry in the matrix is the covariance between two assets.
- The diagonal entries are the variances of each asset.

Once you have a covariance matrix and a vector of portfolio weights, the variance of the portfolio return can be obtained by a sequence of vector and matrix multiplications. Intuitively, the covariance matrix encodes all the interaction terms between assets, and the weights tell you how much each interaction matters.

Computationally, evaluating portfolio risk for many portfolios means applying the covariance matrix repeatedly to many weight vectors. This is essentially a batched matrix–vector multiplication, one of the core operations in GPU-accelerated linear algebra.

Factor Models and Exposure Matrices

While a full covariance matrix for many assets can be large and hard to estimate, factor models provide a more structured representation of risk.

Common Factors and Idiosyncratic Risk

A factor model assumes that each asset's return is driven by:

- A set of common factors, such as market, size, value, or sectors.
- An idiosyncratic component unique to the asset.

Each asset has *factor loadings* that describe its sensitivity to each factor. These loadings can be collected into a factor loading matrix:

- Each row corresponds to an asset.
- Each column corresponds to a factor.
- Entries tell you how strongly an asset is exposed to a factor.

Factor Covariance and Asset Covariance

If you know how the factors move together (the factor covariance matrix) and you know the factor loadings, you can reconstruct a large part of the asset covariance structure:

- Factor loadings say how each asset responds to changes in each factor.
- Factor covariance describes how the factors themselves co-move.

Multiplying the factor loading matrix, the factor covariance matrix, and the transpose of the loading matrix produces a structured approximation to the full asset covariance matrix. You may also add an idiosyncratic risk matrix, usually diagonal, to capture asset-specific variance.

This chain of matrix multiplications is a perfect example of what GPUs handle well:

- A dense matrix times another dense matrix, then times a transpose.
- Potentially repeated many times for different universes, risk horizons, or scenarios.

Portfolio Factor Exposures

Given the factor loadings and a portfolio's asset weights, you can also compute the portfolio's exposure to each factor. This is simply another matrix–vector multiplication: the transpose of the factor loading matrix times the portfolio weight vector.

From a practitioner's perspective, this gives immediate insight:

- How much market exposure does the portfolio have?
- How loaded is it on a value factor, a momentum factor, or sector tilts?

From a computational perspective, factor exposures for many portfolios can be computed in a batched way, again aligning with GPU strengths.

Positions, Factors, and Covariances as a Flow of Matrices

We now have the main objects:

- A position vector for each portfolio.
- A factor loading matrix linking assets to factors.
- A factor covariance matrix, and by extension, an implied asset covariance matrix.

Before diving into matrix decompositions, it is useful to visualize how these pieces fit together as a flow of linear algebra operations.

This diagram emphasizes three key computational patterns:

- Matrix multiplication to build asset covariances from factors.
- Matrix–vector multiplication to project positions into factor space.
- Applying a covariance matrix to a weight vector to obtain portfolio risk.

All of these are operations that mature GPU libraries, such as cuBLAS and cuSOLVER, are designed to accelerate.

Dense and Sparse Representations

So far we have implicitly treated all matrices as dense, meaning we store every entry. In practice, some matrices are sparse: many entries are zero.

Sparse Exposure Matrices

In large universes, a given factor may apply only to a subset of assets. For example, a sector factor matrix may have nonzero entries only within each sector, or an execution cost model may link each order only to a few liquidity buckets. This structure leads naturally to sparse matrices.

Storing and operating on sparse matrices can be much more efficient than treating them as dense:

- Less memory is required.
- Computations can skip the many zero entries.

On GPUs, sparse linear algebra has its own specialized routines. Recognizing sparsity in your problem can therefore unlock further speedups and memory savings.

When Dense Makes Sense

By contrast, covariance matrices and factor loading matrices are often treated as dense, especially when the number of assets or factors is moderate and correlations are widespread. Dense matrices map directly onto classic GPU-accelerated primitives, and for many portfolio and risk problems, this is the dominant workload.

A good modeling habit is to ask, for each matrix in your pipeline:

- Is it mostly full, or mostly zero?
- Should I use dense or sparse representations on the GPU?

Answering these questions correctly can make the difference between an implementation that merely runs and one that truly exploits the hardware.

Matrix Decompositions in Finance

Once you describe your problem in terms of matrices, you often need to transform or factor those matrices to understand their structure or to perform calculations efficiently and stably. Matrix decompositions are standardized ways of doing this.

Eigenvalue Decomposition and Principal Components

An eigenvalue decomposition expresses a matrix as a combination of special directions (eigenvectors) and associated strengths (eigenvalues). For a covariance matrix, the eigenvectors can be interpreted as principal components of risk:

- The first principal component might represent a broad market movement.
- Subsequent components might capture sector swings, curve steepening, or other common patterns.

In practice, you often use only the leading principal components to build a low-dimensional representation of risk. This can simplify risk reporting and also reduce the size of certain computations: instead of working in the full asset space, you operate in a smaller factor space.

On GPUs, eigenvalue decompositions of large dense matrices are demanding but well-supported by specialized routines. For many assets and histories, offloading this work to the GPU can dramatically reduce computation time.

Singular Value Decomposition

The singular value decomposition is related to eigenvalue decomposition but applies to general rectangular matrices, such as return matrices with many assets and fewer time points. In finance, it appears in:

- Dimension reduction for large cross-sectional datasets.
- Identifying latent factors that explain most of the variance in returns.

Again, from a computational standpoint, singular value decomposition is a heavy linear algebra task that benefits greatly from GPU acceleration.

Cholesky Decomposition for Scenario Generation

Cholesky decomposition expresses a positive-definite matrix, such as a covariance matrix, as the product of a lower-triangular matrix and its transpose. In Monte Carlo simulation, this is a key tool:

- Start with independent standard normal random variables.

- Multiply by the Cholesky factor to introduce correlations matching your covariance matrix.

This transforms uncorrelated random shocks into correlated asset returns or factor moves. In other words, Cholesky provides the bridge from simple, independent random draws to realistic, correlated scenarios.

On a GPU, both the Cholesky factorization and the repeated application of the factor to large numbers of random vectors are highly parallelizable. This makes correlated scenario generation one of the most natural use cases for GPU-accelerated linear algebra in risk analytics.

Solving Linear Systems for Factor-Based Portfolios

When you design a factor-based portfolio, you often end up solving systems of linear equations. For instance:

- You may wish to find portfolio weights that achieve a target factor exposure while minimizing risk.
- You may impose constraints, such as neutrality to certain factors or sectors.

In matrix form, these problems often boil down to solving systems where a covariance or normal-equation matrix multiplies a vector of unknown weights to yield a vector of required exposures or conditions.

Solving these systems robustly requires attention to numerical conditioning and stability. From a computational standpoint, solving many such systems for different sets of constraints or parameter choices can be expressed as a batched linear system problem, which GPUs handle efficiently.

Batched and Blocked Computations

The common thread in all of these examples is repetition:

- Many portfolios evaluated against the same covariance matrix.

- Many time slices or scenarios processed with the same factor model.
- Many candidate parameter sets or factor structures tested in parallel.

GPU libraries expose batched and blocked versions of key linear algebra routines for exactly this reason.

Batched Operations

A batched operation takes a collection of small or medium-sized linear algebra problems and processes them together. For instance, you might have:

- Hundreds of covariance matrices, one per region or sector, each of moderate size.
- Thousands of small systems to solve when calibrating execution models for different instruments.

Instead of launching one small GPU operation per problem, which would underutilize the hardware, you use a batched routine that handles all of them in one call. The computation is then internally arranged so that the GPU can keep many threads busy.

Blocked Operations

Blocked operations refer to splitting large matrices into sub-blocks to better use caches and shared memory. Although this is often handled inside libraries, it is conceptually useful to understand that:

- Large matrix operations are divided into smaller tiles.
- Each tile is processed by a group of threads that reuses data efficiently.

When you design your own GPU kernels around linear algebra primitives, thinking in terms of blocks and tiles helps align your logic with how the hardware moves data and schedules threads.

From Theory to GPU Practice

Linear algebra provides the language and structure for much of modern quantitative finance:

- Portfolios become vectors of weights.
- Asset universes and factors become matrices of returns and loadings.
- Risk and dependence are collected into covariance matrices.
- Factor models, decompositions, and optimizations are expressed through systematic matrix operations.

From the probabilistic foundations in the previous section, we know what quantities we want to compute: expected returns, risks, correlations, and factor sensitivities. Linear algebra tells us how to compute them in a structured, scalable way. GPUs, in turn, provide the brute-force parallelism to perform those structured operations quickly across large universes, long histories, and many scenarios.

As you move into later chapters, keep this mapping in mind. When you see a complex-looking backtest or risk model, look for the underlying vectors and matrices. If you can rewrite the core of the computation as a sequence of matrix multiplications, factorizations, and solves, you can usually leverage GPU-accelerated linear algebra libraries to achieve large speedups with relatively little additional complexity.

1.3 Calculus & Numerical Analysis Basics

The previous sections gave us the statistical and linear algebra foundations for modeling portfolios and risk. We described returns as random variables, organized them into vectors and matrices, and used factor models and covariance structures to summarize risk. We now add a third layer: continuous-time thinking and the numerical methods that turn smooth mathematical models into discrete computations that GPUs can execute at scale.

In modern quantitative finance, many models are written as if time were continuous. Prices evolve every instant; interest accrues continuously; option values change smoothly with the underlying and with time. Calculus is the language used to describe such smooth change. However, no computer works in continuous time. To simulate a diffusion or solve a pricing equation, we must approximate continuous-time ideas using discrete time steps and spatial grids. That approximation process is the domain of numerical analysis.

The aim of this section is to connect the continuous-time models you may know from derivatives pricing or stochastic calculus to the discrete, approximate schemes that dominate GPU workloads:

- We first revisit key calculus ideas as they appear in finance: compounding, rates of change, and diffusions.
- We then show how these continuous concepts are approximated using finite differences for derivatives and numerical integration for expectations.
- We move on to time-stepping schemes for stochastic differential equations and partial differential equations, explaining how step size, accuracy, and stability interact.
- Throughout, we highlight how these approximations become large collections of simple, parallel tasks that are natural for GPUs.

Continuous-Time Thinking in Finance

Before diving into approximations, it is helpful to recall why continuous-time models are so popular in finance.

Continuous Compounding and Rates

When interest is compounded continuously, the value of an investment grows smoothly rather than in discrete jumps. Instead of thinking in terms of a periodic interest rate applied at fixed intervals, we think in terms of an instantaneous rate that applies continuously over time.

This continuous viewpoint extends naturally to returns:

- Simple returns measure proportional change over a finite period.
- Continuously compounded returns measure the accumulated effect of many tiny changes, added up over time.

Continuously compounded returns add across time, which is convenient for modeling and for connecting to normal or heavy-tailed distributions. In many pricing models, the logarithm of price evolves smoothly under a continuous-time process, while the price itself remains positive by construction.

Diffusions and Stochastic Differential Equations

In continuous-time models, asset prices are often described as diffusions. A diffusion has two main ingredients:

- A drift term, describing the average rate of change.
- A volatility term, describing the random fluctuations around that average.

Mathematically, this is written as a stochastic differential equation, where the infinitesimal change in price or in log-price over a tiny time interval has a deterministic part (the drift) and a random part (the volatility times a random shock). The random shock is modeled as a very fine-grained noise process with independent increments.

This framework underlies classical derivative pricing models, such as those used for equity options, interest rate derivatives, and credit risk. Greeks, which measure sensitivities of option prices to underlying parameters, are defined as derivatives of pricing functions with respect to inputs.

These continuous descriptions are elegant and powerful, but to compute actual prices or risk measures, we must approximate them numerically.

From Derivatives to Finite Differences

Calculus defines derivatives as instantaneous rates of change. For example, the derivative of an option price with respect to the underlying price, often called delta, tells you how much the option price changes for a very small change in the underlying.

A computer cannot work with truly infinitesimal changes; it can only apply small but finite increments. The basic idea of finite differences is to approximate a derivative by looking at how a function changes over a small step.

Approximating First and Second Derivatives

In practice:

- A first derivative can be approximated by taking the difference in function values at two nearby points and dividing by the distance between them.
- A second derivative, which measures curvature, can be approximated by combining function values at points ahead of and behind the reference point.

These approximations become more accurate as the step size shrinks, up to the point where numerical rounding errors begin to dominate.

In option pricing, second derivatives with respect to the underlying (gamma) and first derivatives with respect to time (theta) appear naturally in partial differential equations that govern the option price. Approximating these derivatives using finite differences is the starting point for many grid-based pricing methods.

Grids and Stencils

To apply finite differences systematically, we set up a grid:

- The horizontal axis might represent the underlying price, divided into many discrete levels.
- The vertical axis might represent time to expiry, divided into time steps.

The option value is then represented by its value at each grid point. Finite difference formulas relate the value at a grid point to values at neighboring points. The pattern of neighbors used is often called a stencil.

On a GPU, this stencil computation is highly parallelizable:

- Each grid point update involves a fixed, small amount of work.
- Updates across different grid points can often be computed independently in each time step, as long as they use only values from the previous time level.

This leads to thousands or millions of nearly identical small calculations, perfectly suited for a massively parallel architecture.

Numerical Integration and Expectations

Calculus also defines integrals, which in finance often represent aggregated quantities:

- The total discounted payoff of a cash flow stream over time.
- The expected value of a payoff under a risk-neutral probability measure.

Just as derivatives are approximated by differences, integrals are approximated by sums.

Quadrature as Weighted Sums

Numerical integration techniques, sometimes called quadrature rules, replace an integral by a weighted sum of function values at discrete points. For example:

- Simple methods approximate the area under a curve by rectangles or trapezoids.
- More refined methods use cleverly chosen sample points and weights to achieve higher accuracy with fewer evaluations.

In derivative pricing, such methods can be used to compute expectations of payoff functions against continuous distributions. Instead of simulating random paths, you evaluate the payoff at selected points in the state space and weight them appropriately.

On a GPU, quadrature can again be parallelized:

- Each evaluation of the function at a quadrature point is independent.
- Aggregating the results into a final sum is a reduction operation, for which optimized parallel patterns exist.

Although Monte Carlo is often more flexible for high-dimensional problems, quadrature methods can be very efficient when the dimension of the integral is low and the structure of the problem is smooth.

Time-Stepping for Stochastic Differential Equations

Continuous-time diffusions are described by stochastic differential equations, but to simulate them we must replace the continuous equation with a step-by-step rule in discrete time.

Basic Time-Stepping Idea

The basic idea is to move forward in time in small increments. At each step:

- You compute how much the state changes due to the drift over that time step.
- You add a random change due to volatility, based on a random draw that represents the noise over that interval.

This gives a recursion: the state at the next time step is computed from the current state plus deterministic and random increments. The simplest incarnation of this approach is often called the Euler–Maruyama method.

Accuracy and Higher-Order Schemes

The smaller the time step, the closer the discrete-time path will mimic the continuous-time model. However:

- Very small steps increase the number of computations and amplify the effect of numerical rounding.

- Larger steps reduce computational cost but introduce bias, because the discrete-time approximation no longer tracks the continuous-time dynamics closely.

Higher-order schemes are designed to achieve more accurate approximations for a given step size by using additional function evaluations or by more cleverly combining random increments. These schemes can reduce bias without shrinking the time step as aggressively, but they may increase complexity per step.

From a GPU perspective, both simple and higher-order schemes share a common pattern:

- You have many independent paths or scenarios.
- Each path evolves through time by applying the same update rule with different random shocks.

This is a prototypical example of an "embarrassingly parallel" computation: each path can be simulated by a separate thread or group of threads, with little interaction between them until final aggregation.

Partial Differential Equations for Pricing

Another route to pricing derivatives is to work directly with partial differential equations that govern how the price of a contract evolves with the underlying and with time.

Pricing as a PDE Problem

Under suitable assumptions, such as no arbitrage and continuous trading, the price of a derivative can be characterized as the solution to a certain partial differential equation with boundary conditions specified by the payoff at expiry and by behavior at extreme values of the underlying.

This view is especially natural for options, where:

- The spatial variable is the underlying asset price (or sometimes a transformed version, such as its logarithm).

- The time variable is the time remaining until expiry.

Solving the pricing PDE numerically involves setting up a grid in space and time, applying boundary conditions, and marching backwards in time from maturity to the present, using finite difference approximations for spatial and temporal derivatives.

Explicit and Implicit Schemes

There are different ways to relate the solution at one time level to the next:

- Explicit schemes compute the solution at the next time step directly from known values at the current time step. They are simple and highly parallel, but may require very small time steps for stability.
- Implicit schemes define the next time step through a linear system that must be solved at each step. They are more stable and can use larger time steps, but involve more complex linear algebra.

From a GPU standpoint:

- Explicit schemes involve stencil updates across the grid, which are straightforward to parallelize.
- Implicit schemes require solving large, structured linear systems, which can also be accelerated using GPU-optimized solvers and matrix factorization routines.

In practice, mixed schemes that combine the advantages of both approaches are common, and they too can be mapped onto GPU-friendly linear algebra patterns.

Truncation Error, Round-Off, and Stability

Whenever we approximate a continuous model with a discrete scheme, two types of error arise:

- Truncation error, due to approximating derivatives and integrals by finite differences and sums.
- Round-off error, due to representing real numbers with finite precision on a computer.

Understanding how these errors behave as you refine your grid or reduce your time step is central to designing reliable numerical methods.

Trade-off Between Accuracy and Cost

Shrinking the step size or making the grid finer usually reduces truncation error: the discrete scheme more closely mimics the continuous model. But this comes at a cost:

- More grid points or more time steps mean more computations, which increases run time.
- Larger arrays of numbers may also increase memory usage and communication overhead.

For GPUs, this trade-off is nuanced. GPUs can handle large numbers of arithmetic operations efficiently, but performance can be limited by memory bandwidth and by how well data access patterns align with the hardware.

Round-Off and Floating-Point Limits

Computers represent real numbers in floating-point format, which has limited precision. When you add or subtract numbers of very different magnitudes, or when you repeatedly apply small updates, rounding errors can accumulate.

On a CPU, these effects may already be nontrivial; on a GPU, which often uses single precision for speed, they can be more pronounced. As you refine a numerical scheme:

- Initially, decreasing the step size reduces overall error.
- Beyond a certain point, further reduction may actually increase total error, because round-off effects become dominant.

Recognizing this behavior helps you choose a sensible step size that balances truncation and round-off, rather than simply assuming that smaller is always better.

Stability Considerations

A numerical scheme is stable if small perturbations in the input or in intermediate steps do not explode as the computation progresses. Instability can manifest as wild oscillations or diverging values, even when the underlying continuous model is well-behaved.

Stability often constrains your choice of step size or scheme:

- Some explicit schemes require very small time steps to remain stable.
- Implicit or semi-implicit schemes may remain stable for much larger steps, making them attractive despite their higher per-step cost.

For GPU-accelerated methods, stability analysis is not optional. A scheme that blows up numerically will fail faster on a GPU, because the hardware faithfully accelerates whatever operations you specify, including unstable ones.

Why GPUs Excel at Numerical Schemes

The numerical methods we have discussed share a common structure:

- They break a continuous problem into many small, similar operations on discrete points in time or space.
- These operations are often local: updating one grid point depends only on nearby points or on local random draws.
- There are many independent paths or grid points to update, especially when simulating many scenarios, pricing many instruments, or sweeping across parameter sets.

This structure is ideal for GPUs:

- Each path in a Monte Carlo simulation can be handled by an independent thread.
- Each grid point in a PDE solver can be updated by a separate thread, using values from nearby points.
- Repeated application of the same time-stepping rule, or the same finite difference stencil, leads to predictable, regular memory access patterns that GPU hardware can exploit.

At the same time, the potential pitfalls of numerical analysis—truncation error, round-off, and stability—do not disappear on GPUs. In some cases they become more subtle, because the higher throughput encourages you to push to finer grids or more paths without fully examining the error behavior.

A sound workflow therefore looks like this:

- Start from a continuous-time financial model with clear economic meaning.
- Choose a numerical scheme with known accuracy and stability properties.
- Analyze how step size and grid resolution affect truncation and round-off error.
- Only then, map the scheme to a GPU implementation that respects data locality and parallel structure.

Connecting Back to the Big Picture

Calculus and numerical analysis bridge the gap between elegant continuous-time models and the discrete world of computation. In the context of this book:

- **Probability and statistics** gave us a language for uncertainty and estimation.
- **Linear algebra** organized portfolios, factors, and covariances into vectors and matrices.

- **Calculus and numerical analysis**, as discussed here, show how to evolve these quantities in continuous time and then approximate that evolution with schemes that GPUs can run at scale.

As we move on to time-series models, optimization methods, and market microstructure, the same numerical patterns will reappear in different guises: rolling-window estimates, gradient calculations, dynamic programming recursions, and more. Recognizing the underlying calculus and numerical structure will help you design GPU-accelerated research pipelines that are not only fast, but also mathematically sound and interpretable.

1.4 Time-Series Fundamentals

Up to this point, we have focused on cross-sectional structure and continuous-time modeling. We treated returns and P&L as random variables with distributions, organized them into vectors and matrices, and described how they evolve in continuous time through diffusions and numerical schemes. We now add a crucial dimension: time-series behavior.

In real markets, prices and returns do not arrive as isolated draws from a distribution. They appear as sequences: ordered observations through time. The way these sequences behave is central to forecasting, risk measurement, and strategy evaluation. It is also central to GPU acceleration: many workloads in quantitative finance involve computing time-series statistics or fitting models for vast numbers of instruments and scenarios.

In this section we will:

- Define what we mean by a financial time series and introduce the idea of stationarity.
- Explore autocorrelation, partial autocorrelation, and empirical patterns such as mean reversion and volatility clustering.
- Present classical linear time-series models (AR, MA, ARMA/ARIMA) and describe what they capture and miss.

- Introduce conditional heteroskedasticity models (ARCH/-GARCH) for time-varying volatility.
- Highlight which aspects of time-series analysis lend themselves to GPU parallelism and which remain inherently sequential.

Throughout, we will keep an eye on how these concepts feed into GPU-intensive tasks such as large-scale forecasting, scenario generation, and volatility simulation.

What Is a Financial Time Series?

A financial time series is simply a quantity indexed by time. Typical examples include:

- Daily closing prices of a stock.
- Intraday midquotes, best bids, or best offers from a limit order book.
- Returns computed from prices over fixed intervals.
- Trading volume, bid-ask spread, or realized volatility measured over time.

The key feature is ordering: observation at time one comes before time two, which comes before time three, and so on. The order matters because the future can depend on the past, but the past cannot depend on the future.

From a modeling perspective, we think of a time series as a sequence of random variables, one for each time point. The joint behavior of these variables over time encodes both distributional properties (such as mean and variance) and dynamic properties (such as dependence on past values).

Stationarity: Stable Behavior Over Time

To make progress, we usually assume that the statistical behavior of a time series is stable in some sense. This idea is called stationarity.

Intuition for Stationarity

A stationary time series is one whose basic statistical properties do not change over time. Informally, this means:

- The average level of the series is roughly constant.
- The variability around that level is roughly constant.
- The way the series depends on its past does not change over time.

Returns are often modeled as stationary, at least over moderate horizons and in the absence of structural breaks. Prices, by contrast, tend to drift and trend over long periods, making them less suitable for stationary modeling in raw form. A common practice is therefore to transform prices into returns or log-returns before fitting time-series models.

Why Stationarity Matters

Stationarity is important because many time-series tools, including autocorrelation analysis and ARMA models, rely on it. When a series is stationary:

- We can use past data to infer patterns that we expect to persist into the future.
- The parameters of a model fitted on one part of the series are expected to be valid for another part.

For GPU-accelerated workflows, stationarity also has a practical benefit. If we assume similar dynamics across time, we can apply the same model structure to many overlapping windows, many instruments, or many simulated paths, and parallelize those calculations aggressively.

Autocorrelation and Partial Autocorrelation

Once we regard a series as stationary, we want to understand how its current values relate to its past values. Autocorrelation provides a simple, powerful diagnostic.

Autocorrelation Function (ACF)

Autocorrelation measures how similar the series is to a shifted version of itself. For a given lag, we look at the correlation between current values and values that are that many steps in the past.

If returns have zero autocorrelation at all positive lags, they resemble white noise: knowing the past gives no linear predictive power for the next observation. If autocorrelation is nonzero at some lags, there is linear dependence across time:

- Positive autocorrelation suggests persistence or momentum: high returns tend to be followed by high returns.
- Negative autocorrelation suggests mean reversion: high returns tend to be followed by lower returns, and vice versa.

The autocorrelation function (ACF) plots autocorrelation as a function of lag. It is a central tool for diagnosing time-series behavior.

Partial Autocorrelation Function (PACF)

While the ACF measures overall correlation with past values, the partial autocorrelation function measures correlation at a given lag after accounting for the influence of shorter lags.

Intuitively, the partial autocorrelation at lag two tells you how strongly the current value depends on the value two steps back, once you have already adjusted for the effect of the value one step back.

The PACF is especially useful for determining the order of autoregressive models, which we will introduce shortly.

Empirical Patterns: Mean Reversion and Volatility Clustering

Real financial time series exhibit several recurring patterns:

- **Weak autocorrelation in raw returns:** For many liquid assets, daily or intraday returns show little linear autocorrelation beyond very short lags. This is consistent with markets working to eliminate easy linear predictability.

- **Stronger autocorrelation in squared or absolute returns:** Measures of volatility, such as squared returns, tend to show much stronger and more persistent autocorrelation. Periods of high volatility tend to cluster, as do periods of low volatility.

Volatility clustering is a key motivation for time-varying volatility models like GARCH, which we will discuss later. It is also one of the reasons that volatility simulation and forecasting are natural targets for GPU acceleration: they often involve evaluating volatility recursions across many series and scenarios.

A Running Example: Returns, Autocorrelation, and Volatility

To make these ideas concrete, it is useful to work with a visual example: a simple return series, its autocorrelation function, and a measure of conditional volatility over time.

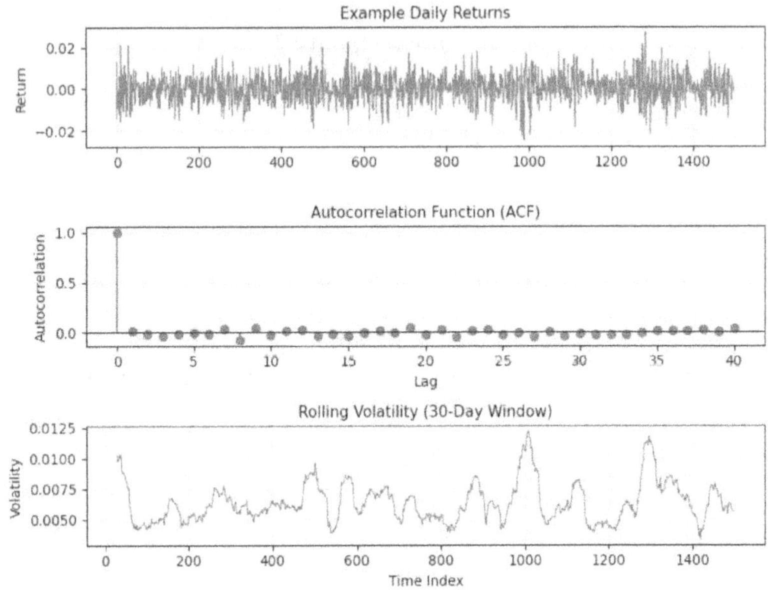

This example illustrates three key observations:

- The return series itself looks noisy and does not show obvious trends.
- The autocorrelation function for raw returns is close to zero at most lags, suggesting limited linear predictability.
- Rolling volatility varies over time, with clusters of high and low volatility, reflecting the persistent behavior often seen in markets.

These features motivate different modeling choices for the conditional mean (expected return) and conditional variance (volatility) of the series.

Linear Time-Series Models: AR, MA, ARMA, ARIMA

A natural starting point for modeling dynamics in the mean of a series is the family of linear time-series models.

Autoregressive (AR) Models

In an autoregressive model, the current value of the series is expressed as a linear combination of its recent past values plus an unpredictable shock. For example, in an AR(1) model:

- The current return depends on its immediately previous value and a new shock.
- The degree of dependence is governed by a single parameter.

AR models capture persistence or mean reversion in a straightforward way:

- A positive coefficient produces momentum-like behavior.
- A negative coefficient produces mean reversion.

Higher-order AR models incorporate more lags, allowing richer dynamics. The PACF is especially useful in diagnosing how many lags are needed: a sharp cutoff in partial autocorrelations suggests a suitable order.

Moving-Average (MA) Models

In a moving-average model, the current value depends on current and past shocks, but not directly on past values. MA models often arise when white-noise shocks are smoothed or filtered over time.

For example, executing a signal over multiple days can transform an underlying white-noise signal into a return series with moving-average structure. The ACF for an MA process usually cuts off after a certain lag, making the ACF a useful diagnostic.

ARMA and ARIMA Models

Autoregressive moving-average (ARMA) models combine both autoregressive and moving-average components. They are flexible enough to capture many patterns in stationary series.

When a series is not stationary in levels but becomes stationary after differencing, we use autoregressive integrated moving-average (ARIMA) models. The "integrated" part refers to the fact that the original series can be recovered by summing the stationary differenced series over time.

In finance, AR and ARMA models are sometimes used to model returns, spreads, or residuals from factor models. While their predictive power can be limited in highly efficient markets, they remain a useful baseline and can be extended or combined with other features.

GPU Angle: Many Small Models, Many Series

From a GPU perspective, fitting a single ARMA model to one series is often a sequential task, because estimation involves recursions and iterative optimization. However, practical research pipelines rarely stop at one series:

- You may need to fit AR models to thousands of stocks or risk factors.
- You may estimate models across many rolling windows to capture potential structural changes.
- You may evaluate different candidate orders or hyperparameters across a grid.

Each such problem is independent of the others, making the workload embarrassingly parallel across the cross-section or across model configurations. GPUs can be used to accelerate the evaluation of likelihood functions, residual calculations, and forecast generation for large panels of time series.

Conditional Heteroskedasticity: ARCH and GARCH Models

As noted earlier, volatility in returns tends to cluster over time: periods of elevated volatility follow each other, as do calm periods. While a linear model for the mean might assume constant variance for the shocks, this is often unrealistic.

ARCH and GARCH models address this by allowing the conditional variance of returns to depend on past information.

ARCH: Autoregressive Conditional Heteroskedasticity

In an ARCH model, today's volatility depends on past squared shocks. Intuitively:

- Large shocks in the recent past increase current volatility.
- Small shocks in the recent past decrease current volatility.

This simple mechanism can produce volatility clustering even if the underlying shocks themselves are independent.

GARCH: Generalized ARCH

The generalized ARCH (GARCH) model extends this idea by allowing volatility to depend both on past squared shocks and on past volatility itself. This produces more persistent volatility behavior and often matches financial data more closely.

In a GARCH model:

- Volatility evolves through a recursion: each new value is a weighted average of a long-run level, recent squared returns, and recent volatilities.
- Weights are chosen to ensure that volatility stays positive and that the process remains stable.

This recursion directly reflects the intuition behind volatility clustering: a big shock today increases volatility tomorrow, which then decays gradually back toward a long-run level.

Estimating and Using GARCH Models

Estimating a GARCH model involves:

- Choosing a parametric form for the volatility recursion and for the distribution of shocks.
- Finding parameter values that make the observed returns most likely under the model.

Once estimated, the model can be used to:

- Forecast future volatility over short horizons.
- Generate volatility scenarios for Monte Carlo simulation.
- Adjust risk metrics and position sizing based on current volatility conditions.

Because the volatility recursion is inherently sequential within a single series, we cannot parallelize it freely along time. But we can exploit parallelism along other dimensions:

- Many assets: each asset's volatility recursion is independent.
- Many parameter sets: for calibration or sensitivity analysis, multiple candidate parameter values can be tested in parallel.
- Many simulated paths: when using GARCH to simulate scenarios, different paths can be evolved in parallel across Monte Carlo replications.

These cross-sectional and scenario-based dimensions make volatility modeling a rich target for GPU acceleration.

Time-Series Workloads on GPUs: What Parallelizes and What Does Not

Not all time-series computations parallelize in the same way. It is helpful to distinguish between inherently sequential operations and those that decompose across series, windows, or scenarios.

Inherently Sequential Components

Certain recursions tie each time step to the previous one in a way that is hard to break:

- The update of a GARCH volatility depends on the immediately previous volatility and return.
- The filtered estimate in a Kalman filter depends on the previous filtered estimate.
- State-space models and dynamic programming recursions often have similar dependencies.

Within a single series and model, these recursions force you to proceed step by step in time. GPUs can still help by executing the work within each time step faster (through vectorized operations), but they cannot fundamentally break the serial dependency.

Embarrassingly Parallel Dimensions

By contrast, many other aspects of time-series analysis are embarrassingly parallel:

- **Cross-sectional panels:** Returns, volumes, and volatilities for thousands of instruments can be processed independently or in large blocks. Rolling means, volatilities, and other statistics are the same operation applied across many columns of a data matrix.

- **Rolling windows:** For each instrument, you may wish to compute statistics or refit models on overlapping windows. While windows overlap along time, windows across instruments or scenarios are independent.
- **Monte Carlo scenarios:** When simulating future paths of returns or volatilities, different Monte Carlo paths for the same model parameters are independent after you fix the random seeds.
- **Model grids and hyperparameters:** Trying many combinations of model orders, hyperparameters, or alternative specifications is easily parallelizable. Each combination can be evaluated on a GPU thread block.

Recognizing these parallel dimensions is crucial when designing GPU-accelerated time-series pipelines. The core temporal recursion may remain sequential, but almost everything else can be fanned out across hundreds or thousands of threads.

From Time-Series Intuition to GPU-Intensive Tasks

Let us tie the main threads together and connect them to concrete GPU-intensive tasks.

Large-Scale Forecasting

Suppose you are building a forecasting engine that predicts next-day or next-minute returns, volatilities, or spreads across a large universe of instruments. Your workflow might involve:

- Computing rolling features such as moving averages, recent volatilities, or lagged returns.
- Fitting or updating simple time-series models (AR, ARMA, or more complex structures) for each instrument.
- Generating forecasts and confidence intervals.

Each of these steps involves repeating similar operations across many series. GPUs excel at this kind of repeated arithmetic on large arrays, especially when data are laid out in a way that promotes coalesced memory access.

Volatility Simulation for Risk and Pricing

For risk management and derivative pricing, you often need realistic volatility scenarios:

- Simulating returns under GARCH or related volatility models.
- Simulating multi-asset volatility dynamics using factor structures.
- Feeding simulated volatilities into pricing models or P&L projections.

This combines the continuous-time and numerical insights from the previous section with the time-series structure discussed here. GPUs can:

- Evolve many simulated paths in parallel, each with its own volatility recursion.
- Apply batched linear algebra operations to propagate factor structures and correlations.
- Aggregate results into risk measures or scenario distributions.

Backtesting Dynamic Strategies

Many trading strategies depend explicitly on time-series patterns: moving-average crossovers, volatility scaling, mean-reversion signals, and so on. Backtesting such strategies requires:

- Computing indicators or signals that are functions of historical data.

- Applying trading rules that adjust positions based on these signals.
- Accounting for time-varying volatility and correlations when assessing risk.

On a GPU, you might:

- Compute signals for many instruments and parameter choices in parallel.
- Simulate execution and P&L across many scenarios or bootstrapped time series.
- Evaluate performance and risk metrics in parallel across strategies and horizons.

The time-series perspective ensures that you are modeling realistic dynamics, while GPU acceleration ensures that you can explore a broad space of possibilities within practical time constraints.

Time-series fundamentals provide the dynamic complement to the distributional and cross-sectional tools developed earlier in the chapter. We have:

- Treated returns and related quantities as sequences indexed in time, with attention to stationarity and autocorrelation.
- Identified empirical features of financial time series, such as weak autocorrelation in raw returns and strong autocorrelation in volatility.
- Introduced classical linear models for the conditional mean (AR, MA, ARMA, ARIMA) and conditional heteroskedasticity models for the variance (ARCH, GARCH).
- Highlighted where time-series computations are fundamentally sequential and where they offer massive parallelism across series, windows, and scenarios.

These ideas form the basis for GPU-intensive tasks like large-scale forecasting, volatility simulation, and dynamic backtesting. In the next section, we will build on this foundation by studying optimization principles, which underlie portfolio construction, calibration, and execution scheduling. Together, probability, linear algebra, calculus, numerical analysis, and time-series modeling equip you to design research pipelines that are both mathematically coherent and computationally efficient on modern GPU hardware.

1.5 Optimization Principles

We have now assembled several key ingredients: probability and statistics to describe uncertainty, linear algebra to organize portfolios and risks, calculus and numerical analysis to evolve models in time, and time-series tools to capture dynamics. The next step is to make decisions with these ingredients. That is the role of optimization.

In quantitative finance, many core tasks can be phrased as optimization problems:

- Constructing portfolios that trade off expected return and risk.
- Calibrating models so that they fit market data as closely as possible.
- Designing execution schedules that minimize implementation shortfall or market impact.

Each of these examples involves choosing variables (weights, parameters, trade sizes) to minimize or maximize some objective function, subject to constraints. Once we express these tasks in a structured mathematical form, they map directly to linear algebra operations that GPU solvers can accelerate.

This section builds that bridge. We will:

- Introduce the basic vocabulary of optimization: objectives, constraints, and feasible sets.

- Explain gradients, Hessians, and local versus global minima in intuitive terms.
- Highlight convex optimization, where local reasoning is safe and powerful.
- Describe common algorithms (gradient-based and coordinate-based), focusing on their computational structure.
- Show how these structures translate into large-scale or batched problems well suited for GPUs.

Formulating Optimization Problems in Quant Finance

At a high level, an optimization problem has three components:

- A set of decision variables that you are free to choose.
- An objective function that scores each choice as better or worse.
- Constraints that restrict which choices are allowed.

In portfolio construction, the decision variables are portfolio weights for each asset. The objective might be to maximize expected return minus a penalty for risk, or to minimize portfolio variance for a given target return. Constraints encode budget, leverage, regulatory limits, or risk exposure caps.

In model calibration, the decision variables are model parameters: for example, volatility levels, mean-reversion speeds, or factor loadings. The objective is often a measure of misfit between model-implied prices or moments and observed data, such as the sum of squared errors between model and market option prices.

In execution scheduling, the variables are the sizes and timing of child orders. The objective might minimize a model of trading cost that includes spread, impact, and risk of price moves during execution.

In each case, once you write the objective and the constraints in terms of vectors and matrices, the problem becomes a structured numerical task. That structure is what GPU-accelerated solvers exploit.

Objectives, Gradients, and Hessians

To understand and solve optimization problems effectively, we need to talk about how objective functions change when we vary the decision variables.

Objective Functions as Landscapes

A useful mental image is to think of the objective function as a landscape over the space of decisions. Each point in this space corresponds to a specific choice of weights or parameters. The height of the landscape at that point is the value of the objective.

- In minimization problems, you want to find valleys: points where the objective is as low as possible.
- In maximization problems, you want to find peaks: points where the objective is as high as possible.

In high-dimensional problems, we cannot draw this landscape directly, but the analogy remains helpful. Gradients and Hessians tell us about the local shape of this terrain.

Gradients: Direction of Steepest Change

The gradient is a vector that points in the direction of steepest increase of the objective. If you move a small step in the opposite direction of the gradient, you move downhill most rapidly.

For portfolio optimization, the gradient of a mean-variance objective with respect to weights tells you:

- Which assets, if increased slightly, would improve the risk-return trade-off.
- Which assets, if decreased, would decrease risk more than return (or vice versa).

From a computational point of view, computing gradients usually involves matrix–vector products and vector operations:

- Multiplying a covariance matrix by the weight vector.

- Combining expected return and risk terms.

These are basic linear algebra operations that GPUs can accelerate efficiently.

Hessians: Curvature and Second-Order Information

The Hessian is a matrix that summarizes the curvature of the objective function. It tells you how the gradient changes when you move in different directions.

Intuitively:

- If curvature is gentle (small Hessian entries), the landscape is relatively flat and broad around a minimum.
- If curvature is steep in some directions (large entries), the objective changes rapidly when you move along those directions.

In quadratic objectives, such as those used in classical mean-variance portfolio optimization, the Hessian is constant and often equals a scaled covariance matrix. This is particularly convenient because we already know how to store and operate on covariances.

Second-order optimization methods, such as Newton-type algorithms, use Hessian information to choose better search directions and step sizes. This typically leads to faster convergence in terms of iterations, at the expense of heavier computations per iteration.

Local vs Global Optima and the Role of Convexity

Not every valley in the landscape is equally good. A local minimum is a point where the objective is lower than in its immediate neighborhood, but there might be an even deeper valley elsewhere. A global minimum is a point where the objective reaches its lowest possible value across all feasible decisions.

Why Local Minima Matter

In high-dimensional, nonconvex problems (for example, with complex constraints or non-linear objectives), many optimization algorithms can get stuck in local minima. Different starting points can lead to different solutions. This is a common concern in calibration problems with highly non-linear mappings from parameters to market observables.

However, not all problems are this difficult. In many important financial applications, especially those based on quadratic or linear objectives with linear constraints, the problem is convex.

Convex Functions and Sets

A problem is convex if:

- The feasible set of decisions forms a convex region, meaning that if two decisions are allowed, any weighted average of them is also allowed.
- The objective function is convex, meaning that the line segment between any two points on its graph lies above or on the function.

Convexity has a powerful consequence: any local minimum is also a global minimum. This means:

- We can safely use local gradient-based methods without worrying about missing better, distant solutions.
- We can design efficient algorithms that are guaranteed to converge to the global optimum under mild conditions.

Convex Optimization in Finance

Many canonical quant problems are convex:

- Mean-variance portfolio optimization with linear constraints (such as budget, no short-selling, or sector limits) is a quadratic program, typically convex when the covariance matrix is positive semidefinite.
- Risk-parity or minimum-variance portfolios with non-negative weights and linear budget constraints fall into the same class.
- L1-regularized regression problems used to build sparse factor models or sparse signals are convex: the objective is a sum of a squared error term and an L1 penalty on coefficients.

Because these problems are convex, we can rely on robust, scalable optimization techniques and GPU solvers to handle large universes, rich constraint sets, and batched problem instances.

Constraints: Budgets, Limits, and Real-World Structure

Real-world decisions are rarely unconstrained. Constraints encode the difference between a mathematically elegant portfolio and one you can actually trade.

Common Constraint Types

Several constraint types appear repeatedly in practice:

- **Budget constraints:** The sum of weights must equal one, or leverage must lie within certain bounds.
- **Box constraints:** Each asset's weight must lie between lower and upper bounds, reflecting limits on shorting or concentration.
- **Exposure constraints:** Net exposure to certain factors, sectors, or regions must stay within prescribed ranges.
- **Turnover constraints:** Changes in weights from one rebalancing to the next must be limited to manage transaction costs.

Mathematically, these constraints are often linear or can be expressed as simple bounds. This keeps the optimization problem in the realm of linear or quadratic programming, where powerful solvers exist.

Feasible Sets and Projections

The set of all decisions that satisfy the constraints is the feasible set. When you apply an iterative optimization algorithm, intermediate steps may land outside this set. To enforce constraints, many algorithms use projections:

- Starting from a tentative update, you project back onto the feasible set by finding the closest allowed point (according to some distance measure).

- For simple constraints like box bounds or normalization, projection is straightforward and can be applied independently across assets or portfolios.

On GPUs, projection operations are natural candidates for parallelization: each coordinate or each portfolio can be handled independently within an iteration.

Core Algorithms: Gradient Descent and Its Variants

With objectives, derivatives, and constraints defined, we turn to algorithms. Many popular methods share the same skeleton: start from an initial guess, compute a search direction, choose a step size, update the variables, and repeat.

Gradient Descent

In gradient descent, you repeatedly move in the opposite direction of the gradient, scaled by a step size:

- If the step size is too large, you may overshoot or cause instability.
- If it is too small, convergence will be slow.

Gradient descent is conceptually simple and easy to implement. Each iteration requires:

- Evaluating the objective and its gradient.
- Updating the variables by subtracting a scaled gradient.

In portfolio problems with quadratic objectives, computing the gradient amounts to multiplying the covariance matrix by the weight vector and adding or subtracting linear terms. This is a matrix–vector product plus vector additions: operations that GPUs handle very efficiently.

Projected Gradient Methods

When constraints are present, pure gradient descent may yield updates that violate them. Projected gradient methods address this by:

1. Taking a gradient step as if unconstrained.
2. Projecting the result back into the feasible set.

For example, for a long-only portfolio with a budget constraint, a projection might consist of:

- Setting any negative weights to zero.
- Renormalizing the weights to sum to one.

Both steps operate coordinate-wise or involve simple reductions (sums and rescaling), which are highly parallelizable. Thus, projected gradient methods are well suited for large-scale constrained optimization on GPUs.

Newton and Quasi-Newton Methods

Newton-type methods use second-order information to refine the search direction. Instead of following the gradient, they solve a local quadratic approximation of the objective around the current point to determine an update.

In practice:

- Newton's method can converge in fewer iterations than gradient descent, particularly for well-behaved, convex problems.
- Each iteration is more expensive, because it involves solving a linear system using the Hessian (or an approximation).

Quasi-Newton methods, such as BFGS, build approximate Hessians from gradient information without computing second derivatives explicitly. They strike a balance between gradient descent and full Newton methods.

From a GPU perspective, Newton-type methods involve heavier linear algebra per iteration:

- Systems of equations that require matrix factorizations or iterative solves.

- Repeated matrix–vector products and vector updates.

These are precisely the operations that cuBLAS and cuSOLVER accelerate. When you have many similar optimization problems (for example, calibrating a model across many assets), batched Newton or quasi-Newton methods can leverage GPUs effectively.

Coordinate Descent

Coordinate descent optimizes one variable or a small group of variables at a time, holding the others fixed, and cycles through all coordinates:

- For some problems, especially those with separable or sparse structure, each coordinate update is simple and often has a closed form.
- L1-regularized problems, such as those used to construct sparse factor portfolios or signals, often benefit from coordinate descent.

Implemented naively, coordinate descent can be sequential, as updates for one coordinate depend on the current values of others. However, in structured problems where blocks of coordinates are loosely coupled, block coordinate descent allows simultaneous updates of multiple groups, opening doors to parallelization.

On GPUs, coordinate descent is most natural when:

- You solve many independent small problems in parallel (for instance, one per asset or one per cluster).
- Within each problem, group updates can be implemented as vector operations.

Conditioning, Regularization, and Numerical Stability

Even with a well-formulated optimization problem, numerical issues can degrade performance or lead to unreliable solutions.

Conditioning and Ill-Posedness

Conditioning measures how sensitive the solution is to small changes in input data. An ill-conditioned problem is one where tiny changes in returns or covariances lead to large changes in optimal weights or parameters.

In portfolio optimization, conditioning is heavily influenced by the covariance matrix:

- Highly correlated assets can make the covariance matrix nearly singular.
- Inverting such a matrix amplifies estimation noise, leading to unstable weights.

On GPUs, ill-conditioned problems are not inherently worse in terms of performance, but they can produce numerically questionable results, especially in single precision. It is therefore essential to address conditioning at the modeling level.

Regularization Techniques

Regularization introduces additional terms or constraints that stabilize the solution and prevent overfitting. Common techniques include:

- **Ridge-type penalties:** Adding a small multiple of the identity matrix to the covariance before inversion. This shrinks weights toward more balanced allocations and improves conditioning.
- **L1 penalties:** Encouraging sparsity in weights or factor loadings, which can reduce transaction costs and improve interpretability.
- **Constraint-based regularization:** Imposing bounds on weights, exposures, or turnover to avoid extreme solutions driven by noisy inputs.

Regularization not only improves robustness but can also simplify computations by reducing effective dimensionality or imposing structure that solvers can exploit.

Batched and Large-Scale Optimization on GPUs

The most compelling gains from GPU acceleration appear when you solve many related optimization problems or a few very large ones.

Batched Optimization Problems

In practice, you often face families of similar optimization tasks:

- Rebalancing portfolios across many accounts or strategies, each with its own constraints.
- Calibrating a volatility model separately for each asset in a large universe.
- Fitting factor models for different regions, sectors, or risk horizons.

Each instance shares the same structure but has different data (returns, covariances, constraints). Batched GPU routines allow you to:

- Factorize many small covariance matrices in parallel.
- Solve many linear systems simultaneously.
- Apply gradient or Newton updates across a grid of portfolios or parameter sets in one unified call.

By aligning data in memory and structuring calls to GPU libraries, you can convert thousands of modest-size problems into a single large, efficient GPU workload.

Large-Scale Single Problems

In some cases, the problem itself is huge: a portfolio with tens of thousands of assets and many constraints, or a calibration problem with a massive parameter space and data set.

Here, the challenge is to:

- Exploit sparsity in matrices to reduce memory and computation.
- Use iterative solvers that avoid full matrix factorizations when possible.

- Organize computations into blocks or tiles that fit well into GPU memory hierarchies.

The linear algebra primitives that underlie optimization—matrix–vector products, factorizations, triangular solves—are already implemented in GPU libraries with blocking and tiling strategies. By framing your optimization algorithm around these primitives, you inherit these performance benefits without micro-managing low-level GPU details.

From Optimization Theory to GPU Practice

Optimization principles provide the decision-making layer on top of our probabilistic and numerical foundations:

- We use probability and time-series models to estimate expected returns, covariances, and volatilities.
- We organize these estimates into the matrices and vectors that define our objectives and constraints.
- We apply calculus-based optimization algorithms to find weights, parameters, or trade schedules that best meet our goals.

GPU acceleration enters when these tasks are repeated across many assets, portfolios, scenarios, or parameter sets. The same patterns of computation appear repeatedly:

- Gradient evaluations reduce to matrix–vector products and simple nonlinear operations.
- Constraint handling relies on projections and reductions across arrays.
- Second-order methods and constrained solvers rely on factorizations and solves that are at the heart of GPU linear algebra libraries.

By understanding optimization at this structural level, you can design research and production systems that offload the heaviest numerical workloads to GPUs while retaining mathematical clarity and stability. This, in turn, allows you to explore richer models, larger universes, and more nuanced constraint sets than would be practical on CPUs alone, without sacrificing rigor in how you make and justify trading and risk decisions.

1.6 Market Microstructure & Risk/Return Measures

The earlier sections of this chapter equipped us with probabilistic tools, linear algebra, numerical methods, time-series models, and optimization algorithms. We can now simulate returns, build factor models, forecast volatility, and solve portfolio optimization problems at scale, especially on GPUs. But none of this is useful if the numbers we optimize do not reflect how markets actually trade.

This final foundational section connects the math to market reality. We focus on two intertwined themes:

- **Market microstructure:** How orders become trades, and why prices, spreads, and liquidity behave the way they do.
- **Risk and return measures:** How we summarize performance and risk in terms that portfolio managers, risk committees, and clients actually care about.

Our goal is to build a clear pipeline from raw high-frequency events to the aggregated measures that drive optimization and risk decisions. Understanding this pipeline is essential when you design GPU-accelerated backtests and risk engines: it tells you what must be modeled carefully, which parts can be approximated, and where massive parallelism is both possible and meaningful.

Core Elements of Market Microstructure

At the microstructure level, markets are not smooth diffusions. They are discrete systems where individual orders arrive, interact, and form trades. The key building blocks are:

- **Order types:** Market orders, limit orders, cancellations, and more complex instructions.
- **Limit order book:** The queue of resting buy and sell limit orders at different prices.
- **Bid-ask spread:** The difference between the best available buy and sell prices.
- **Depth and liquidity:** How much volume can be traded at or near the best bid and offer.
- **Transaction costs:** Explicit fees and implicit costs such as spread and market impact.

Most trading strategies interact with this microstructure, even if their models are written at daily or longer horizons. For example, a seemingly profitable intraday strategy can be untradeable once spread, slippage, and market impact are accounted for.

From Orders to Trades

A limit order specifies a price and quantity at which you are willing to buy or sell. It sits in the order book until it is matched by an incoming order or cancelled. A market order specifies a quantity but not a price; it trades immediately against the best available limit orders on the other side of the book.

Trades occur whenever a new order crosses the spread or when two compatible limit orders meet. The result is:

- A change in positions for the participants in the trade.
- A realized transaction price and volume.
- An update to the order book, reflecting consumed or remaining liquidity.

At high frequency, this process generates a stream of order events and trade prints. Turning this stream into usable backtest and risk inputs is a data engineering and modeling problem, not just a statistical one.

From Events to Positions and P&L: A Conceptual Pipeline

When we evaluate a strategy, we rarely work directly with raw order events. Instead, we summarize them into positions, cash balances, and P&L. To anchor this discussion, it helps to visualize the conceptual pipeline from raw microstructure data to aggregated risk and return measures.

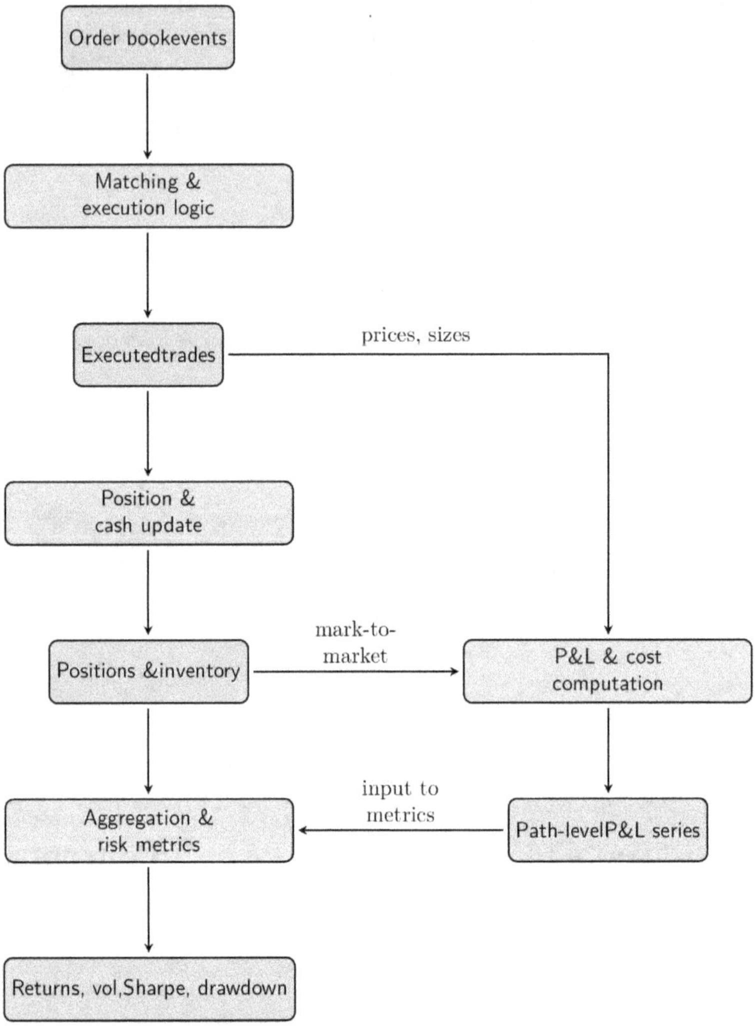

Reading this diagram from left to right:

- Raw order book events are transformed by matching and execution logic into executed trades.

- Executed trades update positions and cash, forming an inventory process.
- Positions and trades together generate a detailed P&L path once you account for prices and transaction costs.
- The P&L path and positions are then aggregated into returns, volatility, Sharpe ratios, drawdowns, and other risk/return measures.

A GPU-accelerated research platform often touches every stage of this pipeline, especially when simulating alternative execution policies or running many backtests in parallel. Getting the pipeline right conceptually ensures that speed does not come at the expense of realism.

Transaction Costs and Slippage

One of the biggest gaps between stylized models and real trading is transaction costs. When you buy and sell at midprices without friction, a strategy can look extremely profitable. Once you introduce realistic costs, performance may deteriorate sharply.

Explicit and Implicit Costs

Transaction costs come in two broad categories:

- **Explicit costs:** Commissions, fees, and taxes that are directly charged by brokers and exchanges.
- **Implicit costs:** Spread, slippage, and market impact that arise from interacting with the order book.

Spread cost is incurred when you cross the bid-ask spread with a market order: you buy at the ask and sell at the bid. Slippage refers to getting a worse price than expected, for example because your order is large relative to available depth. Market impact captures the idea that your trading activity can move the price, especially in less liquid markets.

Modeling Costs in Backtests

To make GPU-accelerated backtests realistic, you must embed a cost model in the event-to-P&L pipeline:

- If you backtest at the bar level (for example, using minute bars), you may use simple rules: a fixed fraction of the spread, or a cost proportional to volatility and traded volume.
- If you backtest at higher frequency with simulated order books, you can model execution more precisely: which queue positions your limit orders get, how partial fills arrive, and how your market orders walk the book.

The more detailed the cost model, the more computationally intensive the backtest, and the more it benefits from GPU acceleration, especially when you simulate many scenarios or strategies in parallel.

From Prices to Returns

Once trades and costs are mapped into positions and cash, the next step is to define returns. In practice, several notions coexist, and each has its uses.

Simple vs Log Returns

A *simple return* over a period is the percentage change in value. A *log return* is the logarithm of the ratio of ending value to starting value.

Log returns have two attractive properties:

- They add across time: the log return over multiple periods is the sum of the log returns of each subperiod.
- For small moves, log and simple returns are numerically close, but log returns are more convenient in some statistical models.

In a GPU-accelerated pipeline, returns are typically computed as vectorized operations across time and assets: each thread or block can handle a segment of the time series or a subset of instruments.

Cumulative Returns and Equity Curves

Cumulative return over a horizon is the total growth of capital, often visualized as an equity curve. To obtain it, you compound period-by-period returns along the P&L path.

Cumulative returns can be computed for:

- A single strategy or portfolio.
- Many strategies, parameter variations, or Monte Carlo scenarios, in parallel.

The latter case is where GPUs shine: computing equity curves for thousands of backtest variants can be done as a collection of independent prefix products or cumulative sums.

Risk and Performance Measures

Risk and return measures summarize the rich, path-dependent information in positions and P&L into a set of numbers that are easier to compare, optimize, and communicate.

Volatility

Volatility is the standard deviation of returns over a chosen horizon. From earlier sections, we know it is directly linked to variance, one of the central moments of the return distribution.

In a backtest or risk engine, volatility can be:

- Estimated from historical returns using rolling windows or exponential weighting.
- Forecast from time-series models such as GARCH.
- Aggregated across assets using covariance matrices in a factor framework.

Each of these estimators and forecasts can be computed in parallel across assets, portfolios, or scenarios, making them natural GPU workloads.

Sharpe and Sortino Ratios

The Sharpe ratio measures mean excess return per unit of volatility. It answers the question: how much return do we earn for each unit of risk, where risk is proxied by standard deviation?

The Sortino ratio refines this idea by penalizing only downside volatility. It measures mean excess return relative to the standard deviation of negative returns, focusing on harmful risk.

From a computational standpoint, evaluating these ratios requires:

- Averages of returns (means).
- Measures of variability (standard deviations), with or without conditioning on sign.

These are simple reductions over arrays of returns and can be performed for many strategies or scenarios in parallel on a GPU.

Drawdowns

Drawdown measures the peak-to-trough decline in an equity curve. Maximum drawdown over a period is especially salient: it quantifies the worst percentage loss an investor would have experienced if they had entered at the worst possible time within the sample.

Drawdown is path-dependent, not fully captured by volatility. Two strategies might have similar volatility but very different drawdown profiles.

Calculating drawdowns involves:

- Tracking running maxima of cumulative returns or equity values.
- Measuring the difference between current value and the running maximum.

This too is a sequential operation along time for each equity curve, but parallel across strategies, parameter sets, or Monte Carlo paths. GPUs can exploit this cross-sectional parallelism effectively.

Turnover and Capacity

Turnover is the rate at which a portfolio's holdings change over time. High turnover implies more trading, higher transaction costs, and potentially limited capacity, because scaling up the strategy could overwhelm market liquidity.

Turnover is typically computed as the sum of absolute changes in weights or positions over a rebalance interval, normalized by portfolio size. Capacity analysis then combines turnover with microstructure estimates of market depth and impact.

These computations require:

- Differences of position vectors across time.
- Aggregation of absolute changes.

Again, they are linear algebra and reduction operations across many assets and periods, well suited to GPU acceleration.

Hit Rates and Other Diagnostics

Hit rate is the fraction of periods with positive returns. It captures the frequency of gains, but not their magnitude. A strategy with modest hit rate but large wins when it is right can still be attractive.

Other diagnostics include skewness, kurtosis, and tail quantiles of the return distribution. Many of these are computed by sorting or scanning arrays of returns, tasks that GPU libraries also support efficiently.

Risk Decomposition and Horizon Dependence

Portfolio risk is not monolithic. Decomposing it into components and understanding how it scales with horizon are central to robust risk management.

Factor vs Idiosyncratic Risk

Factor models, introduced earlier in the chapter, separate return variation into:

- Systematic components driven by broad factors such as market, sectors, styles.
- Idiosyncratic components specific to each asset or strategy.

Risk decomposition uses the covariance structure of factor returns and idiosyncratic terms to attribute total portfolio variance to each source. This tells you how much of your risk comes from, say, market beta versus sector tilts, and how much is stock-specific.

In GPU-accelerated systems, factor-based risk decomposition involves repeated matrix–vector and matrix–matrix operations across portfolios or scenarios, aligning neatly with GPU linear algebra routines.

Risk Scaling Across Horizons

Risk and return measures depend on the time horizon:

- Volatility typically scales with the square root of time when returns are independent, but this breaks down with autocorrelation or volatility clustering.
- Sharpe ratios and drawdowns look very different at daily, weekly, monthly, or intraday horizons.

Accurately scaling risk across horizons requires time-series models and simulations that reflect observed dependencies. GPUs are particularly useful here:

- Simulating many long paths to study multi-horizon risk.
- Aggregating returns over different block sizes to estimate horizon-specific volatility and drawdown distributions.

By combining microstructure-aware models at short horizons with appropriate aggregation and simulation, you can produce risk measures that remain consistent across the time scales that matter to your stakeholders.

Parallelism Along the Pipeline

At every stage of the microstructure-to-metrics pipeline, there are opportunities for GPU acceleration:

- **Event processing:** Parsing and basic filtering of large streams of order events can be parallelized across instruments, time buckets, or simulation scenarios.

- **Execution simulation:** When evaluating many strategies or parameter settings, you can simulate order matching and fills in parallel for each variant or Monte Carlo path.
- **Position and P&L updates:** Position updates and mark-to-market calculations are vector operations that can be carried out across many portfolios or scenarios simultaneously.
- **Metric evaluation:** Returns, volatilities, Sharpe ratios, drawdowns, and risk decompositions can all be evaluated in batched form, calling into GPU-optimized reduction and linear algebra routines.

At the same time, certain aspects remain sequential along time within each path, such as tracking queue positions in a limit order book or computing running maxima for drawdowns. For these, parallelism must be exploited across paths, not within a single path.

A well-designed GPU-accelerated research platform therefore:

- Treats the entire pipeline from events to metrics as a first-class object, not just the mid-steps like covariance estimation or optimization.
- Identifies and exploits cross-sectional and scenario-based parallelism wherever possible.
- Keeps microstructure realism in view, ensuring that the risk/return measures it ultimately optimizes are grounded in how markets trade, not just in how models behave.

Closing the Loop: From Metrics Back to Models and Optimization

Risk and return measures are not the end of the story. They feed back into model design and optimization:

- If a backtest shows attractive mean returns but poor Sharpe or deep drawdowns under realistic costs, the strategy may need rethinking.

- If risk is dominated by a small set of factors, you may impose new constraints or revise your factor model.
- If turnover and impact erode performance, you may adjust execution rules, holding periods, or universe selection.

In this way, the microstructure-aware metrics you compute become targets and constraints in the optimization problems discussed earlier. Those optimizations, in turn, rely on the probabilistic, linear algebra, numerical, and time-series foundations laid in prior sections.

Bringing these elements together on modern GPU hardware allows you to explore richer strategies, more detailed cost models, and more realistic risk scenarios without sacrificing timeliness. The result is not just faster backtests, but better-informed trading and risk decisions rooted in both market mechanics and solid quantitative reasoning.

Chapter 2

Research & Backtesting Methodology

Most backtests lie-some subtly, some spectacularly. This chapter shows you how to make yours tell the truth. We'll design a research workflow that can survive compliance, rereading your results a year later, and porting the same idea from a laptop prototype to a GPU farm-without changing the answer. You'll learn how to slice time without look-ahead, translate elegant signals into messy execution, and measure performance in a way that makes CPU and GPU implementations directly comparable.

2.1 Research Workflow & Hypothesis Design

GPU acceleration changes the tempo of quantitative research. What once took hours now runs in minutes, and full parameter sweeps that were previously unrealistic become routine. This is a gift and a risk. With more compute, you can explore the space of ideas more thoroughly; but you can also overfit faster, bury mistakes under layers of complexity, and lose track of what was actually tested. In this section we build a disciplined, audit-ready research workflow that moves from a loose idea to a precise, falsifiable trading hypothesis, and then into a sequence of experiments that can be reproduced on both CPU and GPU pipelines.

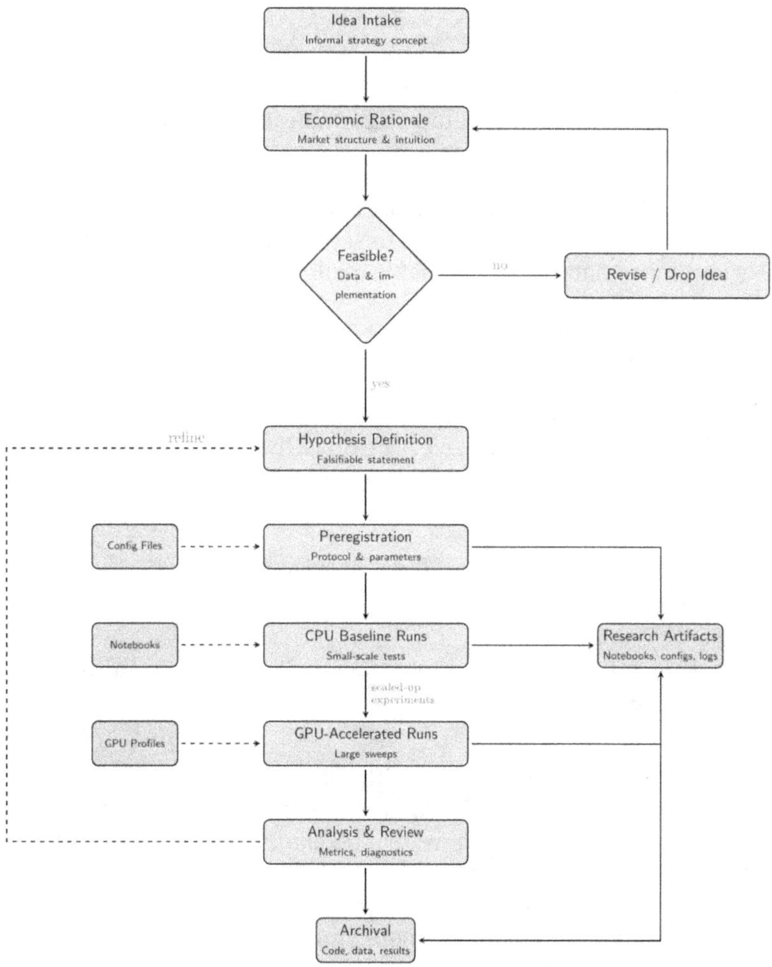

From Loose Idea to Falsifiable Hypothesis

Most research efforts start with an intuition: "momentum works in mid-cap tech," "small caps overreact to earnings surprises," or "option order flow anticipates volatility spikes." Intuitions are useful, but they are also vague. To turn them into something that can be tested, reproduced, and audited, we need to reshape them into clear hypotheses.

A useful mental checklist for this transformation is:

- **Define the economic story.** What behavior or friction in markets could make this profitable? Are you exploiting investor biases, structural constraints, information delays, or risk compensation?
- **Specify what is observable.** Which signals, prices, or fundamental variables stand in for the economic idea? Can you actually get those data with reasonable quality?
- **Fix the unit of decision.** Are you making daily stock picks, intraday futures trades, monthly allocation shifts, or something else?
- **State a directional prediction.** Given your inputs, what do you expect to happen to returns or risk, in which direction, and over what horizon?
- **Make it falsifiable.** Under what conditions would you say, "this idea did not work"?

Suppose the initial idea is: "momentum works in mid-cap tech stocks." A falsifiable version might be:

> In U.S. technology stocks with market capitalizations between 2 and 10 billion dollars, selecting the top 20% of stocks by 6-month past return (excluding the most recent month) and holding them for 1 month will, after realistic costs, deliver a higher risk-adjusted return than an equal-weighted portfolio of all eligible mid-cap tech stocks, over the period 2010–2024.

This statement is not perfect, but it already has:

- **Scope:** U.S. tech, mid-cap, specified years.
- **Signal definition:** 6-month past return with a 1-month skip.
- **Decision frequency:** Monthly rebalancing.
- **Benchmark:** Equal-weighted universe portfolio.
- **Outcome measure:** Risk-adjusted return (for example, Sharpe ratio) after costs.

If, after proper testing, the strategy fails to beat the benchmark on the chosen metric, the hypothesis is rejected. You may still choose to revise and try again, but you do so knowing that the original claim did not hold under scrutiny.

Why GPUs Raise the Bar for Methodology

On a CPU, running 50 variations of this strategy might already feel ambitious. On a GPU, running 5,000 variations—different lookback windows, holding periods, universes, cost assumptions—becomes normal. This power is only valuable if you can answer basic questions afterwards:

- Which variations were planned in advance, and which were added as you went along?
- How many total variations did you test before picking the "winner"?
- Did CPU and GPU implementations actually test the same thing, just faster, or did subtle differences in data handling creep in?

If you cannot answer these, then your impressive GPU speedup is a mirage. The workflow we build next is designed to keep these questions answerable.

Designing the Research Workflow

The workflow in the diagram can be thought of as a loop with several gates. Each gate forces you to write something down, make a decision, and leave a trace that auditors (including your future self) can follow.

We will walk through the key stages:

1. Idea intake and economic rationale.
2. Feasibility and scoping.
3. Formal hypothesis definition.
4. Preregistration of the research plan.
5. Creation of research artifacts.
6. CPU baseline experiments.
7. GPU-accelerated experiments.
8. Analysis, review, and archival.

Idea Intake and Economic Rationale

Research ideas come from many places: academic papers, practitioner blogs, market events, or simple pattern spotting. At this stage, it is enough to record the idea in a short, human-readable form:

- The informal description.
- The supposed source of edge (for example, "slow reaction to earnings surprises").
- The approximate trading frequency and instruments.

The next step is to articulate the *economic rationale*. This is more than a slogan. Ask:

- Who is on the other side of these trades?

- Why would they systematically misprice this risk or information?
- What prevents them from arbitraging it away?

If you cannot answer these questions, the idea may still be worth exploring, but you should label it as highly exploratory and treat any positive results with extra skepticism.

Feasibility and Scoping

Before turning an idea into a full hypothesis, you must check feasibility:

- **Data availability:** Do you have the necessary prices, volumes, corporate actions, and other features for a long enough period?
- **Data quality:** Are survivorship biases, stale quotes, or missing records likely to distort results?
- **Implementation complexity:** Does the idea require modeling limit order books, complex options structures, or other features that your current backtest engine cannot yet handle?
- **Compute implications:** Roughly how many assets, time points, and parameter combinations do you expect to test?

This is a decision point in the workflow. If feasibility fails, you either revise the idea (narrow the universe, simplify the signal, adjust horizons) or drop it. Systematically recording dropped ideas is valuable; it prevents you from revisiting the same infeasible concept later without remembering why you abandoned it.

Formal Hypothesis Definition

Once an idea passes the feasibility gate, you convert it into a formal hypothesis. A simple internal template might include:

- **Title:** A concise name that conveys the core concept.
- **Universe:** Instruments, markets, and inclusion rules.

- **Signal:** How inputs are combined into trading decisions.
- **Trading rules:** Rebalancing frequency, position sizing, risk limits.
- **Cost model:** Slippage, fees, and other frictions to be used.
- **Time period:** Historical span for development and testing.
- **Primary metric:** The main success criterion (for example, annualized Sharpe ratio).
- **Secondary metrics:** Drawdowns, turnover, capacity, and so on.
- **Rejection criteria:** Thresholds that define failure.

The important feature is that these elements are written down *before* you see the final out-of-sample performance. This is where preregistration enters.

Preregistration for Quant Research

Preregistration means documenting your research plan in advance. In medicine and social sciences, this is done to limit p-hacking and selective reporting. The same logic applies to trading strategies, especially under GPU acceleration.

You do not necessarily need a public registry, but you *do* need an internal one. A lightweight preregistration record should include:

- The hypothesis template described above.
- The planned data splits: which period is for training or calibration, which for validation, and which for final testing.
- The parameter ranges you will explore (for example, lookback windows from 1 to 12 months).
- The number of variations you expect to run, at least roughly.

- The decisions you commit to in advance: for example, "If the validation Sharpe exceeds 0.8 and the maximum drawdown is less than 25%, we will proceed to test; otherwise we will not."

The goal is not to forbid exploratory work. You will still discover new twists and follow up on surprising patterns. Preregistration simply creates a clear line between:

- **Confirmatory tests:** Those that were planned in advance and can support strong claims about performance.
- **Exploratory tests:** Those that were added afterwards and require more cautious interpretation.

This distinction becomes particularly important when many parameter combinations are tried on the GPU. If your "best" strategy was chosen after trying thousands of combinations, its impressive backtest may be mostly luck unless you validate it properly on truly untouched data.

The Research Artifact Stack

A good hypothesis and a preregistration document are necessary but not sufficient. You also need a consistent way to store and link all the ingredients of a study: data, code, configurations, and results. This is your *research artifact stack*.

At minimum, this stack should contain:

- **Version-controlled notebooks:** These hold the narrative of your experiments—data inspections, sanity checks, and summary tables. They should not hard-code critical parameters.
- **Configuration files:** These separate logic from parameters. For example, a configuration file might specify the universe definition, date ranges, signal parameters, and cost settings. Both CPU and GPU backtest pipelines should read from the same configuration formats.
- **Experiment logs:** Each experiment run should produce a machine-readable record capturing:

- The configuration used.
- The code version (for example, a commit hash).
- The data version or snapshot identifier.
- The hardware profile: CPU type, GPU model, driver and library versions.
- The random seeds or other stochastic settings.

- **Results bundles:** For each experiment, store key outputs together: equity curves, daily or intraday PnL, risk metrics, and any diagnostics.

The central principle is that, given an experiment identifier from your log, another researcher should be able to reconstruct everything needed to reproduce the run, regardless of whether it was executed on CPU or GPU.

CPU Baseline Before GPU Scaling

Even in a GPU-centric environment, it is wise to start with a CPU baseline. There are several reasons:

- **Debuggability:** CPU implementations are often easier to step through and inspect.
- **Numerical consistency:** Differences in precision and parallel execution order can cause small discrepancies between CPU and GPU results. Establishing a baseline helps you understand and control these.
- **Sanity checks:** You can start with a small universe and short time window where everything is easy to reason about.

In practice, the workflow looks like this:

1. Take the preregistered configuration and fix a relatively small set of parameter combinations for a pilot run.

2. Run these on the CPU engine, using the same data and cost models that the GPU engine will use later.
3. Inspect signals, positions, trades, and PnL line by line for a few sample assets and dates. Confirm that they match your expectations.
4. Verify that your metrics and logging behave as intended.

Only after this baseline is stable do you scale up to the GPU, increasing the number of assets, the historical length, and the breadth of the parameter grid.

GPU-Accelerated Experimentation with Guardrails

When you move to GPU-accelerated experimentation, the temptation is to "turn all the knobs"—to explore every combination of lookback window, threshold, and stop-loss rule. You should certainly take advantage of the hardware, but within a controlled framework.

A disciplined approach includes:

- **Parameter schemas:** Define parameter spaces in a structured way and link them back to the preregistration document. Distinguish between the core grid (planned) and any extensions (exploratory).
- **Batching and identifiers:** Group related experiments into named batches. Each batch corresponds to a separate entry in your experiment log.
- **Resource budgeting:** Decide in advance how much GPU time you are willing to allocate to this hypothesis. If results are weak, avoid endlessly expanding the search just because you can.
- **Consistency checks:** Periodically select a sample of GPU runs and rerun them on the CPU with identical settings. Compare outputs to ensure the two paths remain aligned within acceptable tolerances.

The goal is not to limit exploration artificially, but to make exploration legible. You should be able to answer, months later, exactly what was tested and where the "best" configuration came from.

Analysis, Review, and Decision Making

Once experiments are complete, the workflow moves to analysis and review. At this stage, the temptation is to focus on headline metrics—Sharpe ratios, annualized returns, maximum drawdowns. Those are important, but within a disciplined workflow they are embedded in a broader set of questions:

- **Are the results consistent across data splits?** A strategy that performs well in one regime and fails badly in another may still be useful, but only if you understand why.
- **Are the results robust to reasonable changes in parameters and cost assumptions?** GPU sweeps are particularly useful here; they can show whether performance is concentrated in a narrow, suspiciously specific region of parameter space.
- **Do CPU and GPU paths agree?** Any systematic discrepancy needs investigation before you can trust the GPU results.
- **Do the trades and exposures make sense given the economic rationale?** If your "value" strategy behaves like a momentum strategy in factor attribution, something is off.

Decisions at this stage should be recorded along with justifications:

- Proceed to further development or paper trading.
- Revise the hypothesis and preregister a new version.
- Archive as a negative result and move on.

Negative results are not failures; they are the price of honest research. Properly logged, they prevent you from circling back to the same unproductive ideas and overestimating your true hit rate.

Archival and Audit Readiness

The final stage in the workflow is archival. For each hypothesis and its associated experiments, you should preserve:

- The original preregistration record and any subsequent amendments.
- All configurations used, including those that produced poor results.
- The code versions and hardware profiles.
- The key outputs: performance summaries, diagnostic plots, and any notes from review meetings.

This archival layer serves several purposes:

- **Internal audit:** Risk managers and senior researchers can review the path from idea to decision, checking for process violations.
- **Knowledge reuse:** Future projects can learn from past experiments—both successes and failures—without repeating work.
- **Regulatory defense:** For institutions subject to external oversight, a clear record of how trading models were developed and tested can be crucial.

Because CPU and GPU runs share the same configuration formats, data definitions, and logging conventions, your archival store becomes hardware-agnostic: it captures *what* was tested, not just *where* it ran.

A Lightweight Checklist for Everyday Use

To make this workflow practical, condense it into a checklist that every new strategy must pass before you burn serious compute:

1. **Idea recorded** with economic rationale and basic scope.

2. **Feasibility assessed** for data, implementation, and compute.
3. **Hypothesis written** in a falsifiable form with clear metrics.
4. **Preregistration completed** including parameter ranges and data splits.
5. **Artifacts set up:** version-controlled notebooks, configuration files, and logging templates.
6. **CPU baseline run** completed and validated.
7. **GPU experiments planned and executed** with clear batch identifiers and resource limits.
8. **Results analyzed** with attention to robustness, consistency, and economic sense.
9. **Decision recorded** and all materials archived.

This checklist is not bureaucratic overhead; it is a protective layer between you and the seductive power of modern hardware. GPUs will happily accelerate any computation you feed them. The workflow you design now ensures that what you accelerate is worth computing, and that the knowledge you generate can stand up to scrutiny, both from colleagues today and from your future self months or years from now.

2.2 Temporal Data Splitting & Walk-Forward Validation

In the previous section we built a disciplined, hypothesis-driven research workflow and insisted on preregistration, shared configurations, and experiment logs for both CPU and GPU runs. That framework ensures we know *what* we are testing. We now turn to an equally important question: *how* we test, given that financial data arrive over time and exhibit dependence, regime shifts, and delays.

Many standard machine learning tools assume that data points are independent and identically distributed. They also assume we are free to shuffle observations when we create training and test sets. In markets, these assumptions fail. Returns are serially correlated, volatility clusters, and information released at one time can affect prices later. If we ignore this and treat time like a deck of cards to be shuffled, we introduce look-ahead bias and label leakage. Our models then perform unrealistically well in backtests and disappoint in production.

This section introduces three time-aware validation schemes designed for financial data:

- Temporal train/validation/test splits that respect chronology.
- Purged K-fold cross-validation with embargo periods.
- Walk-forward (rolling) validation that mimics live deployment.

We will also emphasize a practical theme: all of these schemes should be implemented in a way that both CPU and GPU backtests consume the *same* split definitions. You want differences in performance to reflect models and ideas, not accidental differences in data slicing.

Why Random Splits Fail in Markets

In a typical machine learning course, you might randomly split your dataset into 70% training, 15% validation, and 15% test. This is fine for many problems where each row is an independent observation. In finance, this approach breaks down for at least three reasons.

1. Time dependence. Returns today are related to returns yesterday and tomorrow. Volatility regimes can last weeks or months. If you randomly interleave past and future observations, information from the future will leak into the training set that is supposed to represent only the past.

2. Overlapping labels. Many financial labels, such as returns over the next day, week, or month, overlap in time. For example, if you define a two-day return label from day 1 to day 3, and another from day 2 to day 4, the labels share a day. If these overlapping labels end up in both training and validation sets, the model effectively sees most of the validation information during training.

3. Regime shifts. Market behavior in one period can differ sharply from another (for example, pre- and post-crisis, calm versus stressed conditions). A random split that blends all periods together will hide these differences. Your model might look great on average but fail in the regimes that matter most to you.

Naive random splitting, especially when accelerated on a GPU and scaled to many assets and labels, can silently produce overly optimistic performance. To avoid this, we need validation schemes that respect the order of time.

Basic Temporal Splits

The simplest time-aware approach is to split the historical period into contiguous blocks:

- A **training period** where you calibrate model parameters or tune strategy rules.
- A **validation period** where you compare variations and select hyperparameters.
- A **test period** that you leave untouched until the very end as a final check.

All training data occur *before* validation data, which all occur *before* test data. You never train on data that come after what you are trying to predict.

Even this simple scheme requires choices:

- How long should each period be?
- Do you want a single validation and test period, or multiple?
- Should the split boundaries align with business cycles (for example, pre- and post-regulation, bull and bear markets)?

For a low-frequency allocator that trades monthly and cares about behavior across decades, it may be reasonable to use multi-year blocks.

For a high-frequency strategy, you might choose shorter blocks aligned with important microstructure changes or technology upgrades at exchanges.

Temporal splits are a starting point, but they do not yet address overlapping labels or the desire to use the data more efficiently. That is where purged K-fold and embargo enter.

Purged K-Fold Cross-Validation for Time Series

In standard K-fold cross-validation, you split your dataset into K parts (folds), train on $K - 1$ parts, and validate on the remaining part, rotating through all possibilities. This uses the data more efficiently than a single train/validation split and provides a sense of variability across folds.

For financial time series, we can adapt this idea, but we must preserve the temporal order and remove overlaps between training and validation labels. The usual adaptation is called *purged K-fold cross-validation.*

The process, in conceptual terms, is:

1. Divide your time axis into K contiguous blocks (folds), ordered in time.
2. To create fold i:
    - Use some blocks as training data and one block as validation, ensuring that you never train on data that occur after the validation period.
    - Remove ("purge") any training samples whose labels overlap in time with the validation period.

Purge means: if a label for a training sample extends into the validation window, you drop that training sample, even if its time index falls outside the strict validation dates. This prevents near-duplicate information from appearing in both sets due to label overlap.

For example, suppose each label is a five-day return. If your validation period spans trading days 100 to 120, then any training sample whose label interval touches days 100 to 120 should be removed from the training set for that fold. Without this step, the model could effectively see future price moves during training that are supposed to be reserved for validation.

Purged K-fold has several advantages:

- It uses most of the data for training across different folds.
- It gives you a distribution of performance metrics across different time segments rather than a single point estimate.
- It reduces the optimism caused by overlapping labels.

It also has costs: some samples are discarded from training in each fold due to purging, especially when labels span long horizons. The next enhancement, embargo, addresses another subtle source of leakage.

Embargo Periods to Prevent Information Bleed

Even if labels do not strictly overlap, information can often bleed across fold boundaries. This is common when:

- There are delayed price reactions to news or events.
- Corporate actions (splits, dividends, mergers) affect prices over a window of time.
- Your labeling scheme uses events (for example, earnings announcements) whose effects persist.

To protect against this, we can add an *embargo* period around the validation window. The idea is simple: for each validation block, you exclude training samples whose labels are too close in time to the validation dates, even if they do not strictly overlap.

You can think of the embargo as a safety buffer. For instance:

- Suppose your validation block is days 100 to 120.
- You choose an embargo of five days.

- Then you drop from the training set any samples whose labels end within five days before the start of the validation period or begin within five days after its end.

This reduces the chance that the model inadvertently "sees" patterns that are essentially the same as those in the validation window. The exact length of the embargo depends on your label construction and the typical duration of event effects.

In combination, purged K-fold with embargo gives you a much more realistic estimate of how well a strategy might generalize to unseen periods. This is especially important when using GPUs to run many folds and many parameter combinations; you do not want speed to multiply the effect of subtle leaks.

Walk-Forward Validation: Mimicking Live Deployment

Purged K-fold is primarily a statistical tool for assessing generalization across time segments. Walk-forward validation focuses more directly on mimicking how a strategy would operate in production. The idea is to repeatedly:

1. Train or calibrate the model on a historical window.
2. Move the window forward in time.
3. Re-train and test on the next period, always using strictly past data.

There are two common versions:

- **Expanding window:** The training set starts at a fixed point and grows over time as new data arrive. For example, you might train on 2010–2014, then 2010–2015, and so on.
- **Rolling window:** The training set has a fixed length and slides forward. For example, always the last three years of data are used for training, then tested on the following month or quarter.

Walk-forward validation is particularly helpful when:

- You expect regime changes and want the model to focus on more recent data.
- Your strategy will be periodically re-estimated in live trading.
- You care about the time profile of performance: how the strategy would have evolved if you had been running it in real time.

In practice, a walk-forward test produces a sequence of pseudo-live returns: at each step, you simulate how the model would have traded using only information available up to that date. When concatenated, these returns give an equity curve that resembles a real deployment, with the advantage that you can analyze its behavior across different environments.

Precomputing Temporal Partitions for CPU and GPU

To make temporal splitting practical at scale, especially when using GPUs, you should avoid ad-hoc, scattered logic in your backtest code. Instead, precompute and store the indices that define:

- Train, validation, and test blocks for basic temporal splits.
- Fold assignments and purged training sets for purged K-fold with embargo.
- Training and testing windows for each step of walk-forward validation.

These partitions can then be passed into both CPU and GPU pipelines as part of the configuration or as separate index arrays. This approach has several benefits:

- **Consistency:** Every implementation uses the same time splits, so performance is comparable.

- **Reproducibility:** You can store these partitions alongside experiment logs, making it clear exactly how data were divided.
- **Efficiency:** GPUs can operate on pre-defined subsets of data without needing to make complicated time-based decisions inside performance-critical kernels.

In your research artifact stack, it is helpful to assign identifiers to particular split schemes (for example, "TS_SPLIT_V1", "PKFOLD_K5_EMBARGO2D", "WF_ROLLING_36M_STEP1M") and log which scheme each experiment used.

Choosing Between Schemes

Which validation scheme should you use? There is no one-size-fits-all answer, but a few guidelines help:

Sample size and frequency.

- For daily or lower-frequency strategies with moderate data volume, purged K-fold with embargo can provide a good balance between efficient use of data and robustness.
- For very high-frequency strategies with vast amounts of data, you may rely more on walk-forward validation over shorter windows, as you can afford to reserve entire days or weeks for testing without sacrificing sample size.

Turnover and horizon.

- If your strategy holds positions for long periods (weeks or months), labels will overlap more, making purged K-fold and carefully chosen embargo periods more critical.
- If your strategy trades intraday with short holding periods, overlap may be less of a concern, but microstructure changes and venue behavior across time become more important.

Business questions.

- If the main question is "Does this strategy work across different historical regimes?", purged K-fold with folds aligned to known regimes can be informative.
- If the main question is "How would this strategy have behaved if we had been running it live?", walk-forward validation, especially with an expanding or rolling window, is the more natural choice.

In practice, mature research pipelines often use a combination: for early idea screening, basic temporal splits or a few walk-forward steps; for more serious assessment, purged K-fold with embargo; and prior to deployment, a detailed walk-forward analysis.

Visualizing Time-Aware Validation Schemes

To make these concepts concrete, it helps to see how different schemes slice a common time axis. The following diagram contrasts naive random splits with temporal splits, purged K-fold with embargo, and a rolling walk-forward window.

Logging Split Logic as Part of the Research Stack

In the previous section we stressed the importance of experiment logs that tie together data versions, code commits, and hardware profiles. Temporal splitting logic belongs in the same audit trail. For each experiment or batch of experiments, you should record:

- Which splitting scheme was used (for example, temporal split, purged K-fold with specified K and embargo length, walk-forward with defined window and step).
- The exact date ranges in each train, validation, and test block.
- Any purged or embargoed intervals, ideally as explicit date ranges.
- The identifier of the partition set or index file used by both CPU and GPU backtests.

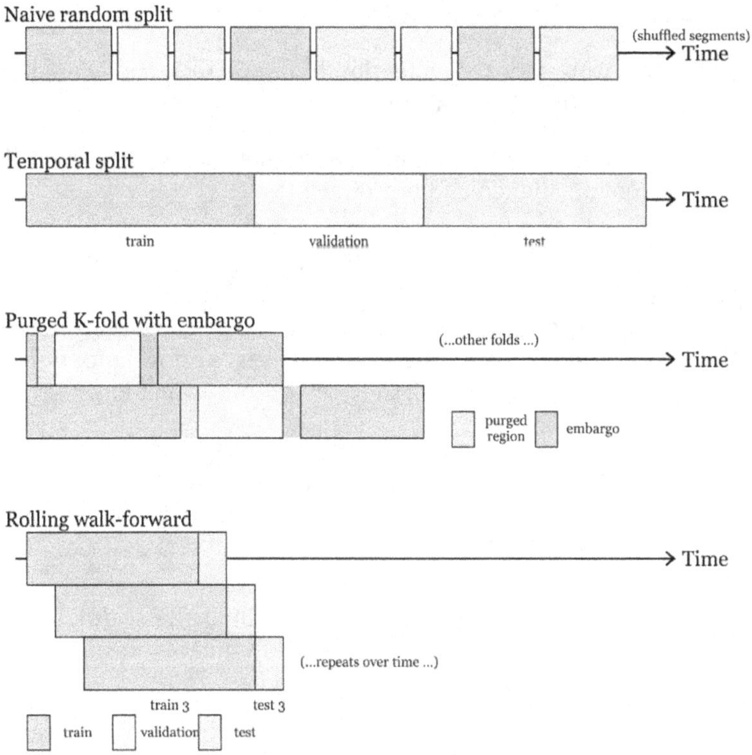

This information can be stored in configuration files and in the experiment log. It ensures that anyone revisiting the results can understand the context: not just that a strategy achieved a certain Sharpe ratio, but under which temporal assumptions and validation scheme.

Time-aware validation is one of the main defenses against overfitting in quantitative finance. When combined with the hypothesis-driven workflow and artifact stack introduced earlier, it forms the backbone of a research culture in which GPUs are used wisely. Instead of shuffling time and letting speed amplify hidden leakage, you:

- Respect chronology with basic temporal splits.

- Use purged K-fold with embargo to handle overlapping labels and information bleed.
- Employ walk-forward validation to mimic real deployment and study behavior over evolving regimes.
- Precompute and log temporal partitions so that CPU and GPU runs remain aligned and reproducible.

In the next section we will build on this foundation to design realistic backtests that translate signals into trades, including slippage, transaction costs, and corporate actions. These backtests will rely directly on the temporal splits defined here, so that every performance number you see is grounded in a careful, time-respecting evaluation.

2.3 Backtest Design, Slippage & Transaction Costs

In the first two sections of this chapter we built the scaffolding for sound research: a hypothesis-driven workflow and time-aware validation schemes that avoid look-ahead and leakage. You now know *what* you are testing and *how* to slice time correctly on both CPU and GPU. In this section we move one level closer to reality: turning abstract trading signals into a simulated trading book with orders, executions, and profit-and-loss (PnL) paths that you can trust.

A backtest is not just a function that takes in signals and outputs an equity curve. It is an engine with several layers, each of which can be modeled more or less realistically:

1. Signal generation.
2. Portfolio construction (desired positions).
3. Order creation (what you ask the market to do).
4. Execution simulation (what the market *actually* does for you).
5. Portfolio accounting (how positions, cash, and PnL evolve).

GPU acceleration tends to live in the numerically heavy parts of this stack: running thousands of signal variations, portfolio optimizations, or execution scenarios in parallel. But if the surrounding backtest engine is naive, faster computation simply produces misleading results more quickly. Our goal here is to design an engine that is both realistic enough to avoid major pitfalls and structured enough to be implemented consistently on CPU and GPU.

From Signals to Positions: The Logical Flow

It is helpful to think of a backtest as a pipeline of transformations:

- **Signals** are model outputs: for example, an expected return, a ranking score, or a probability of upward move for each asset and time.
- **Portfolio construction** turns signals into target positions. This might be as simple as "go long the top 50 names and short the bottom 50" or as complex as solving an optimization with risk and turnover constraints.
- **Order creation** compares current positions to targets and generates orders: buy 5,000 shares of A, sell 2 futures contracts on B, and so on.
- **Execution simulation** models how those orders interact with market prices and liquidity. This is where slippage and market impact enter.
- **Portfolio accounting** updates cash, positions, and realized/unrealized PnL, including transaction costs and corporate actions.

For GPU acceleration, you want each transformation to be clearly defined and parameterized. That way, you can easily run many versions in parallel by changing parameters, rather than rewriting logic.

Research-Grade vs Production-Grade Backtests

Not every idea requires the same level of realism. It is useful to distinguish between:

Research-grade approximations.

These are simplified models you use early in the research funnel to decide if an idea has any promise. For example:

- Assuming you can trade at the midpoint between bid and ask.
- Applying a simple, fixed fee per trade.
- Ignoring partial fills and intraday price paths.

These approximations are often easy to vectorize and therefore easy to accelerate on a GPU. They are useful, but they can be dangerously optimistic if used as the sole basis for investment decisions.

Production-grade realism.

As you move closer to deployment, you need to capture more features of real trading:

- Limited liquidity and its effect on achievable size.
- The spread between bid and ask prices.
- Order types (market, limit, participation).
- Latency and the fact that the market moves while you are trading.
- Corporate actions and changes in tradable universe.

Some of these elements are harder to simulate at scale and may not map cleanly onto simple vectorized GPU kernels. You therefore want an engine that can support both: a research mode that is fast and approximate, and a production mode that is slower but much more realistic. Crucially, both modes should share as much logic and data handling as possible so that differences in results are attributable to modeling choices rather than implementation drift.

Modeling Slippage: How Prices Move Against You

Slippage is the difference between the price you *intend* to trade at and the price you *actually* receive. It can arise from:

- The bid-ask spread.
- Market impact from your own trading.
- Market moves between the time you decide to trade and the time it executes.

There are several practical ways to model slippage in a backtest, each with its own trade-offs.

Fixed basis point slippage.

You assume that every trade suffers a constant penalty, such as 5 basis points (0.05%) of the traded notional. This is simple and easy to apply:

- **Advantages:** Very easy to implement and scale; just subtract a fixed cost from each trade.
- **Limitations:** Ignores liquidity differences across assets and time; does not distinguish between trading inside the spread and across the spread.

This model is often acceptable for early research on liquid instruments, but it should be refined later.

Spread-based slippage.

Here you explicitly model the bid and ask:

- Buying at or near the ask price.
- Selling at or near the bid price.

If you only have mid-quote or last-trade data, you can approximate the spread as a function of volatility, price level, or liquidity bucket. This approach ties slippage more directly to observable market features:

- **Advantages:** Captures the basic cost of crossing the spread; allows differentiation across assets.
- **Limitations:** Still crude regarding order size and market impact; assumes that full size can be executed at those quotes.

Volume participation and impact models.

For more realistic modeling, especially for larger orders, you can relate slippage to how aggressively you trade relative to typical volume:

- Specify a maximum participation rate, such as 10% of average daily volume.
- Spread the order over time (for example, over the trading day).
- Model impact as a function of traded volume and volatility.

In this framework, larger and faster trades incur higher costs. The exact functional form can vary (linear, square-root, and so on), but the key is that slippage is no longer a fixed constant; it scales with how you choose to execute.

From a GPU perspective, volume-based slippage models are attractive because you can simulate many execution schedules in parallel, for many instruments and days, as long as you structure your data and computations carefully.

Transaction Costs: Beyond Slippage

Slippage is only one piece of trading friction. A realistic backtest must include other transaction costs:

Brokerage and exchange fees.

These are explicit charges per share, per contract, or per notional amount traded. In many markets you pay:

- A fee to your broker for routing and clearing.
- A fee or rebate from the exchange, depending on whether you add or remove liquidity.

In a backtest, you can model these as:

- Per-share or per-contract charges.
- Percentage of notional traded.

You can also make them depend on the order type and venue.

Taxes and levies.

Some jurisdictions apply transaction taxes, stamp duties, or financial transaction levies. These may:

- Apply only on certain instruments (for example, equities but not futures).
- Apply only on certain sides (for example, buys but not sells).

Even if you do not plan to trade those markets directly, modeling them in backtests can prevent you from being surprised later.

Financing and borrow costs.

If you take leveraged or short positions, you incur financing costs:

- Interest on borrowed cash for leveraged longs.
- Stock borrow fees for shorts, which can be especially high for hard-to-borrow names.

These costs accumulate over time, not per trade. For short positions, for example, you might:

- Assign a borrow rate per asset.
- Apply it daily to the short notional outstanding.

In a GPU-accelerated environment, you can easily scan multiple cost scenarios—high borrow, low borrow, different fee schedules—to understand how sensitive your strategy is to these frictions.

Corporate Actions: Keeping Prices and Positions Honest

Corporate actions—splits, dividends, rights issues, mergers, spin-offs, symbol changes—can dramatically change prices and share counts. Ignoring them leads to distorted return series and incorrect PnL. Handling them correctly is essential.

Price and volume adjustments.

Most historical price vendors provide adjusted prices and volumes that:

- Smooth out discontinuities caused by splits and certain dividends.
- Preserve the economic meaning of returns over time.

Your backtest should use a consistent adjustment scheme:

- If you use adjusted prices for signals, you must also use them for PnL calculations, or carefully track the relationship between adjusted and unadjusted series.
- The same adjustments must be applied in both CPU and GPU pipelines, ideally via a shared preprocessing step.

Cash flows and share counts.

Beyond price adjustments, you must also model:

- Dividend payments as cash credited to your portfolio on ex-date or pay date, depending on your convention.
- Changes in share count for splits or consolidations (for example, a 2-for-1 split doubles shares and halves price).
- Events such as mergers where positions may be converted into new securities or cashed out.

These events affect both PnL and the universe of tradable instruments. A sloppy implementation might simply treat a merger as a price jump and lose track of what happened to the position. A disciplined engine will centralize corporate action handling so that:

- The same event feed is used to adjust prices, volumes, and positions.
- Both CPU and GPU backtests see identical adjusted data and updates to holdings.

Execution Simulation: Bridging Orders and Fills

Between portfolio construction and portfolio accounting lies the execution simulator: the part of the engine that converts desired trades into fills at specific prices and times.

At a minimum, an execution simulator must decide, for each order:

- If and when the order is executed.
- At what price or prices.
- For what quantity (full fill, partial fill, or no fill).

There is a spectrum of complexity:

Bar-based execution.

If you only have daily or bar data (open, high, low, close, volume), you might:

- Assume that trades happen at the open, close, or volume-weighted average price.
- Enforce liquidity limits, such as "do not trade more than 10% of daily volume".

Within this framework, you can still model slippage by moving execution prices away from the chosen reference (for example, paying slightly above the open for buys).

Order book and tick-based execution.

For more granular strategies, you may have access to intraday quotes and trades. Then you can:

- Simulate limit and market orders interacting with a synthetic order book.
- Model queue priority and the probability of getting filled at each price.
- Include latency, so that orders see a slightly stale view of the book.

These simulations are more realistic but also more demanding computationally. GPU acceleration can help by processing many simulated paths in parallel, but only if your data structures and algorithms are designed with parallelism in mind.

Portfolio Accounting: Building Believable PnL Paths

Once you know which trades were executed and at what prices and sizes, portfolio accounting keeps track of:

- Positions in each instrument.
- Cash balance and financing.
- Realized and unrealized PnL.
- Transaction costs and fees.
- Corporate action effects.

A simple but robust approach follows these steps at each time step:

1. Start from last period's positions and cash.
2. Apply corporate actions to positions and prices.

3. Apply market price changes to compute unrealized PnL.
4. Apply trades and transaction costs to update positions and cash.
5. Apply financing and borrow costs.
6. Record total portfolio value and any risk metrics of interest.

It is important that this accounting be deterministic: given the same sequence of trades, prices, and events, both CPU and GPU implementations should produce the same PnL path within acceptable numerical tolerances. That means:

- Using consistent rounding rules.
- Applying fees and taxes in the same order.
- Defining clearly when in the time step each event occurs.

Parametrizing Frictions for Stress Testing

To make the backtest engine useful for robust research, you should expose key assumptions as parameters:

- Slippage rates or impact coefficients.
- Fee schedules and tax rates.
- Borrow cost levels and financing spreads.
- Maximum participation rates and execution horizons.

With these parameters centralized in configuration files, you can:

- Run baseline tests with conservative estimates of costs.
- Stress-test the strategy by varying costs across a realistic range.
- Understand how performance changes across different market environments.

This parametrization is particularly natural for GPU workloads: you can launch large grids of experiments where each combination of parameters is one point in a cost-scenario space. Because the rest of the engine is identical, differences in performance can be attributed cleanly to the cost assumptions.

Data Structures Friendly to Vectorization and GPUs

To support both event-driven realism and GPU acceleration, you must choose data structures that:

- Represent orders, trades, and positions clearly.
- Are easy to slice and batch across assets and time.
- Can be transferred efficiently between CPU and GPU memory.

Some practical guidelines:

Tabular layouts.

Store core objects (orders, executions, positions) in table-like arrays with:

- One row per event or time-asset combination.
- Columns for timestamps, instrument identifiers, sizes, prices, and flags.

On the CPU, these may be data frames; on the GPU, you may convert them into columnar arrays. The key is to maintain a consistent schema so that both sides interpret fields in the same way.

Time-major or asset-major ordering.

Decide whether your primary index is time or asset, depending on the dominant access pattern:

- Time-major (all assets at time t together) is convenient for strategies that make cross-sectional decisions (for example, ranking all stocks each day).

- Asset-major (all times for one asset together) is convenient for time-series models and some execution logic.

For GPU computations, contiguous memory access is important. You may choose one ordering for GPU kernels and another for CPU analysis, with carefully controlled transformations between them.

Shared identifiers and metadata.

Use consistent identifiers for instruments, venues, and events across your entire stack:

- A mapping from vendor symbols to internal numeric IDs.
- Standardized representations of order types and side (buy/sell).
- Clear flags for events such as corporate actions or trading halts.

These details ensure that your backtest remains interpretable even when you scale up to millions of events across many instruments.

Tying It Back to the Research Workflow

All the design choices in this section should plug cleanly into the research workflow and temporal validation schemes established earlier:

- Hypotheses specify not just signals and universes, but also the cost and slippage models to be used.
- Preregistration documents the chosen level of backtest realism for each stage (for example, "phase 1 uses spread-based slippage, no impact; phase 2 adds volume-based impact").
- Temporal splits (including purged K-fold and walk-forward) define which time periods feed into the backtest engine for training, validation, and testing.
- Experiment logs record the exact cost parameters, corporate action feeds, and execution assumptions used in each run.

This alignment ensures that when you compare two strategies, or CPU and GPU implementations of the same strategy, you are making a fair comparison: same data, same splits, same frictions, same accounting rules. Differences in PnL paths then reflect differences in ideas and algorithms, not in hidden implementation quirks.

In the next section we will focus on how to measure the performance of these backtests—what metrics to compute, how to perform attribution, and how to keep those calculations consistent across CPU and GPU. But all of those performance numbers will only be as meaningful as the backtest engine underneath them. A carefully designed engine, with realistic slippage, transaction costs, and corporate actions, is therefore not a luxury; it is the foundation on which credible GPU-accelerated research is built.

2.4 Performance Metrics & Attribution

The previous sections gave us a disciplined research workflow, time-aware validation schemes, and a realistic backtest engine that turns signals into executed trades and PnL. We are now in a position where backtests produce detailed paths of portfolio value, positions, and cash flows on both CPU and GPU. The natural question is: *how do we measure and compare what we see?*

In this section we build a metrics and attribution framework designed for two goals:

- To evaluate strategies fairly, making explicit how much risk is taken to earn observed returns.
- To compare different implementations of the *same* strategy (for example, CPU vs GPU engines, different slippage models, or execution choices) in a transparent way.

The emphasis is on clarity and reproducibility. We want a configuration-driven metrics layer that can be applied identically to any PnL stream, no matter where it came from or how it was computed, and that breaks down performance into understandable sources.

Three Families of Metrics

It is useful to organize performance statistics into three broad families:

- **Return statistics:** How much money did we make?
- **Risk measures:** How bumpy or fragile was the path that produced those returns?
- **Risk-adjusted ratios:** How much return did we earn per unit of risk?

In addition, we will introduce *path-dependent* metrics that capture aspects of the experience of holding the strategy, and then move to attribution: understanding where returns came from.

Throughout, keep in mind that financial returns are often non-normal, serially correlated, and influenced by overlapping trades. Naively applying textbook formulas without reflection can mislead you-especially when accelerated GPU experiments give you thousands of results to sift through.

Return Statistics: First Look at Performance

Return statistics should be simple and robust. Typical examples include:

- **Total return:** The percentage change in portfolio value over the evaluation period.
- **Annualized return (CAGR):** The constant annual growth rate that would turn the starting value into the ending value over the length of the period.
- **Hit rate:** The fraction of periods (days, weeks, months) with positive returns.
- **Payoff asymmetry:** Average gain on winning periods versus average loss on losing periods.

When computing these, you must decide:

- **Return frequency:** daily, weekly, monthly, or trade-by-trade.
- **Compounding convention:** whether you treat returns as simple or compounded.
- **Calendar assumptions:** for example, how many trading days per year.

In a GPU-aware framework, these choices should not be scattered inside kernels. Instead, they belong in a centralized metrics configuration. Then CPU and GPU can both feed PnL series into the same computation with the same conventions, ensuring comparability.

Risk Measures: Understanding the Journey, Not Just the Destination

Returns alone do not tell you whether a strategy is attractive. Two portfolios can have the same average return but very different levels of risk. We therefore need to measure variability and downside.

Volatility.

Volatility is the variability of returns over time. In practice, you might compute:

- The standard deviation of daily or weekly returns.
- An annualized version based on an assumption such as 252 trading days per year.

However, volatility has limitations:

- It treats upside and downside moves symmetrically.
- It can be distorted by serial correlation: when returns are autocorrelated, the naive standard deviation underestimates true uncertainty over longer horizons.

Drawdowns.

A drawdown is the percentage drop from a peak in portfolio value to a subsequent trough. Key drawdown metrics include:

- **Maximum drawdown:** the worst peak-to-trough decline over the period.
- **Average drawdown:** the typical size of a drawdown.
- **Time under water:** how long the portfolio spends below a previous peak.
- **Recovery time:** how long it takes to recover from major drawdowns.

These metrics are path-dependent: they cannot be derived from average returns and volatility alone. They describe the investor's lived experience and are crucial when judging whether a strategy is tolerable for real capital.

Tail risk.

Tail risk measures focus on extreme negative outcomes. Common choices are:

- **Value at Risk (VaR):** a threshold loss level such that losses worse than this level occur only a small fraction of the time (for example, 1% or 5%).
- **Expected Shortfall (ES):** the average loss in the worst fraction of cases (for example, average of the worst 5% of outcomes).

In a backtest context, these are often estimated empirically from the distribution of returns, but you must be cautious with small samples and non-stationary data.

Risk-Adjusted Ratios: Return Per Unit of Risk

Risk-adjusted ratios bring return and risk together into single-number summaries. Common examples include:

- **Sharpe ratio:** average excess return divided by volatility.
- **Sortino ratio:** average excess return divided by downside volatility (volatility of negative returns only).
- **Information ratio:** excess return relative to a benchmark divided by tracking error (volatility of the difference).
- **Calmar ratio:** annualized return divided by maximum drawdown.

These ratios are heavily used in practice, but they hide assumptions:

- That volatility is a good measure of risk.
- That returns are reasonably stable over time.
- That the evaluation period is representative of what might happen in the future.

When comparing CPU and GPU implementations, or different configurations of the same strategy, you must ensure that:

- Ratios are computed over the exact same time period and using the same frequency of returns.
- Any risk-free or benchmark rates used are identical.

Again, a centralized metrics configuration file is the easiest way to enforce this.

Path-Dependent Measures: The Shape of the Equity Curve

Path-dependent measures complement ratios by focusing on the shape and stability of the equity curve. We have already mentioned drawdown-related metrics; here we broaden the view.

Equity curve diagnostics.

Beyond simply plotting cumulative returns, you can compute:

- **Skewness of returns:** capturing asymmetry between big gains and big losses.
- **Clustering of losses:** for example, average run length of consecutive negative days.
- **Autocorrelation of returns:** indicating trends or mean-reversion in PnL.

These diagnostics can reveal whether a high Sharpe ratio is driven by a steady trickle of small gains punctuated by occasional large losses, which may be unacceptable in practice.

Turnover and capacity.

Operationally, you care about how much trading is required to achieve the PnL path:

- **Turnover:** the fraction of portfolio value traded over a given period.
- **Capacity:** an estimate of how much capital the strategy can absorb before market impact and liquidity constraints erode performance.

These measures connect directly to the backtest design choices in the previous section: execution models, slippage, and transaction costs.

A Metrics Configuration File

To keep all of this under control, especially in a GPU-accelerated environment, you should define metrics through a configuration file rather than scattered code. Such a configuration might specify:

- Which metrics to compute (for example, total return, annualized return, volatility, Sharpe, max drawdown, time under water).
- The return frequency (daily, weekly, monthly) for each metric.
- The conventions: trading days per year, compounding methods, definition of risk-free rate, whether to use simple or log returns.

- Which benchmarks to use for relative measures (information ratio, tracking error).
- Which horizons to report (for example, full sample, last year, last month, by regime).

This configuration becomes part of your research artifact stack:

- It is stored under version control.
- It is referenced in experiment logs so you know which metrics definitions were used for each run.
- It is shared across CPU and GPU implementations so that both paths feed into the same metrics engine.

With this in place, you can confidently say that a Sharpe ratio of 1.2 means the same thing whether it was computed from a baseline CPU backtest or a large GPU parameter sweep.

Attribution: Where Do Returns Come From?

Metrics tell you how a strategy performed; attribution tells you *why*. Good attribution breaks total performance into understandable components so that you can answer questions like:

- Did we make money by choosing the right assets within sectors, or mainly by being in the right sectors?
- How much of our performance can be explained by exposure to known risk factors?
- Did timing decisions (when to increase or decrease risk) help or hurt?

We will focus on three complementary lenses:

- Allocation versus selection effects.
- Factor exposure analysis.
- Timing and residual (idiosyncratic) effects.

Allocation vs Selection

In a portfolio divided into groups (for example, sectors, countries, styles), it is common to decompose returns into:

- **Allocation effect:** the impact of overweighting or underweighting groups that performed differently from the benchmark.
- **Selection effect:** the impact of picking better or worse assets than the group averages.

A simple intuitive view is:

- If you overweighted a sector that outperformed the market, that contributes positively to the allocation effect.
- If, within a sector, your chosen stocks outperformed the sector average, that contributes positively to selection.

In practice, there are several formal attribution schemes (for example, Brinson-like methods), but they share the same spirit: explain portfolio return relative to a benchmark in terms of where you placed your weights and which names you chose.

In a GPU-aware setting, allocation and selection calculations can be performed across many portfolios and time windows in parallel. For example, you might attribute performance:

- By calendar period (monthly, quarterly).
- By regime (bull versus bear markets).
- Across thousands of parameter combinations in a grid search.

As long as the attribution logic is deterministic and documented, you can use GPUs to make it fast without turning it into a black box.

Factor Exposure Analysis

Factor models view portfolio returns as a combination of exposures to systematic risk factors plus idiosyncratic residuals. Common factors include:

- Broad market indices.
- Style factors such as value, momentum, size, quality, and low volatility.
- Sector or industry factors.

To perform factor-based attribution, you typically:

- Obtain or construct time series of factor returns.
- For each period, express the portfolio as exposures to these factors (by regression, by holdings-based mapping, or using predefined factor loadings).
- Decompose portfolio returns into:
  - The portion explained by factor exposures.
  - The unexplained residual (idiosyncratic alpha).

This analysis helps you understand:

- Whether your "alpha" strategy is in fact just a levered bet on common factors.
- Which factors contributed most to gains and losses.
- How stable factor exposures are across time and regimes.

Factor-based attribution is naturally vectorizable and thus well suited to GPUs:

- You can run regressions or panel calculations for many strategies and sub-periods in parallel.

- You can simulate alternative factor definitions and see how attribution changes.

However, you must be careful to keep the attribution model itself simple and transparent. Researchers and risk managers should be able to understand:

- Which factors were used.
- How exposures were computed.
- Over which windows and frequencies the analysis was carried out.

These details, like everything else, belong in your metrics configuration and experiment logs.

Timing and Residual Effects

Beyond allocation and factor exposures, many strategies involve timing: dynamically increasing or decreasing risk based on signals. Attribution should separate:

- **Static effects:** what you would have earned if you had maintained average exposures over time.
- **Timing effects:** incremental gains or losses from changing exposures.

One way to think about this is:

- Compute the return your portfolio would have earned if its weights were fixed at their long-term averages while factors and assets evolved as in reality.
- Compare this to the actual return from your time-varying weights.

The difference reflects the contribution of timing decisions. In practice, there are many technical choices (for example, discrete time approximations, rebalancing frequency), but the goal remains the same: attribute performance not only to *what* you held but also to *when* and *how* you changed it.

The remaining residual after accounting for allocation, selection, and factor exposures is sometimes labeled “alpha”. Treat this term cautiously. A non-zero residual may reflect model misspecification, omitted factors, or lucky timing during the evaluation period.

Designing a GPU-Aware Attribution Engine

To integrate attribution into a GPU-accelerated research stack, consider the following design principles:

Separation of concerns.

- The backtest engine produces time series of portfolio returns, holdings, and possibly factor exposures.
- The metrics and attribution engine consumes these outputs and computes statistics.

This separation allows you to reuse the same attribution logic across different backtest implementations and even across different research teams.

Batch-oriented computation.

As with metrics, attribution should accept batches of portfolios and time windows, not just single runs. For example:

- A batch might consist of all parameter combinations in a grid search.
- Another batch might group different markets or asset classes.

On the GPU, each batch can be processed in parallel, greatly speeding up large-scale exploration of attribution patterns.

Configuration-driven logic.

Attribution choices-such as which groups to use for allocation/selection, which factors to include, and which time windows to analyze-should be specified in configuration files. That way, you can easily:

- Re-run attribution under different assumptions.
- Compare attribution results across experiments.
- Ensure that CPU and GPU paths use identical logic.

Dashboards and Summary Tables

Raw metrics and attribution numbers can be hard to digest, especially when you have many strategies, time periods, and configurations. It is therefore helpful to define a standard set of summary views, such as:

- A table of key risk and return metrics for each strategy and implementation (CPU, GPU).
- An equity curve and drawdown chart for each strategy, perhaps with CPU and GPU variants overlayed.
- Attribution tables showing allocation/selection effects by sector or region, and factor contributions by style.
- Regime-based panels: performance broken out by volatility regime, interest-rate regime, or crisis vs non-crisis periods.

These dashboards serve as the first line of defense against overfitting and implementation error:

- Large discrepancies between CPU and GPU equity curves suggest numerical or logic issues.
- Performance concentrated in a single regime or factor exposure warns of fragility.
- Strategies that look strong on headline ratios but weak on drawdown and tail metrics may not be acceptable in practice.

Logging and Reproducibility

Finally, metrics and attribution must be tied into the same logging and archival practices as the rest of your research:

- Each experiment log should reference the metrics configuration version and attribution configuration version used.
- Summary statistics and attribution outputs should be stored alongside raw PnL series and holdings.
- Any reports or dashboards generated should be reproducible from configuration files and raw data.

This infrastructure turns your GPU-accelerated research platform into an *evidence-generating machine*: for each hypothesis and implementation, you can answer not only "How did it do?" but also "Where did the performance come from, under what risks, and how do CPU and GPU implementations compare under identical measurement conventions?"

With this metrics and attribution framework in place, we are ready for the final methodological step of the chapter: event-driven backtesting engines. There we will see how to architect the overall system so that strategies, execution simulators, and performance reporters remain modular-and so that heavy numerical tasks, including the metrics and attribution computations we have just described, can be offloaded to GPUs without sacrificing transparency or control.

2.5 Event-Driven Backtesting Engines

Up to this point in the chapter we have treated backtests mostly as transformations on time series: signals become desired positions, positions imply trades, trades generate PnL. This view works well for daily or lower-frequency strategies and for many GPU-accelerated research tasks. However, as soon as you care about realistic execution—partial fills, intraday liquidity, latency, multiple venues—the simple time-series picture becomes strained.

Real markets are not smooth functions of time; they are streams of *events*. Quotes update, trades print, orders are submitted, modified, and canceled. Corporate actions take effect, end-of-day processes roll positions, and risk limits fire. An execution-focused backtest that ignores this event structure will miss important dynamics.

In this section we introduce *event-driven* backtesting engines: architectures that process one event at a time, updating strategy state, orders, executions, and portfolios step by step. We will:

- Contrast vectorized and event-driven approaches.
- Define a simple but powerful event model for backtesting.
- Lay out an engine architecture with clear component boundaries.
- Discuss how to instrument such an engine for logging and metrics.
- Indicate where GPU kernels naturally plug into this architecture.

The goal is not to replace vectorized backtests, which remain extremely valuable for early-stage research and large-scale GPU sweeps, but to complement them with an engine that can handle the fine structure of trading while still being GPU-friendly in its numerically intensive parts.

Vectorized vs Event-Driven: Two Views of the Same Market

A **vectorized** backtest sees the world as arrays: prices, signals, and positions indexed by time and asset. Operations are applied across these arrays in bulk. For example:

- Compute yesterday's momentum score for all stocks in parallel.
- Update all positions at the close based on a ranking.
- Apply slippage and transaction costs using simple formulas.

This style is:

- Efficient for cross-sectional strategies with regular trading schedules.
- Naturally aligned with GPUs, which excel at operations on large arrays.
- Convenient for high-level research and parameter sweeps.

However, it can struggle with:

- Intraday order placement and cancellation.
- Partial fills and queue priority in order books.
- Latency and asynchronous data from multiple venues.
- Complex event logic such as conditional orders or algorithmic execution schedules.

An **event-driven** backtest, by contrast, treats everything as a sequence of discrete events ordered in time:

- A new quote arrives.
- A trade is printed in the market.
- The strategy receives a bar or signal and decides to send an order.
- The simulated broker receives the order and interacts with the market stream.
- A fill is generated, and the portfolio is updated.

Each event triggers updates to internal state machines: the strategy, broker, portfolio, and metrics modules. This architecture:

- Mirrors how live trading systems operate.
- Handles asynchronous, irregular data naturally.
- Allows detailed modeling of execution and microstructure.

On the surface, this style is less obviously GPU-friendly, because it introduces control flow, branching, and dependencies between events. However, as we will see, much of the heavy lifting inside an event-driven engine—pricing, risk, large scenario fans, factor calculations—can still be offloaded to GPUs as separate kernels, while the event loop itself runs on the CPU.

An Architectural Overview

Before diving into details, it is useful to fix a mental picture of the components in an event-driven backtester and how they interact. At the center is an *event queue* feeding a set of modules:

- **Data adapters:** turn raw market data into standardized market events.
- **Strategy:** consumes market and portfolio events, decides on trading actions, and emits order events.
- **Broker / execution simulator:** receives order events, simulates their interaction with the market, and emits fill events.
- **Portfolio:** updates positions, cash, and PnL in response to fills, corporate actions, and market events.
- **Metrics / logging:** listens to events and state changes, computes statistics, and records everything needed for audit and analysis.
- **GPU services:** on-demand numerical engines (for example, optimizers, risk calculators, pricing models) called from strategy, broker, or portfolio modules.

All communication flows through a shared event queue and state objects with well-defined interfaces. This separation of concerns makes the architecture easier to maintain and naturally supports GPU integration.

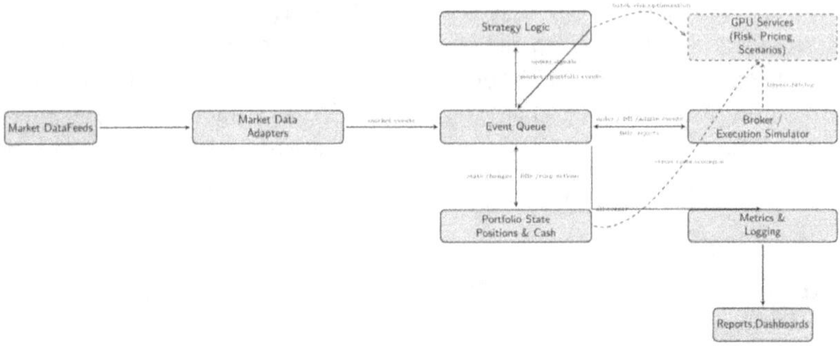

Defining the Event Model

An event is a small, self-contained record representing something that happens at a point in time that matters to the backtest. A pragmatic event model for trading research typically includes:

- **Market events:** quotes, trades, bars (for example, 1-minute or daily OHLCV), and reference data updates.
- **Signal events:** outputs from your models indicating new forecasts or ranking updates.
- **Order events:** requests to buy or sell specific quantities of instruments with specified instructions (side, type, time-in-force).
- **Fill events:** confirmations that an order has (partially) executed at a price and size.
- **Admin events:** corporate actions, trading halts, start/end-of-day markers, risk limit triggers.

Each event minimally carries:

- A timestamp.
- An event type.
- An instrument or portfolio identifier if applicable.

- A payload of fields relevant to that type (for example, price, size, side).

By standardizing the event schema, you ensure that:

- Strategy code can be written against a stable interface, independent of whether the underlying data came from a CPU preprocessing step or a GPU-accelerated model.
- The broker simulator can focus on order handling logic, not on idiosyncratic data formats.
- Metrics and logging modules can subscribe to a unified event stream and remain agnostic to the details of any particular strategy.

The Event Queue and Processing Loop

At the heart of the engine lies an event queue. Conceptually, it works as follows:

1. Initialize the queue with a stream of market events and any initial admin events (for example, portfolio start state).
2. While the queue is not empty:
   (a) Pop the next event in time order.
   (b) Dispatch it to modules that have registered interest in that event type.
   (c) Modules may update internal state and optionally emit new events (for example, the strategy emits an order, the broker emits a fill).
   (d) Push any emitted events back onto the queue at the appropriate timestamps.

Although the main loop is simple, it can represent highly complex interplay between modules. For example:

- A new bar event triggers the strategy to compute signals (possibly calling GPU kernels for cross-sectional scoring), which generates order events.
- The broker receives order events, checks simulated order books, and emits fill events.
- The portfolio processes fill events, updating positions and generating portfolio-state events.
- The metrics module processes all these events, updating PnL curves and risk statistics incrementally.

Because the queue enforces chronological ordering, you preserve temporal causality: no component can react to information from the future. This property aligns naturally with the temporal data splitting and walk-forward validation schemes introduced earlier.

Strategy Module: From Events to Orders

The strategy module receives market and portfolio events and decides what to do. In an event-driven engine, your strategy logic often looks conceptually like:

- On receiving a new bar or signal event:
  - Update internal model state (for example, rolling features, forecasts).
  - Consult risk budgets and portfolio state.
  - Decide on target positions or directly construct orders.
- On receiving portfolio or risk events:
  - Adjust aggressiveness based on drawdowns or volatility.
  - Pause trading under certain conditions (for example, risk limits).

GPU integration naturally appears where the strategy needs heavy computation:

- Computing large cross-sectional signals from many features.
- Solving portfolio optimization problems across many scenarios.
- Running Monte Carlo risk or scenario fans before making allocation decisions.

In practice, the CPU loop triggers these GPU tasks asynchronously or in batches, receives the results, and then emits order events based on them. This pattern keeps the control logic simple while still exploiting GPU power for the numerically intensive steps.

Broker / Execution Simulator: Realistic Fills

The broker or execution module approximates the behavior of a real broker and market venue. It receives order events from the strategy and interacts with market events to produce fills. Depending on the level of realism required, you can model:

- Different order types: market, limit, stop, iceberg, participation.
- Queue position for limit orders and partial fills over time.
- Slippage and impact based on order size and liquidity.
- Latency: delays between order generation and arrival at the simulated venue.
- Multiple venues, routing logic, and smart order routing policies.

At a minimum, the broker must:

- Track outstanding orders and their remaining quantities.
- Decide whether each order gets filled, partially filled, or left unfilled when relevant market events occur.
- Emit fill events capturing executed quantity, price, and fees.

Again, numeric sub-tasks inside the broker—like evaluating impact functions or simulating many execution schedules—can be offloaded to GPUs, especially when you are running large batches of backtests or scenario analyses.

Portfolio State: Positions, Cash, and Risk

The portfolio module maintains the current state of holdings and cash. It responds to:

- Fill events: updating positions and cash balances.
- Market events: updating mark-to-market valuations and unrealized PnL.
- Corporate action events: adjusting share counts and recording dividends, splits, and other actions.

From a methodological standpoint, it is important that:

- Portfolio accounting is deterministic and consistent with the backtest design rules you defined earlier (slippage, costs, corporate actions).
- The same accounting logic is used whether the engine is running with or without GPU acceleration.
- Intermediate portfolio states are visible to the strategy and metrics modules at the right times.

For GPU integration, the portfolio module is often the primary consumer of risk services:

- On-demand calculation of factor exposures and risk contributions.
- Scenario analysis (for example, shocks to curves, spreads, or volatility).
- Aggregation of positions by sector, currency, or other dimensions.

These tasks frequently involve large matrix and vector operations, which GPUs handle efficiently when data are laid out appropriately.

Metrics and Logging: Instrumenting the Engine

An event-driven engine is a rich source of information. The metrics and logging module should subscribe to the event stream and record everything needed to:

- Reconstruct PnL paths and drawdowns.
- Attribute performance to signals, sectors, factors, and timing decisions.
- Diagnose execution quality (fill rates, slippage relative to benchmarks).
- Audit strategy decisions and risk limit interactions.

In practice, this means:

- Logging key events (orders, fills, major state changes) with timestamps and identifiers.
- Aggregating statistics incrementally as events are processed, rather than in a separate pass.
- Respecting the metrics configuration file introduced earlier so that statistics are computed consistently across experiments.

Because metrics and attribution themselves can be computationally heavy—especially when computed for many strategies and long histories—this module is another natural place to use GPUs. For example:

- Batch computation of performance metrics for hundreds of strategy variants.
- Parallel factor regressions for attribution.
- Aggregation of drawdowns and path-dependent statistics across multiple scenarios.

The event-driven engine thus becomes not only a trading simulator but also a data generator feeding GPU-accelerated analysis pipelines.

Handling Practical Realities: Partial Fills, Cancellations, and Latency

One of the main reasons to invest in an event-driven architecture is to handle practical trading details that vectorized backtests often gloss over. Among these:

Partial fills.

Orders may not be filled in one go. The broker simulator should:

- Allow orders to be partially filled over multiple events and times.
- Update remaining quantities and possibly strategy state based on fill progress.

Cancellations and modifications.

Strategies often modify or cancel orders in response to new information:

- A cancellation event removes or reduces an existing order from the broker's book.
- A modification may be implemented as cancel-and-replace, generating new order identifiers.

Proper handling of these flows requires that the broker track order lifecycles, and that strategy and metrics modules understand which orders correspond to which intentions.

Latency and asynchrony.

In real markets, orders are not executed instantaneously, and data from different venues can be delayed relative to each other. A realistic simulator can:

- Assign time delays to orders before they affect the simulated order book.
- Model jitter in market data arrival timestamps.
- Reflect the impact of delayed information on strategy decisions.

These features complicate the event logic but significantly enhance realism for intraday strategies.

Scaling Event-Driven Engines with GPUs

At first glance, event-driven engines and GPUs seem at odds: GPUs flourish on regular, data-parallel workloads, whereas event loops involve branching and sequential decisions. The key to reconciling them is to:

- Keep the event loop and control flow on the CPU.
- Identify numerically heavy sub-tasks that can be batched and mapped to GPUs.
- Structure data so that GPU-bound tasks operate on contiguous, well-organized arrays.

Some examples of GPU-friendly workloads inside an event-driven engine include:

- Repricing large universes of options or other derivatives whenever market states change.
- Running Monte Carlo simulations to estimate risk measures or price path-dependent instruments.
- Solving portfolio optimization problems across many scenarios or candidate parameter sets.
- Computing factor exposures and attributions across many portfolios simultaneously.

From an architectural point of view, this suggests:

- Designing clear, asynchronous interfaces between CPU modules and GPU services.
- Allowing the CPU event loop to continue handling light tasks while the GPU processes heavy jobs.

- Capturing GPU configuration (such as kernel versions, device models, and numerical settings) in experiment logs, just as you do for backtest configurations.

In this way, the event-driven engine you build today will not need to be torn apart tomorrow when you introduce more GPU acceleration; instead, you will plug increasingly powerful numerical engines into a stable, well-defined architecture.

Bringing It All Together

Event-driven backtesting engines complete the methodological arc of this chapter:

- A hypothesis-driven workflow defines what you are testing and how you will judge success.
- Temporal data splitting and walk-forward validation ensure that you respect time and avoid leakage.
- Realistic backtest design, including slippage, transaction costs, and corporate actions, anchors PnL in plausible trading mechanics.
- Performance metrics and attribution frameworks let you understand results and compare implementations fairly.
- Event-driven engines tie these elements together in a flexible, scalable architecture that can handle real-world trading complexity and interface gracefully with GPU-accelerated analytics.

As your research stack evolves, you may start with simple, vectorized daily backtests and gradually move toward more event-driven, intraday simulations. The discipline you build now—standardized event models, clear module boundaries, configuration-driven behavior, and careful logging—will determine whether that evolution yields robust, trustworthy insights or merely more elaborate illusions. GPUs will happily accelerate either. The design of your engine decides which one they serve.

Chapter 3

GPU Architecture & CUDA Fundamentals

Most quants learn CUDA by copy-pasting kernels and hoping they run faster. In this chapter, you'll do the opposite: you'll step inside the GPU, understand how thousands of threads really execute, see why some memory access patterns are effectively "free" while others are disastrous, and learn how precision choices quietly move P&L. By the end, you won't just launch kernels-you'll design them to exploit the hardware for backtests and Monte Carlo analytics with intent.

3.1 GPU Architecture: SMs, Warps & Memory Hierarchy

In the rest of this book we will write CUDA kernels, tune parameters, and look at profiler output. All of that becomes far easier if you first carry around a simple mental picture of what a GPU actually is. In this section we build that picture with the specific goal of understanding how many operations per second you can realistically expect for typical quant workloads, and what will limit you: raw arithmetic throughput, or the rate at which you can move data.

At a very high level, an NVIDIA GPU consists of several identical *Streaming Multiprocessors* (SMs). Each SM is a small "factory floor" that executes groups of threads called *warps*. Underneath the code you write, the SMs constantly fetch data from a layered *memory hierarchy*: very fast, tiny storage right next to the arithmetic units; medium-sized, medium-speed storage shared within the SM; and large, relatively slow storage shared by the whole GPU. In this section we unpack these three concepts—SMs, warps, and the memory hierarchy—and connect them to concrete finance examples like Monte Carlo paths, scenarios, factor loadings, and covariance matrices.

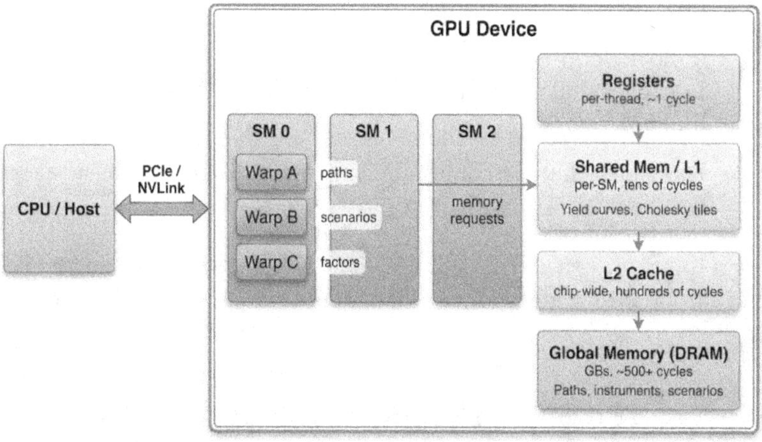

From CPU Cores to GPU SMs: Many Small Factories

If you are used to CPUs, you may think of performance in terms of "how many cores do I have?" Each core is powerful and can run a whole thread of execution with complex control flow and a large private cache. A modern desktop CPU might have 8 to 32 such cores.

A contemporary NVIDIA data-center GPU instead has on the order of 50 to 100 SMs. Each SM is weaker than a CPU core in terms of single-thread performance, but it can host and rapidly switch among thousands of lightweight GPU threads. The design philosophy is different: rather than making each individual thread fast and sophisticated, GPUs aim to keep an enormous number of simple threads in flight, so that as soon as some threads wait for data, others can take their place.

An SM contains:

- Arithmetic units for integer and floating-point operations.
- A pool of registers, which are very fast storage slots for each thread's working variables.
- A block of on-chip memory (often called shared memory and/or L1 cache) that can be accessed quickly by all threads running on that SM.
- Hardware that schedules and manages *warps*, the basic execution units.

For a quant, it is useful to picture each SM as a small pricing engine that can process many paths or instruments in parallel, as long as they all follow roughly the same sequence of operations.

Warps: The Basic Execution Grain

A GPU does not execute threads one by one. Instead, each SM groups threads into fixed-size batches called *warps*. On NVIDIA hardware, a warp is 32 threads. The warp executes as a single entity: all 32 threads issue the same instruction at the same time, just on different data values.

You can think of a warp as a 32-lane highway. Each lane carries a car (a thread), but at any point all cars travel in lockstep: if the next step is "multiply position by return," all 32 threads perform that multiplication concurrently. If some threads need different control flow (for example, taking an early-exercise branch in an American option payoff while others do not), the warp will execute both branches sequentially and mask out threads that should not take a given path. This is called warp divergence, and later chapters will show how to avoid it where it matters.

Finance maps naturally to warps because many tasks are "same instruction, different data." Consider:

- Pricing a path-dependent option under Monte Carlo: each thread simulates one path; a warp handles 32 paths.
- Evaluating credit losses under many macro scenarios: each thread processes one scenario for a given portfolio; a warp handles 32 scenarios.
- Applying a factor model to a universe of assets: each thread computes factor exposures or scenario P&L for one asset; a warp handles 32 assets.

In each of these, the algorithm for each path, scenario, or asset is identical. That is exactly what the warp-based Single Instruction, Multiple Threads (SIMT) model wants.

Latency Hiding: Why So Many Threads?

On a CPU, a cache miss that goes to main memory can stall a core for hundreds of cycles. CPUs hide this latency using deep caches, sophisticated branch predictors, and out-of-order execution. GPUs use a different trick: they keep many warps *ready to run* on each SM.

When one warp issues a memory load and has to wait, the SM's scheduler instantly switches to another warp that already has data. This context switch is essentially free because all state is already in registers and shared memory. The more independent warps per SM, the more latency the hardware can hide.

For you, this means that when you design a kernel to simulate millions of paths, you want enough total threads (hence warps) so that each SM always has something to do. Later, when we talk about *occupancy*, we will formalize this intuition: using too many registers or too much shared memory per thread can limit how many warps fit on an SM, which in turn reduces the GPU's ability to hide latency.

The Memory Hierarchy: From Registers to Global Memory

To understand throughput limits, you must know how far data has to travel. The GPU's memory hierarchy has several levels, each larger but slower than the one before it.

Registers: Per-thread workbench.

Registers are the fastest storage on the GPU. Every thread gets its own set of registers where it holds loop counters, intermediate payoffs, discount factors, and similar temporary values. Accessing a register is effectively a one-cycle operation.

In a Monte Carlo kernel, you want most of the inner-loop state for a path to live in registers: current underlying price, running sums, flags for barrier hits, and so on. As long as those values stay in registers, the SM can crunch numbers at very high speed.

The trade-off is that register space is limited per SM. If each thread uses many registers, the SM cannot host as many threads at once. This is where "register pressure" comes from and why sometimes a slightly more compact data representation improves performance by allowing more warps to coexist.

Shared memory and L1: Fast, small, and per-SM.

Shared memory is an on-chip memory region that all threads within a block (and therefore within one SM) can read and write quickly. Depending on the GPU generation and configuration, shared memory is combined with or sits alongside an L1 cache. Conceptually, you can view this level as:

- Controlled by you: shared memory is explicitly managed in CUDA kernels; you decide what to store there.

- Much faster than global memory: typically an order of magnitude or more lower latency, with very high bandwidth.
- Visible only within one SM: data in shared memory is not directly seen by other SMs.

Shared memory shines when many threads in the same block need to reuse the same data. Finance examples include:

- A small yield curve table used repeatedly to discount cash flows for many paths.
- A tile of a covariance or Cholesky matrix used to correlate random shocks for a batch of factors.
- Factor loadings for a segment of a portfolio, reused while computing P&L across many scenarios.

Rather than having each thread fetch these repeatedly from global memory, a few threads can cooperatively load the data into shared memory once, and then all threads access it cheaply many times.

L2 cache: Shared across the GPU.

Below shared memory/L1 sits an L2 cache that is shared by all SMs. You do not manage it directly; the hardware populates it as data is read and written. L2 helps when different SMs or warps access overlapping regions of data, such as:

- Accessing the same instrument definitions or risk factor histories from different kernels.
- Iterating over time slices of the same scenario set in separate kernel launches.

L2 is much larger than shared memory but also significantly slower. You should not rely on it for tight inner loops where every cycle matters. Instead, think of L2 as a helpful buffer that smooths traffic to global memory.

Global memory (device DRAM): Big but slow.

Global memory is the main memory of the GPU. It holds:

- Large arrays of Monte Carlo paths or random numbers.
- Instrument data for entire portfolios.
- Scenario and factor histories spanning many dates.

Global memory is measured in gigabytes, but accessing it costs hundreds of cycles. The bandwidth is high when many threads access it in a coordinated way, but latency per access is still large compared to arithmetic or on-chip memory accesses.

You can think of global memory as your "database" on the GPU: you need it to fit your dataset, but pulling data from it is expensive unless done in large, well-organized chunks. Later, when we discuss memory coalescing, we will see that how 32 threads in a warp read from global memory can mean the difference between one large, efficient request and many small, inefficient ones.

Where Do Quant Data Structures Live?

With this hierarchy in mind, it is helpful to assign common quant objects to rough "homes":

- **Registers:** Path-local state in a simulation (current spot, running payoff, flags), loop counters, coefficients used only by one thread.
- **Shared memory / L1:** Small tables reused across many threads in a block: slices of yield curves, tiles of correlation matrices, local aggregations of P&L before writing to global memory.
- **L2:** Implicit cache for widely shared data such as portfolio-level parameters or scenario metadata touched by multiple SMs; you do not plan around it explicitly, but you benefit from it when access patterns are friendly.
- **Global memory:** Bulk storage for paths, scenarios, instruments, historical time series, and result arrays returned to the host.

When you read a kernel, try to visualize the journey of data: loaded in bulk from global memory into registers or shared memory, used heavily in arithmetic operations, and then written back, ideally only once per result.

Throughput Versus Bandwidth: Two Different Ceilings

Now we can return to the central theme: reasoning about throughput limits before writing code. On a GPU, two broad ceilings compete:

1. **Compute throughput:** How many floating-point operations per second the SMs can perform if they are fully fed with data.
2. **Memory bandwidth:** How many bytes per second can be moved to and from global memory.

Your kernel will usually be limited by one of these:

- If each byte of data loaded from global memory feeds many arithmetic operations in registers, the kernel is *compute-bound*. This is common in heavy path simulation where each random draw is reused many times along the path.
- If you do very little arithmetic for each byte you load (for example, reading a yield curve point, discounting a single cash flow, and moving on), the kernel may be *memory-bound*. In this case, the shape and pattern of your loads from global memory dominate performance.

Without any math formulas, you can still develop a feel for this:

- Ask: "How much work do I do with each path or instrument after I fetch it?"
- If the answer is "a lot," then the GPU's arithmetic units are more likely to be the limiting factor.
- If the answer is "hardly anything; I mostly read and write," then global memory bandwidth and access patterns will probably dominate.

In later chapters, we will show you how to use profiling tools to confirm this. For now, the mental model is enough to guide high-level design. For example, if you suspect a kernel is memory-bound, you immediately know that reorganizing data to improve coalescing or using shared memory to cache hot data is worth exploring.

Occupancy, Register Pressure, and Active Warps

We have hinted at *occupancy*: the fraction of the SM's theoretical capacity for hosting warps that you actually use. Occupancy depends on:

- The number of threads per block in your kernel launch.
- The number of registers each thread uses.
- The amount of shared memory each block reserves.

The SM has fixed budgets for registers and shared memory. If each thread uses many registers, or each block uses a lot of shared memory, fewer blocks (and therefore fewer warps) can reside on the SM simultaneously. Low occupancy means fewer warps available to hide global memory latency.

Consider two conceptual designs for a path simulation kernel:

- Design A uses many temporary variables per path, keeping everything in registers and shared memory. Each thread is "fat," and you can only fit a handful of warps per SM.
- Design B is more frugal with per-thread state, perhaps recomputing some cheap quantities instead of storing them. Each thread is "slimmer," so the SM can host more warps.

Which is better? If the kernel is compute-bound and spends most of its time in arithmetic with little global memory traffic, Design A's rich register use may be fine. But if you are memory-bound and need many warps to cover latency, Design B can perform better even though each thread does a bit more work.

The point is not to memorize any specific rule, but to connect resource usage to the SM's ability to keep warps in flight. When reading or designing a kernel, ask:

- "Am I using so many registers or so much shared memory per thread/block that I might be starving the SM of warps?"
- "Given that this kernel appears memory-heavy, should I favor slightly simpler per-thread state to allow more concurrency?"

We will return to occupancy with quantitative tools later. For now, think of it as the "crowdedness" of the SM's factory floor: enough workers (warps) to cover waiting times, but not so many that each worker has no tools (registers, shared memory) to be effective.

Putting It Together: A Monte Carlo Thought Experiment

To solidify this mental model, imagine you are pricing an exotics book with a Monte Carlo engine:

1. You copy large arrays of initial prices, volatilities, and correlations from the CPU to GPU global memory. These become the base data in global memory.
2. You launch a kernel where each thread will simulate one path for one instrument.
3. On each SM, hundreds or thousands of threads are resident, organized into warps.
4. For each time step, a warp of 32 threads:
    - Reads a small batch of random numbers from global memory, ideally in a coalesced way.
    - Uses shared memory to hold a small tile of the Cholesky factor for correlating shocks across factors.
    - Updates path state held in registers: current price, running payoff, barrier flags.
5. When the path is finished, each thread writes a single discounted payoff into a results array in global memory.

If you visualize this flow, you can already reason about performance:

- If random number loads dominate runtime, you are likely memory-bound, and you might consider generating random numbers on the fly in registers instead of reading them from global memory.

- If the Cholesky operations dominate, you are closer to compute-bound, and your focus should be on keeping data close (in shared memory) and minimizing unnecessary instructions.

- If profiling shows low occupancy, you might reduce per-thread register use or per-block shared memory to allow more warps per SM and better latency hiding.

None of this required writing a line of CUDA yet. It came directly from understanding SMs, warps, and the memory hierarchy.

Mental Checklist Before Coding

Whenever you consider moving a financial algorithm to the GPU, run through a short mental checklist based on this architecture:

1. **What is the natural mapping of work to threads and warps?** Paths, scenarios, instruments, or time steps?

2. **For each unit of work, how much arithmetic happens versus how many bytes are read or written?** This hints at compute-bound versus memory-bound behavior.

3. **Which data are reused heavily across threads in a block?** These are candidates for shared memory.

4. **Which data are local to a thread and stay live throughout a loop?** These belong in registers; watch for excessive state that might hurt occupancy.

5. **Does the algorithm require irregular control flow that will cause warp divergence?** If so, can you restructure it so threads in a warp behave more similarly?

Armed with this mental model, you can walk into the subsequent chapters on the CUDA programming model, memory coalescing, and optimization with a clear sense of what the GPU is trying to do under the hood. The goal is not to turn you into a hardware engineer, but to ensure that when you look at a kernel or a profiling trace, you see more than lines of code: you see SMs scheduling warps, juggling registers and shared memory, and streaming data through a hierarchy whose strengths and limitations you now understand.

3.2 CUDA Programming Model & Execution

The previous section gave you a hardware-first view of GPUs: Streaming Multiprocessors (SMs), warps, and the memory hierarchy. You now know that the GPU wants to run many simple threads in parallel, grouped into warps, and that those warps live on SMs and draw data from different levels of memory.

In this section we move one layer up, from hardware to programming model. CUDA gives you a way to describe your financial algorithm in terms that map directly onto that hardware:

- You write *kernels*, which are functions meant to run on the GPU.
- A kernel is executed by a large number of *threads*.
- Threads are organized into *blocks*, and blocks form a *grid*.
- A kernel launch is requested by the CPU (the *host*) and runs on the GPU (the *device*).

By the end of this section, you should be able to look at a quant problem—say, pricing a million options across thousands of scenarios—and immediately sketch how kernels, grids, and blocks should be structured.

From Hardware Concepts to CUDA Abstractions

Recall the hardware view:

- The GPU has multiple SMs.
- Each SM runs warps of 32 threads.
- Threads see a hierarchy of memories: registers, shared memory, caches, and global memory.

CUDA's abstractions line up with this:

- **Thread:** The smallest unit of work in your program. Each thread executes the same kernel code on different data.
- **Block:** A group of threads that can cooperate via shared memory and synchronization. All threads in a block run on the same SM.
- **Grid:** The full collection of blocks launched for one kernel invocation.

A kernel launch is therefore: "Run this function on a grid of blocks, each block containing many threads." The hardware then takes blocks from the grid and schedules them onto SMs. Within each block, the SM groups threads into warps and runs them in lockstep, as described earlier.

This mapping is what makes CUDA both powerful and conceptually simple: you focus on defining the work for a single thread and describing how threads are arranged; the GPU driver and hardware handle the details of scheduling blocks on SMs and threads into warps.

Kernels: Functions That Run on the Device

A kernel is just a function written in C++-like CUDA syntax, but it is special in two ways:

- It runs on the GPU (the device), not on the CPU.
- It is executed by many threads in parallel, not just one.

Conceptually, you can think of a kernel as:

> "The algorithm a single thread will apply to one unit of financial work."

What counts as a "unit of work" depends on the problem:

- Monte Carlo pricing: one thread per path.
- Cross-sectional factor model: one thread per instrument.
- Historical risk measure: one thread per (instrument, scenario) pair.

When you design a kernel, your first decision is: *What is my per-thread job?* The answer should mirror the embarrassingly parallel structure of your quant task: independent paths, scenarios, instruments, or contracts.

Inside a kernel, each thread can discover "who it is" by reading its indices within its block and grid. These indices are provided by CUDA and allow each thread to select its own slice of the global data. We will not show code here, but keep in mind that you always have a way to say: "This thread handles path number i and scenario number j."

Threads, Blocks, and Grids: A Geometric View

CUDA organizes threads into a one-, two-, or three-dimensional layout. This may sound abstract, but it is simply a convenient way to label work items that naturally live in 1D, 2D, or 3D structures.

Threads within a block.

A block contains a fixed number of threads. For finance, you most often use:

- A 1D block when indexing along a single axis, such as "path index" or "instrument index."
- Occasionally a 2D block if each thread naturally needs two indices, such as (time step, factor) in some matrix operations.

Threads in the same block:

- Share access to the same on-SM shared memory.
- Can synchronize at well-defined points so they move together through certain parts of the algorithm.

This is ideal for patterns like "cooperatively load a tile of a covariance matrix into shared memory, then have each thread use it to update its own path state."

Blocks within a grid.

A grid is a collection of blocks. Like blocks, it can be 1D, 2D, or 3D.

Examples:

- **1D grid:** You have 10 million paths. You choose blocks of 256 threads. Your grid then contains enough blocks so that the total thread count covers all 10 million paths.
- **2D grid:** You price a surface of options for many underlyings and maturities. One dimension of the grid can index underlyings; the other can index maturities. Each thread handles a particular combination.

The grid describes the entire problem size. CUDA gives every block and every thread within a block its own set of indices, so you can map them cleanly to paths, instruments, scenarios, or time buckets.

How blocks meet SMs, and threads meet warps.

Blocks are the unit of scheduling onto SMs:

- When you launch a kernel, the GPU does not assign all blocks at once. Instead, it gradually takes blocks from the grid and places them on SMs as resources become available.
- A block runs on a single SM from start to finish; it is never split across SMs.

Within a block:

- The SM groups threads into warps of 32.

- Warps execute the kernel code in lockstep, as discussed previously.

This leads to some practical guidance:

- Choose block sizes that are multiples of 32, so that all warps are fully occupied.

- Make blocks "large enough" so that each SM can host multiple warps from one or more blocks to hide memory latency, but not so large that per-block resource usage (shared memory, registers) squeezes out other blocks.

Visualizing Threads, Blocks, Grids, SMs, and Warps

It is useful to visualize this structure for a simple but realistic task: pricing many options where each thread handles one contract or one path. Imagine:

- A 2D grid of blocks: one dimension for options, another for scenarios.

- Each block is a small 2D tile of that (option, scenario) space.

- Inside each block, threads form a matching 2D grid, each thread computing the price or P&L for its own (option, scenario) combination.

- The GPU maps blocks onto SMs; each SM further divides a block's threads into warps.

The following diagram sketches this mapping.

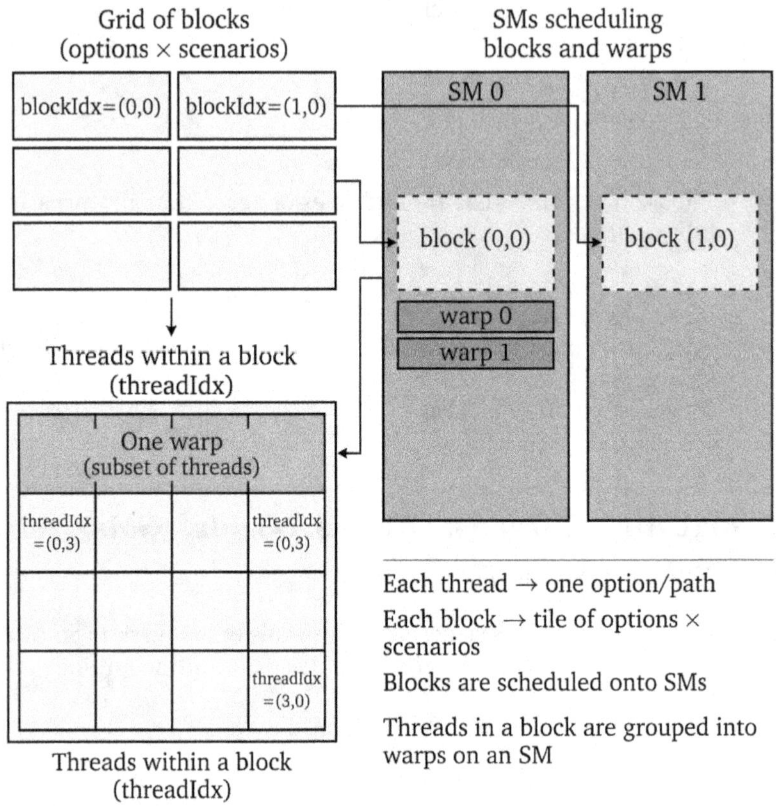

You should read this diagram as follows:

- The leftmost grid shows many blocks, each identified by its block indices.
- The central enlarged block shows a grid of threads, each with its own thread indices; a subset of these threads forms a warp.
- The right side shows how blocks are assigned to SMs, and how warps live inside SMs.

Keeping this picture in mind will make the rest of CUDA much easier to reason about.

Host-Device Interaction: Who Does What?

So far we have described what happens on the GPU. But your program always begins on the CPU. In CUDA terminology:

- The CPU (and its memory) is the *host*.
- The GPU (and its memory) is the *device*.

Most CUDA-based quant routines follow a life cycle with a few standard steps.

1. Prepare data on the host.

You usually start with market data, trade data, and model parameters already in CPU memory:

- Arrays of underlyings, strikes, maturities.
- Volatility surfaces or curves.
- Correlation matrices or factor loadings.
- Historical scenarios or generated Monte Carlo shocks.

You may also allocate arrays on the host for the results you want back, such as option prices or portfolio P&L per scenario.

2. Allocate memory on the device.

Next, you ask CUDA to allocate corresponding arrays in GPU global memory:

- Device arrays for input data: prices, volatilities, correlations, initial states.
- Device arrays for outputs: prices per contract, P&L per path, risk measures per scenario.

This is akin to booking shelf space in the GPU's global memory "warehouse" to hold your data while kernels execute.

3. Transfer data from host to device.

You then copy the necessary input data from host memory to device memory. This is a physical transfer over PCIe or NVLink. It has non-trivial cost, so in performance-sensitive code you often:

- Transfer only the data you need.
- Reuse data that does not change (for example, static portfolio definitions) across many kernel launches.

Think of this as loading the GPU with all the information it needs to do its work without returning to the CPU for more pieces mid-calculation.

4. Launch the kernel.

Once data is in place, you launch a kernel. When you do this, you specify:

- Which kernel to run.
- The *grid* size: how many blocks, possibly in 1D or 2D.
- The *block* size: how many threads per block, also possibly 1D or 2D.

Behind the scenes:

- The launch parameters and a reference to the kernel code are passed to the GPU driver.
- The GPU creates the requested grid of blocks.
- SMs start pulling blocks, storing their state, and running their threads as warps.

From the host's perspective, this is a single asynchronous call: "Please start running this work on the GPU." Depending on how you configure it, the host may wait for completion or proceed to do other tasks.

5. Transfer results back to the host.

After the kernel finishes, the contents of device output arrays are copied back to host memory. For example:

- Per-path discounted payoffs.
- Per-instrument Greeks for each scenario.
- Aggregated P&L buckets per risk factor.

With the results in CPU memory, you can perform further operations: aggregation, reporting, storing to disk, or feeding into other systems.

6. Clean up.

Finally, you free the device memory you allocated once it is no longer needed. In long-running systems, careful memory management on the GPU is just as important as on the CPU.

Choosing Grid and Block Sizes for Quant Problems

Designing a CUDA kernel is partly about the algorithm and partly about choosing a good grid and block configuration. For quant workloads, a few patterns show up repeatedly.

Embarrassingly parallel tasks: one thread per unit.

For tasks like Monte Carlo path simulation, scenario-wise pricing, or instrument-wise factor exposure, the natural mapping is one thread per:

- Path,
- Scenario,
- Instrument,
- Or pair like (path, instrument) if you want a 2D view.

If you have N units of work and you choose a block size of B threads, you will have roughly N/B blocks in your grid. CUDA offers a great deal of flexibility here, but a few simple rules help:

- Use block sizes that are multiples of 32 (a warp).
- Start with block sizes in the range of 128 to 1024 threads, depending on the device and kernel complexity.

- Ensure that the total number of threads is at least several times the total number of SMs times a few warps, so that the hardware has ample parallel work.

Matching problem geometry: 2D and 3D grids.

When data naturally lives in two or three dimensions, it can be helpful to mirror that in the grid:

- A 2D grid where one dimension indexes instruments and the other indexes scenarios.
- A 2D block inside a grid where one dimension indexes time and the other indexes factors or underlyings.

This choice can simplify index calculations inside the kernel and can improve memory access patterns when data is laid out correspondingly in memory.

Occupancy and per-thread resources.

As discussed earlier, occupancy is how many warps per SM are actually active. Grid and block sizes influence this, but so do:

- The number of registers each thread uses.
- The amount of shared memory each block reserves.

From a high-level design perspective:

- For memory-bound kernels common in finance (such as payoff evaluation over many instruments with simple formulas), higher occupancy is usually beneficial.
- For compute-heavy kernels (such as dense linear algebra on factor models), you may tolerate lower occupancy if each thread uses more registers and shared memory to hold intermediate data and reuse it.

You do not need to perfect this on the first attempt. Start with reasonable block sizes, profile, and adjust. The important thing is to understand that block size is not just a cosmetic parameter: it interacts with hardware resources to shape performance.

Basic Synchronization: Staying in Step Where Needed

CUDA provides simple primitives to coordinate threads, which you will use increasingly as you design more sophisticated quant kernels.

Within a block: barrier synchronization.

Threads in the same block can rendezvous at certain points in the kernel. Conceptually, you can say:

> "All threads in this block must reach this point before any of them can proceed."

This is crucial whenever threads cooperate:

- Cooperatively loading a tile of a covariance matrix into shared memory.
- Computing partial sums for a block-level aggregation of P&L or risk measures.

The pattern is typically:

- Each thread loads or computes its own small piece into shared memory.
- All threads synchronize, ensuring the shared data is ready.
- Then all threads proceed to use that shared data safely.

Across blocks: implicit kernel boundaries.

Threads from different blocks cannot synchronize directly inside a single kernel. The only global synchronization point you have is the end of a kernel launch. Once a kernel finishes, you know:

- All blocks have completed.
- All writes to global memory performed by that kernel are visible to subsequent kernels.

You use this to build multi-stage pipelines:

- First kernel: simulate paths and store states in global memory.
- Second kernel: compute payoffs from those states.
- Third kernel: aggregate payoffs into portfolio-level risk measures.

Each kernel launch serves as a global barrier between stages.

Error Handling and Device Properties at a High Level

Although this book focuses on performance, production-quality CUDA code must also handle errors and adapt to the specific GPU it runs on.

Error handling.

Every major CUDA operation—memory allocation, memory copy, kernel launch—can succeed or fail. In a research environment, you may initially ignore detailed error handling; in a trading or risk system, you must:

- Check the status of CUDA calls.
- React appropriately when the device runs out of memory, or when an invalid launch configuration is used.
- Guard against silent failures that might corrupt results.

Querying device properties.

GPUs differ in:

- Number of SMs.
- Maximum threads per block.
- Available shared memory per SM.
- Relative performance of single versus double precision.

CUDA lets you ask the device for these properties at runtime. This is useful for:

- Choosing block sizes that make sense on the specific GPU.
- Adapting algorithms to take advantage of more shared memory or different precision capabilities.

As you progress in this book, you will see patterns for writing code that is both efficient and portable across multiple GPU generations.

From Algorithm Sketch to CUDA Launch: A Quant Example

Let us tie the concepts together with a simple mental walk-through: pricing a large book of options under many stress scenarios.

1. **Define the per-thread job.** Decide that each thread will price a single (option, scenario) pair. It will:
    - Read the option's static data (strike, maturity, type).
    - Read the scenario's underlying level and implied volatility.
    - Run a closed-form pricing formula or a very short Monte Carlo to obtain a price or P&L.
2. **Lay out threads, blocks, and grid.** Suppose you have one million options and 1000 scenarios. You might:
    - Use a 2D grid where the x-dimension indexes options and the y-dimension indexes scenarios.
    - Inside each block, use a 2D thread layout that covers a small tile of (options, scenarios), such as 16 by 16 threads.
3. **Move data from host to device.** On the host, you place the option list and scenario data in arrays. You allocate corresponding arrays on the device and copy the data over. You also allocate an output array on the device to hold one price or P&L per (option, scenario) combination.

4. **Launch the kernel.** You configure the grid and block to cover the full (option, scenario) space, then ask the GPU to run the kernel. The GPU:
   - Schedules blocks onto its SMs.
   - Forms warps from threads in each block.
   - Runs the kernel code for each thread, performing the pricing calculations.
5. **Retrieve results.** After the kernel finishes, you copy the output array back to the host. You then aggregate these per-(option, scenario) prices into portfolio-level measures, such as scenario P&L distributions or risk factor sensitivities.

You can carry out this entire design at the whiteboard, using only the concepts in this section:

- Kernels as per-thread algorithms.
- Threads, blocks, and grids to cover the problem domain.
- Host-device data movement and kernel launches as the execution backbone.

The next sections will refine this picture by teaching you how to organize memory accesses (so that those threads and blocks talk to global memory efficiently) and how to use on-chip shared memory and caches to get the most out of the hardware you now understand.

3.3 Memory Coalescing, Shared Memory & Caching

By now you have two complementary views of the GPU. Architecturally, you know that warps of 32 threads execute on SMs and draw data through a layered memory hierarchy. From the programming side, you know how to launch kernels with grids and blocks so that each thread handles a path, a scenario, or an instrument.

In this section we connect those two views to answer a practical question: how do we organize data so that global memory becomes an ally rather than the main bottleneck? For many quant kernels, performance is limited not by how many floating-point operations the GPU can perform, but by how efficiently we move bytes to and from global memory. The main tools you have for this are:

- **Memory coalescing:** designing access patterns so that a warp's global loads and stores are combined into a small number of large, efficient memory transactions.
- **Shared memory:** using on-chip, user-managed memory as a staging area or cache for data that many threads reuse.
- **Caching and read-only paths:** taking advantage of the built-in L1/L2 caches and special memory spaces when explicit tiling is unnecessary or impractical.

We will build these ideas step by step, with concrete examples from Monte Carlo engines, factor models, and scenario-based risk calculations.

Why Coalescing Matters More Than You Think

Recall that global memory sits far away from the SMs. Accessing it is slow in absolute terms, but the GPU compensates with extremely wide memory interfaces. When used well, these interfaces can stream data at hundreds of gigabytes per second. When used poorly, each warp issues many small, scattered requests that underuse bandwidth, forcing the SM to spend most of its time waiting.

The hardware fetches data from global memory in fixed-size chunks called *transactions*. You can think of these as 32-byte or 128-byte aligned "cache lines," depending on the architecture. If all 32 threads in a warp request data that falls inside a small number of such chunks, the GPU can satisfy the entire warp's needs with a few big, coalesced transactions. If instead each thread reaches into a different, far-apart location, the hardware may need to issue many separate transactions.

From the warp's point of view, both patterns "work" functionally. The difference is purely in performance. In a memory-bound kernel, going from well-coalesced to badly scattered access patterns can easily cost you an order of magnitude in effective bandwidth.

A Warp's-Eye View of an Array

To make this concrete, imagine a simple 1D array in global memory: a large vector of path states, instrument attributes, or random numbers. Now imagine a warp of 32 threads reading from this array.

Good pattern: contiguous indices.

Suppose thread 0 reads element 0, thread 1 reads element 1, thread 2 reads element 2, and so on. The warp's collective request looks like:

> "Give me this 32-element slice of the array."

All those elements lie adjacent in memory. The GPU can fetch them using one or a few large transactions. The result:

- High bandwidth utilization.
- Low overhead per element.

Bad pattern: large strides between threads.

Now suppose thread 0 reads element 0, thread 1 reads element 1000, thread 2 reads element 2000, and so forth. The warp's collective request is:

> "Give me 32 elements scattered across the array, each far from the next."

Now each element likely sits in a different chunk of memory. The GPU must issue many separate transactions. The result:

- Much lower effective bandwidth.
- Many more memory operations for the same logical work.

These patterns show up all the time in quant code. For example:

- Reading per-path state in Monte Carlo: coalesced if paths are laid out contiguously and thread indices match path indices.
- Reading per-instrument data: coalesced if instruments' attributes are stored as arrays of values, not embedded in struct fields that are far apart.
- Reading from a time-series matrix: coalesced if the access pattern matches how you laid out time and asset dimensions in memory.

Data Layout: AoS versus SoA

A central design choice is how you represent collections of objects. Two common layouts are:

- **Array of Structures (AoS):** You have a structure that holds all attributes of one instrument or path, and an array of such structures.
- **Structure of Arrays (SoA):** You have one array per attribute: all strikes in one array, all maturities in another, and so on.

On a CPU, AoS is often convenient and can play well with caches. On a GPU, especially when each thread in a warp needs the same attribute of different objects, SoA tends to produce much better coalescing.

Consider pricing many vanilla options, one per thread:

- In AoS layout, each thread reads a small struct with fields *strike*, *maturity*, *type*, etc. If the struct is large or padded, the strikes for consecutive options may be separated by many bytes, causing the warp's strike reads to be poorly coalesced.
- In SoA layout, all strikes sit in one contiguous array. If thread k handles option k, then all threads in the warp read from adjacent strike elements. That is ideal for coalescing.

The same reasoning applies to path states, scenario values, and factor loadings. Ask yourself:

> "When a warp of threads runs this kernel, will they tend to read the same field across different objects, or many fields from one object?"

If it is "same field across different objects," SoA is usually the right choice. If you need many fields from the same object within one thread and access those objects sparsely, AoS may be less harmful. But in heavily parallel quant kernels, SoA-like layouts are often superior.

Thinking in Terms of Warps, Not Threads

A common early mistake is to think only in terms of a single thread: "this thread reads its path state here, then its instrument properties there." You must also think at the level of a warp:

- Where are the 32 threads in this warp reading from at each step?
- Are their addresses adjacent?
- Is the stride between consecutive threads' addresses small?

This warp-centric thinking guides how you:

- Lay out arrays in memory.
- Assign work to threads (for example, mapping thread indices to (path, instrument, time) indices).
- Decide whether to transpose or reorder your data offline to better align with kernel access patterns.

As you begin writing and profiling kernels, you will often find that modest changes to indexing logic and data layout yield large performance gains because they improve warp-level coalescing.

Visualizing Coalesced and Non-Coalesced Access

Before diving into shared memory, let us visualize the difference between coalesced and non-coalesced global memory accesses for one

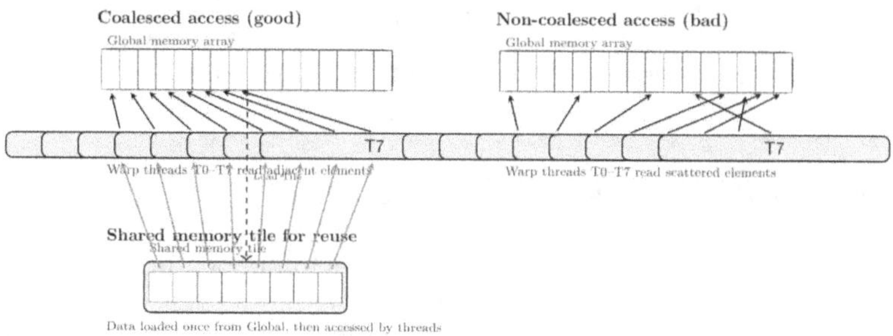

warp, along with the idea of staging data into a shared-memory tile for reuse.

On the left, the warp's arrows line up nicely above adjacent memory slots: this yields coalesced access. On the right, arrows fan out across the array: this causes scattered, non-coalesced access. The inset illustrates loading a small block of data into shared memory with coalesced reads, and then letting many threads reuse that tile cheaply.

Shared Memory: Your On-Chip Scratchpad

Shared memory, which lives on each SM, is much faster than global memory and is fully under your control. Threads within a block can:

- Load data cooperatively from global memory into shared memory.
- Synchronize to ensure the data is ready.
- Perform many computations that repeatedly access that data, all at low latency.

When is shared memory worth using?

Shared memory pays off when:

- Many threads in the same block need to read the same data multiple times.

- That data fits within the limited shared memory budget per block.
- The kernel does enough computation on that data to amortize the cost of loading it from global memory.

Quant examples include:

- **Covariance and correlation:** In factor models or risk calculations, you often multiply random shocks by a Cholesky factor to impose correlations. Rather than each thread repeatedly reading matrix elements from global memory, you can load a small tile of the factor matrix into shared memory and let all threads in the block use it.
- **Yield curves and discount factors:** Many threads might need the same curve for discounting cash flows at various maturities. Caching the relevant segment of the curve in shared memory avoids repeated global accesses.
- **Local aggregations:** When computing per-scenario portfolio P&L, threads can write partial results into shared memory and then perform a reduction (summing them up) before writing a single aggregated result back to global memory.

Tiling: breaking big problems into cache-sized pieces.

Frequently, the data you need is too large to fit in shared memory all at once. You then use a *tiling* strategy:

1. Partition the large dataset (for example, a covariance matrix or a long time series) into smaller tiles that fit into shared memory.
2. For each tile:
    - Have threads in the block cooperatively load the tile into shared memory using coalesced global accesses.
    - Synchronize to ensure the tile is loaded.
    - Perform all computations that use that tile, accessing it from shared memory.
3. Move on to the next tile.

In a Monte Carlo XVA engine, for instance, you might tile the time dimension: load factor dynamics or yield curve data for a subset of time steps into shared memory, process those time steps across many paths, then proceed to the next subset.

Banking and Conflicts: When Shared Memory Slows Down

Shared memory itself is internally divided into *banks*. These banks allow the hardware to serve multiple simultaneous accesses. Each bank can handle one access per cycle, so if threads in a warp all hit different banks, their accesses proceed in parallel. However, if many threads access the same bank but different addresses, the operation is serialized across threads in what is called a *bank conflict*.

The fine details depend on the GPU generation, but the intuitive rule of thumb is:

- Arrange shared memory access so that neighboring threads in a warp read or write neighboring shared-memory addresses.
- Avoid patterns where many threads in a warp stride through shared memory with a step size that causes them to collide on the same bank.

For example:

- Storing a small table as a flat array and having thread k access element k is typically conflict-free.
- Storing data in a 2D fashion and having each thread access a column with a power-of-two stride can sometimes create conflicts; padding rows or adjusting stride can mitigate this.

In practice, you will often start with a simple shared-memory layout, then tune if profiling reveals bank conflicts. The key idea is that shared memory is *very fast when used with care*, but not magically free.

Caches and Read-Only Data Paths

Not all data organization problems require explicit shared memory tiling. GPUs also have hardware-managed caches and special memory spaces that are particularly helpful for read-mostly data.

L1 and L2 caches.

Modern NVIDIA GPUs include:

- A per-SM L1 cache (often combined or configurable with shared memory).
- A chip-wide L2 cache shared by all SMs.

These caches automatically store recently accessed data, speeding up subsequent accesses to the same or nearby locations. When your access patterns are naturally localized—for example, kernels that iterate over consecutive time steps in a scenario or consecutive instruments in a portfolio—the caches can significantly reduce global memory traffic.

However, because the caches are managed by hardware and shared across kernels and SMs, you cannot rely on them with the same predictability as shared memory. Use them as a bonus: if you already have reasonably coalesced accesses and some data reuse, the caches will help.

Constant memory and read-only caches.

CUDA provides memory spaces optimized for data that:

- Is read-only during kernel execution.
- Is accessed by many threads, often in a broadcast-like pattern (all threads read the same element).

These include constant memory and (on newer architectures) specialized read-only paths. They are well-suited for:

- Model parameters that are the same for all paths and scenarios, such as risk-free rates, fixed barrier levels, or calibration coefficients.

- Small, immutable lookup tables used by many threads.

With constant memory, for example, when all threads in a warp read the same address, the hardware can satisfy the request efficiently with a single transaction. This is the opposite of coalescing, which prefers threads reading different but adjacent addresses. The pattern here is *broadcast*: one value, many consumers.

Making Bandwidth a Strength in Quant Kernels

Bringing these ideas together, let us examine how to turn typical quant workloads into bandwidth-efficient kernels.

Monte Carlo payoff evaluation.

In a Monte Carlo engine, one common kernel evaluates payoffs at maturity given simulated underlying prices stored in global memory. To use bandwidth well:

- Lay out simulated prices so that path index varies fastest in memory, and map threads so that thread index matches path index. Then a warp reading prices for a given time step sees contiguous memory and achieves coalescing.
- Store strike and maturity arrays in SoA form so that each thread reads its own strike from a contiguous array. This yields coalesced loads across the warp.
- If many paths share the same static data—for example, all paths for one instrument share a yield curve segment—consider loading that curve into shared memory once per block.

With these design choices, each warp's global memory requests are large and regular, letting you approach the GPU's peak memory bandwidth.

Greeks and risk measures.

When computing Greeks or scenario-based risk, you often:

- Loop over many instruments and scenarios.

- Apply simple formulas per instrument-scenario pair, reading from a handful of input arrays.

To make global memory a strength:

- Use 2D grids and 2D memory layouts that align naturally. For example, store per-scenario underlying prices in a matrix where scenario index is the slow dimension and instrument index is the fast dimension; map threads appropriately.

- Keep instrument attributes in separate arrays so that a warp of threads handling consecutive instruments per scenario reads from contiguous memory.

- If your aggregation is local (for example, per-scenario sums over instruments), use shared memory for partial reductions and write only final aggregates back to global memory, reducing write traffic.

Factor models and covariance operations.

Factor models often involve multiplications with covariance or factor-loading matrices. These operations are naturally heavy in both memory traffic and computation. You can:

- Tile matrices into shared memory so that each tile is loaded once and reused for many multiplications.

- Align tile sizes and thread block shapes to achieve coalesced reads when loading tiles from global memory.

- Use SoA for factor exposures across instruments so that a warp of threads can read exposures or factor shocks contiguously.

These patterns mirror those used in high-performance linear algebra libraries, but anchored in the financial interpretation of "factors," "loadings," and "covariance matrices."

A Practical Workflow for Memory-Aware Kernel Design

Designing memory-efficient quant kernels is iterative, but a simple workflow will keep you on track:

1. **Start from the warp's perspective.** For each major read or write in your kernel, imagine 32 neighboring threads and ask where in memory they will go.

2. **Choose data layouts to favor coalescing.** Prefer SoA over AoS when warps read the same attribute of many objects. Arrange arrays so that the index varied by threads is the fastest-varying dimension in memory.

3. **Identify hot, reusable data.** Determine which small tables, tiles, or segments are read many times by threads within a block. Plan to move these into shared memory.

4. **Design tiling where necessary.** For data too large to fit entirely in shared memory, chop it into tiles that match the shared memory budget and your block structure.

5. **Leverage caches for read-mostly data.** Use constant memory and read-only paths for immutables read by many threads; rely on L1/L2 caches to smooth access to slightly irregular patterns.

6. **Refine based on profiling.** Once you have a working kernel, use profiling tools to check memory throughput, coalescing efficiency, and shared memory behavior. Adjust layouts and tile sizes as needed.

If you follow this process, you will often find that global memory bandwidth becomes a powerful asset: your kernels stream data through the GPU in long, sustained bursts, keeping the arithmetic units busy. Instead of staring at low utilization and wondering why a theoretically simple Monte Carlo or risk computation is slow, you will be able to reason precisely about how data moves and where performance is being lost.

The next section will extend this picture beyond single kernels. We will look at CUDA streams and asynchrony, and show how to orchestrate many kernels and data transfers so that the GPU is nearly always busy doing useful financial work.

3.4 CUDA Streams, Concurrency & Asynchrony

In the previous sections we focused on single kernels: how threads and blocks map to SMs, how to structure data for coalesced accesses, and how to use shared memory and caches to get as much work as possible out of each trip to global memory. That is the right place to start, but it is only part of the performance story.

Real quant systems rarely consist of a single monolithic kernel. A typical workflow might:

- Copy a batch of market or scenario data to the GPU.
- Run one or more kernels on that batch (simulate paths, compute payoffs, aggregate risk).
- Copy results back for further processing or reporting.
- Repeat for the next batch (next day, next time window, next portfolio slice).

If you implement this naively as "copy in, wait; compute, wait; copy out, wait;" the GPU often sits idle while data shuttles over the PCIe bus or while the CPU performs serial work. In other words, you may optimize the kernels yet still see disappointing end-to-end speedups.

CUDA streams and events are designed to solve this problem. They let you:

- Overlap data transfers with kernel execution.
- Run multiple independent kernels concurrently.
- Build pipelined workflows where the GPU and CPU work in parallel.

The goal of this section is to make those ideas intuitive enough that, when you design a backtest or intraday analytics pipeline, you naturally think in terms of overlapping stages rather than executing everything in strict sequence.

What Is a CUDA Stream?

A *CUDA stream* is simply a queue of operations for the GPU. These operations can be:

- Memory copies between host and device.
- Kernel launches.
- Synchronization primitives such as events and waits.

Two key properties define how streams behave:

- Operations in the *same* stream appear to execute in order: a kernel launch will not begin until prior copies or kernels in that stream have been issued, and a later copy will not complete before earlier work is done.
- Operations in *different* streams may run concurrently, if the hardware has enough resources and the operations are compatible (for example, one is a host-device copy while another is a kernel).

You can think of each stream as a conveyor belt passing through the GPU. Items on the same belt must maintain their order, but the factory can process items from several belts at once, provided they do not contend for exactly the same machine at the same time.

By default, if you do nothing special, all your operations go into a single implicit stream. That is why naive CUDA programs are entirely sequential: copy in, then compute, then copy out. To gain concurrency, you must introduce additional streams and consciously assign work to them.

Synchronous vs Asynchronous Operations

To understand concurrency, it helps to distinguish between:

- **Synchronous** operations: The CPU call does not return until the operation has completed on the GPU. While it waits, the CPU thread is blocked and can do nothing else.
- **Asynchronous** operations: The CPU call initiates the operation and returns immediately. The GPU then carries out the operation in the background, while the CPU can continue issuing further commands or doing its own work.

In CUDA:

- Many memory copy and kernel launch functions have asynchronous variants that take a stream parameter.
- Using these asynchronous functions with non-default streams is the primary way to gain overlap between transfers and computation.

From the point of view of a quant workflow, asynchronous operations allow you to say:

> "Start copying the next batch of scenarios to the GPU while the GPU is still busy computing payoffs for the current batch."

Done correctly, this can hide most of the PCIe transfer latency behind computation, reducing overall wall-clock time.

A Simple Sequential Pipeline

Before we introduce streams, let us describe a simple but entirely sequential GPU pipeline, such as a Monte Carlo-based overnight risk run:

1. **Copy inputs to the GPU.** You transfer:

- Portfolio data (positions, instrument definitions).
- Scenario or path seeds.
- Model parameters (volatilities, correlations, yield curves).

2. **Simulate paths.** You launch a kernel to simulate risk factor paths or asset trajectories under each scenario, writing states into global memory.

3. **Compute payoffs and P&L.** You launch a second kernel to evaluate payoffs, compute P&L, or measure sensitivities along those paths.

4. **Aggregate results.** You launch a third kernel to aggregate per-path data into per-scenario or portfolio-level risk metrics (means, quantiles, VaR, expected shortfall).

5. **Copy results back to the CPU.** You transfer the final metrics back for reporting or further analysis.

If you repeat this pattern across many batches (for example, multiple portfolios or time windows), you might do all copies and all computations for batch 0, then move on to batch 1, and so on. During the copies, the GPU's compute units are idle; during calculation, the PCIe bus is mostly idle. Overall utilization is low.

Overlapping Transfers and Computation with Streams

Streams allow you to interleave these stages across batches. The general idea is:

- While batch 0 is being processed on the GPU, begin transferring batch 1's input data.

- When batch 0's computation finishes, begin its result transfer while batch 1's computations start.

- Continue this pattern so that, at any given time, the GPU is either computing for one batch, transferring inputs for another, or returning outputs for a third.

Conceptually, you are turning a strict "copy-compute-copy" sequence into a pipeline. This is exactly what you would do in a production backtesting engine that must process many days of tick data or many scenario sets as quickly as possible.

A classic pattern for this is *double-buffering*:

- You allocate two sets of device buffers and possibly two host-side buffers.
- You create at least two streams, say stream A and stream B.
- While stream A's buffers are being used for computation on batch k, stream B's buffers are filled with inputs for batch $k+1$, and vice versa.

The important point is that each stream preserves order for its own batch, but streams are independent, so operations from different batches can overlap.

Streams in a Backtesting Example

Consider a GPU-accelerated intraday backtest that processes order book snapshots in chunks:

- Each chunk covers one hour of market data for a set of symbols.
- For each chunk, you compute simulated P&L for several strategies (market making, arbitrage, execution algorithms).

A sequential approach would:

1. Copy chunk 0's order book data to the GPU.
2. Run kernels to simulate strategies on chunk 0.
3. Copy chunk 0's P&L and statistics back.
4. Repeat for chunk 1, chunk 2, and so on.

Using streams, you can improve this:

- Assign odd-numbered chunks to stream A, even-numbered chunks to stream B.
- While the GPU runs simulation kernels for chunk 0 in stream A, it can simultaneously copy chunk 1's data in stream B.
- Once chunk 0's computation finishes and its result copy begins in stream A, stream B can start simulation on chunk 1.

From the perspective of the backtest, the logic is the same. But from a performance standpoint, PCIe transfers are now largely hidden: the GPU combines computation and transfers to keep its resources engaged.

Events: Markers and Dependencies

Streams tell the GPU *what* to do and *in what per-stream order*. *Events* let you mark points in that work and create dependencies in a flexible way.

An event is:

- A lightweight object that the GPU can "record" at a certain point in a stream.
- A handle the CPU can later use to check whether that point has been reached or to measure elapsed time between two events.
- A synchronization primitive that other streams can wait on, so that operations in one stream do not start until another stream has completed some work.

In a quant pipeline, events help in several ways.

Measuring performance.

You can:

- Record an event just before launching a Monte Carlo kernel.
- Record another event immediately after.

- Ask CUDA to compute the elapsed time between them.

This is a straightforward way to measure the cost of individual stages, such as “path simulation” versus “payoff evaluation,” without disrupting the asynchronous nature of the pipeline.

Building dependency graphs.

Suppose you have:

- Stream S1 for simulating paths.
- Stream S2 for computing payoffs and risk measures from those paths.

You might want S2’s “compute payoffs” kernels to start as soon as the corresponding “simulate paths” kernels finish, but not earlier. Events let you do this:

1. In S1, after submitting “simulate paths for batch k,” you record event E_k.
2. In S2, before launching “compute payoffs for batch k,” you instruct the stream to wait on event E_k.

Now both S1 and S2 can be active concurrently, but their relative order within each batch is respected: payoffs for batch k never start before paths for batch k are ready.

This pattern scales naturally to more complex workflows, such as:

> simulate paths $\rightarrow$ compute instrument P&L $\rightarrow$ aggregate by risk factor $\rightarrow$ compute portfolio VaR.

Each arrow corresponds to events and stream waits, building a directed acyclic graph of dependencies.

GPU-CPU Overlap: Keeping the Host Busy Too

So far we have focused on overlapping different GPU tasks with each other. But the CPU also has work to do:

- Preparing input data: assembling portfolios, constructing scenario sets, generating seeds.
- Post-processing results: formatting risk reports, computing secondary analytics, storing outputs.

When you rely exclusively on synchronous GPU calls, the CPU is often idle while the GPU works, and vice versa. Asynchronous streams and events allow you to:

- Enqueue work on the GPU.
- Immediately return control to the CPU.
- Have the CPU perform its own tasks while the GPU processes queued operations.

In a production risk system, this means you can:

- Start GPU computation for scenario set k.
- Use the CPU to prepare scenario set $k + 1$ in parallel (for example, generating shocks, assembling curves, or applying business rules).
- Once the GPU finishes k, immediately dispatch $k + 1$ without delay.

Combining GPU-GPU overlap (through multiple streams) and GPU-CPU overlap (through asynchronous operations) is how you approach true end-to-end acceleration, not merely faster isolated kernels.

Practical Patterns: Double-Buffering and Chunking

Let us formalize two patterns that repeatedly show up in quant GPU applications.

Double-buffering.

Double-buffering refers to maintaining two copies of certain buffers (usually for input and sometimes output) so that while one is in use by the GPU, the other can be prepared or consumed by the CPU.

A typical setup for processing many scenario batches is:

- Two host buffers: host_in[0], host_in[1]; two device buffers: dev_in[0], dev_in[1].
- Two streams: stream 0, stream 1.

For batch k:

- Choose index $i = k \bmod 2$, so you alternate between 0 and 1.
- While stream i and dev_in[i] are running kernels on batch k, the CPU can fill host_in[$1 - i$] with the data for batch $k + 1$.
- Initiate an asynchronous host-to-device copy from host_in[$1 - i$] to dev_in[$1 - i$] in stream $1 - i$, overlapping with computation on batch k.

Once you configure the pattern properly, the pipeline "fills up" and, after a brief warm-up, you reach a steady state where the GPU is almost never idle.

Chunked processing for large datasets.

Sometimes your dataset is too large to fit in device memory all at once. For example:

- A long historical backtest across billions of ticks.
- A risk run with tens of millions of scenarios.

In such cases, you must process the data in chunks. Streams and asynchrony let you do this without excessive idle time:

- Divide the input into chunks small enough to fit into device memory.
- For each chunk, asynchronously copy in, compute, and copy out in its own stream.

- Keep several chunks "in flight" at once, so that data transfers and computation overlap.

The overall wall-clock time then scales with the number of chunks and the slowest of "per-chunk compute time" and "per-chunk transfer time," rather than the sum of both.

Concurrency Between Kernels

Beyond overlapping transfers and computation, modern GPUs can often execute multiple kernels concurrently, provided:

- They have been launched in different streams.
- Together they do not exhaust SM resources (registers, shared memory, warp slots).

This is particularly attractive in quant finance when you have:

- Multiple relatively small kernels, such as separate Greeks calculations for different risk factors.
- Several independent portfolios or books whose risk can be computed in parallel.

Instead of serially launching "Greeks for delta," then "Greeks for vega," then "Greeks for rho," you can:

- Launch each Greeks kernel in its own stream.
- Let the GPU interleave or truly overlap their execution, depending on resource availability.

However, there are trade-offs:

- Very large kernels that already saturate the GPU's SMs may not benefit from concurrency; the hardware has no spare capacity to run another kernel alongside.

- If kernels have very different characteristics (for example, one is compute-bound, another is memory-bound), concurrency can sometimes help balance resource usage; but this is hardware- and workload-dependent.

The key is to reason from the mental model you have built: SMs have finite resources, and multiple kernels in different streams share those resources. If each kernel alone underutilizes some part of the GPU, concurrency may help fill the gaps.

Synchronization: Knowing When Work Is Done

When you adopt an asynchronous, stream-based style, you must also think carefully about *when* you need to wait:

- Before reading results on the host, you must ensure the corresponding GPU computations and device-to-host copies in that stream have completed.
- Before reusing a device buffer for a new batch, you must ensure all operations that depend on the old contents in that stream are done.

CUDA lets you synchronize at different granularities:

- **Per-stream synchronization:** Waits only for the operations in a given stream to complete. This is ideal when each stream corresponds to a separate batch or portfolio and you want to manage them independently.
- **Whole-device synchronization:** Waits for all outstanding operations on the device to complete. This is simpler but can be overly conservative, stalling unrelated streams.
- **Event-based synchronization:** Waits for a specific event to be reached, either on the CPU or in another stream.

A good practice in quant applications is to:

- Use event-based or per-stream synchronization to keep different batches as independent as possible.
- Reserve device-wide synchronization for error handling, initialization, or clear global barriers between major phases of computation.

This way, you get concurrency where it is safe and needed, without complicating correctness.

Designing Asynchronous Quant Pipelines: A Checklist

When you design a backtest or intraday analytics pipeline, it is helpful to think in stages and ask, for each one, "Can this overlap with something else?" The following checklist summarizes the design process:

1. **Identify stages.** Break your workflow into logical steps: data preparation, host-device transfers, path simulation, payoff computation, aggregation, and result handling.
2. **Classify stages by resource.** Decide which stages are CPU-bound, GPU compute-bound, or transfer-bound. Aim to overlap stages that use different resources.
3. **Define batches or chunks.** Choose the unit of work you will pipeline (for example, a portfolio slice, a time window, or a subset of scenarios).
4. **Assign streams.** Typically, create at least one stream per concurrent batch. Plan the order of operations within each stream (copy in $\rightarrow$ kernels $\rightarrow$ copy out).
5. **Use double-buffering if needed.** For large or frequently updated inputs, maintain multiple buffers and alternate them across streams so that host preparation and device computation overlap.
6. **Insert events for dependencies.** When the start of one kernel depends on the completion of another (even in a different stream), use events and stream waits to encode that relationship.

7. **Bound concurrency.** Do not create more streams or in-flight batches than your GPU and PCIe link can handle; too much concurrency can lead to contention and overhead. Start with a small number (two to four) and scale based on profiling.

By following this process, you treat the GPU not just as a fast calculator, but as a partner in a broader data-processing pipeline, with transfers, computation, and CPU work all choreographed.

Bringing It All Together

CUDA streams and events extend the mental models from earlier in the chapter:

- At the lowest level, SMs schedule warps to hide memory latency.
- At the kernel level, you structure grids and blocks to make efficient use of those SMs.
- At the system level, you use streams and asynchrony to keep the GPU, the PCIe link, and the CPU occupied at the same time.

For quant finance, the benefit is direct and substantial. Whether you are:

- Running overnight Monte Carlo risk with millions of scenarios.
- Pricing large books under intraday stress in near real time.
- Backtesting high-frequency strategies on terabytes of historical data.

streams and asynchrony let you convert raw GPU throughput into real, end-to-end wall-clock savings.

In the chapters that follow, we will continue to enrich this picture by looking more deeply at numerical precision, determinism, and random number generation. But the ideas you have seen here—queues of work, overlapping stages, and explicit dependencies—will remain central whenever you design GPU-accelerated pipelines for trading and risk.

3.5 Precision, Floating-Point & Determinism

Up to this point the focus has been on performance: how to feed the GPU with enough parallel work, how to move data efficiently, and how to keep the device busy with streams and pipelines. In practice, however, raw speed is only useful if the numbers you produce are stable, interpretable, and auditable.

Financial engines are particularly sensitive in this respect:

- Regulatory models must be explainable and reproducible.
- Risk numbers feed capital allocation and limit-setting decisions.
- Small numerical differences can tip borderline trades or hedges from "pass" to "fail."

On GPUs, most of these issues trace back to three related topics:

- **Floating-point formats:** single precision, double precision, and mixed-precision combinations.
- **Rounding and non-associativity:** why adding or multiplying in different orders can produce different answers.
- **Determinism:** why parallel reductions and compiler choices may give slightly different results across runs or platforms, and what you can do about it.

This section builds a practical mental model of these issues in the context of pricing and risk, and outlines patterns you can apply without turning every project into a numerical analysis research problem.

Floating-Point Formats on GPUs

Modern NVIDIA GPUs support the standard IEEE-754 formats you are used to from CPUs, but with very different performance characteristics.

At a high level:

- **Single precision (FP32):** 32-bit values with roughly 7 decimal digits of precision. On most GPUs, this is the "native" format and runs very fast.
- **Double precision (FP64):** 64-bit values with roughly 15–16 decimal digits of precision. On many GPUs, FP64 operations are significantly slower and consume more memory bandwidth.
- **Mixed and lower precision (for example, FP16, tensor formats):** even smaller formats primarily aimed at machine learning. They can be useful for some intermediate calculations, but care is required in financial contexts.

Three practical consequences matter for quant work:

1. **Throughput:** FP32 can often be an order of magnitude faster than FP64 on a given GPU.
2. **Memory footprint:** FP32 uses half the memory of FP64; with FP32 you can store twice as many paths or scenarios in the same device memory.
3. **Precision and range:** FP64 allows you to represent very small differences and very large or small numbers without losing as much information.

This leads naturally to the idea of *where* you can afford lower precision and *where* you need higher precision.

Where Precision Matters in Pricing and Risk

Not all calculations in a risk engine are equally sensitive to precision. It helps to separate them into categories.

Local path-wise calculations.

These include:

- Updating a simulated underlying price at each time step.
- Computing a payoff given the final state of a path.

- Applying discount factors to cash flows along a path.

These operations usually involve a few arithmetic steps applied to modest-sized values (spot prices, volatility shocks, discount factors close to one). In many models, small rounding errors at the per-step level tend to average out across many paths.

For this kind of work:

- FP32 is often adequate for path evolution and payoff evaluation.
- Using FP32 can substantially improve performance and memory usage, allowing more paths and finer time discretization.

Global aggregations and risk measures.

These include:

- Summing payoffs across millions of paths to estimate expectations.
- Aggregating instrument P&L across a large portfolio for each scenario.
- Computing tail statistics such as VaR and expected shortfall.

Here, you are repeatedly adding large numbers of terms, often with different magnitudes and possibly opposite signs. Rounding error can accumulate, and the order in which you add terms begins to matter.

For these stages:

- FP64, or at least higher-precision accumulation, can significantly improve numerical stability.
- Using mixed-precision schemes—computing per-path values in FP32 but summing them in FP64—is a sensible compromise.

Calibration and optimization.

Risk and pricing engines often include:

- Solving nonlinear optimization problems to calibrate model parameters.

- Fitting yield curves, volatility surfaces, or factor models.

These routines amplify numerical noise because they rely on small differences in objective functions (for example, squared errors or likelihoods) to guide parameter updates. Poor precision can:

- Slow convergence.
- Bias fitted parameters.
- Make results sensitive to implementation details.

For calibration:

- FP64 is frequently the safer choice for core optimization logic and objective evaluation.
- Using FP32 for auxiliary steps (for example, path simulation inside an inner loop) may still be appropriate if errors are well-controlled.

Rounding and Non-Associativity: Why Order Matters

Floating-point arithmetic is not exact; it represents real numbers with discrete binary patterns. Whenever a result cannot be represented exactly, it is rounded to the nearest representable number according to specified rules.

This has a subtle but important consequence: *floating-point operations are not associative.* In plain language:

- Adding numbers in a different order can lead to a slightly different result.
- Multiplying terms in a different sequence can do the same.

On a serial CPU, you typically add a sequence of numbers from left to right. On a GPU, reductions (like summations) are often implemented as tree-like patterns where:

- Pairs of numbers are added in parallel.
- The results are then combined, and so on, until a single value remains.

This tree changes the order of additions, and therefore the pattern of rounding. The end result is numerically close to, but not bit-identical with, the serial CPU result. In many cases this difference is tiny and entirely acceptable. In some audit or regression-testing settings, it can be a source of confusion.

Three observations help make sense of this:

1. The discrepancies are usually small relative to the scale of the values being summed.
2. Well-designed parallel reductions often *improve* numerical stability by summing numbers of similar magnitude together first rather than always adding small numbers to a large running total.
3. Different hardware, compilers, or optimization levels can change the summation pattern and therefore the final few bits of the result.

For a quant, the takeaway is:

> "Do not expect GPU results to match CPU results exactly down to the last bit, especially for large reductions. Instead, define acceptable numerical tolerances and test within those."

We will return to strategies for tighter determinism later. First, we need to examine how these rounding issues manifest in parallel reductions.

Reductions on GPUs: Summing Many Small Pieces

Reductions are everywhere in pricing and risk:

- Summing path-wise payoffs to get expected values.
- Summing cash flows across instruments to get portfolio P&L.
- Computing means, variances, and higher moments across scenarios.

On a GPU, you rarely sum millions of values in a single serial loop. Instead, you:

- Assign subsets of the array to different threads or blocks.
- Have each thread or block compute a partial sum.
- Combine partial sums in a second stage, often using a tree-like reduction.

This parallel decomposition has two main numerical implications:

1. **Loss of strict reproducibility across different decompositions.** Slight changes in block size, grid shape, or hardware scheduling can change the grouping and ordering of terms in the sum.
2. **Potential for improved stability if carefully designed.** Summing similar-sized values together can reduce rounding error compared to always adding small values to a large growing total.

An intuitive way to see this is to imagine summing a large positive number and a large negative number, plus many small adjustments. If you add the big positive and negative numbers first, the partial cancellation leaves you with a smaller intermediate value, and the small adjustments retain more significand bits. If you add all the small adjustments into the large numbers early, many of them are effectively "swallowed" by rounding.

Parallel reductions can mimic the more favorable pattern (combine similar-magnitude values locally first) if you structure them appropriately; this is one reason why tree-based reductions are common.

Compensated Summation: A Simple Stability Tool

When you care deeply about the accuracy of a sum, but still want to exploit parallelism, *compensated summation* schemes can help. The basic idea is:

- Track not only the running sum, but also an estimate of the rounding error introduced at each step.
- Use that error estimate to "compensate" future additions.

The classical Kahan summation algorithm is one example. In practice, for GPU code, you adapt such schemes to reduce overhead while still improving stability, for example:

- Use a simple compensation per thread when summing local chunks.
- Accumulate thread or block-level partial sums in higher precision.

In a Monte Carlo risk engine, this might look like:

- Each thread sums payoffs for the paths it owns, using a compensated scheme in FP32.
- The block or global reduction then combines these partial sums in FP64.

This hybrid approach usually offers:

- Much better numerical behavior than naive FP32 summation.
- Only moderate overhead compared to a completely FP32 implementation.

You do not need to implement sophisticated algorithms everywhere. Reserve compensated techniques for numerically sensitive aggregations: total P&L, tail risk measures, and calibration objectives.

Mixed Precision: Combining Speed and Accuracy

Mixed precision refers to using different floating-point formats at different stages of a computation. On GPUs this is attractive because:

- You can use fast FP32 or even lower-precision formats for bulk, noise-tolerant parts of the calculation (for example, path simulation).
- You can switch to FP64 for sensitive aggregations and final risk metrics.

A common pattern in pricing and risk engines is:

1. Simulate paths and compute path-level payoffs in FP32.
2. Accumulate per-scenario or portfolio-level sums in FP64.
3. Convert final aggregates back to FP32 if desired for storage or further processing.

This gives you much of the speed of FP32 with the numerical stability of FP64 where it matters. The cost is carrying both formats in some parts of your code and moving between them carefully.

From a governance perspective, you should:

- Document which parts of the pipeline run in which precision.
- Justify these choices through testing, showing that key risk numbers (for example, VaR, expected shortfall, sensitivities) are stable across plausible market conditions.

Determinism: Do We Get the Same Answer Every Time?

Determinism in this context means:

> "For the same inputs and configuration, repeated runs of the engine produce bit-identical outputs."

On a serial CPU, determinism is often taken for granted. On a GPU, it can be more subtle because:

- Parallel reductions may combine terms in a different order depending on grid/block configuration, or even run-to-run scheduling.
- Compiler optimizations may reorder operations, fuse or split them, or use different instruction sequences to achieve the same mathematical expression.
- Random number generators in parallel settings must manage seeds and stream assignments carefully, or else the mapping from path index to random stream may change between runs.

In practice, this means:

- Two logically equivalent kernels may not produce identical bits, but their results should be close within well-defined tolerances.
- Upgrading drivers, changing compiler flags, or switching GPU models can subtly shift results even if code is unchanged.

For many trading and risk applications, strict bitwise determinism is not necessary. What matters is:

- Statistical stability: risk numbers should not change materially due to implementation details.
- Regression stability: changes in code or hardware should not introduce unexplained jumps in outputs.

In some settings, however—such as regulatory reporting, risk model validation, or model governance—you may be required to provide stronger guarantees. Let us look at strategies for both scenarios.

When Approximate Determinism Is Enough

In research and many internal production uses, you can accept that:

- Results may differ in the lowest bits between runs.
- Differences are bounded and do not affect decisions.

To operate comfortably in this regime:

- Define numerical tolerances for key outputs: for example, relative differences below a certain basis-point threshold are acceptable.
- Use robust statistical comparisons in regression tests, such as comparing percentiles of P&L distributions within small bands.
- Run parallel CPU vs GPU benchmarks across diverse scenarios to confirm that differences are small and consistent.

When differences fall within agreed thresholds, you can attribute them to benign floating-point effects rather than model flaws.

Designing for Stronger Determinism

If you need tighter control, you can design parts of your engine to be deterministic by construction. This typically involves trade-offs in performance and complexity.

Strategies include:

- **Fixed reduction trees:** Use a consistent grid and block layout and a fixed summation pattern, so that the order of additions does not change between runs.
- **Higher-precision accumulation:** Use FP64 for reductions even if the main computation is in FP32. This reduces the sensitivity of the result to summation order.
- **Compiler control:** Avoid aggressive optimizations that change evaluation order; for example, limit certain re-association or fusion optimizations where determinism is critical.
- **Stable random streams:** Assign random seeds deterministically based on path and scenario indices, and keep that mapping unchanged across code versions.

You do not need to apply these measures everywhere. A pragmatic approach in risk engines is:

- Make final aggregates and reported numbers deterministic and stable.
- Allow more flexibility in intermediate per-path or per-scenario values that are not externally exposed.

This balances auditability with performance.

Precision Choices as Risk Management Decisions

Ultimately, choosing precision levels and determinism strategies is a form of risk management:

- **Model risk:** Too low a precision or poorly controlled rounding can bias risk measures or hide sensitivities.
- **Operational risk:** Inconsistent results across runs or hardware can undermine confidence in the system.
- **Performance risk:** Overly conservative precision choices may prevent you from exploiting the GPU's full potential, leading to slow or incomplete risk coverage.

A defensible workflow for a new GPU-accelerated quant engine is:

1. **Start with high precision.** Implement a reference version of the engine where all numerically sensitive parts run in FP64 and reductions use stable schemes.
2. **Explore mixed precision.** Gradually move less sensitive components (for example, path simulation, intermediate states) to FP32, while keeping aggregations in FP64.
3. **Benchmark carefully.** Compare FP64 and mixed-precision outputs across a wide range of portfolios and scenarios. Focus on tails, Greeks, and calibration parameters.

4. **Set tolerances and policies.** Agree with stakeholders (risk, model validation, trading desks) on acceptable numerical differences and formalize them as test criteria.

5. **Document and monitor.** Record precision choices, test results, and known numerical behaviors. Monitor for drifts when you change hardware, drivers, or compilers.

This approach turns precision from an ad hoc coding choice into an explicit design parameter, managed alongside model assumptions and data quality.

Connecting Back to the Hardware and Execution Model

The themes of this section link directly to earlier material:

- The **SIMT execution model** and parallel reductions make non-associativity visible; understanding warps and blocks explains why summation order changes.
- The **memory hierarchy** and bandwidth constraints motivate mixed precision: smaller formats reduce traffic and increase occupancy, at the cost of numerical detail.
- **Streams and pipelines** affect determinism when they change the relative timing and scheduling of kernels; consistent stream usage helps keep behavior stable.

When you design GPU-accelerated pricing and risk engines, you are therefore juggling three intertwined goals:

1. **Throughput:** Exploit the GPU's parallelism and memory bandwidth.
2. **Numerical stability:** Choose formats and algorithms that keep rounding error within acceptable bounds.
3. **Reproducibility:** Provide enough determinism for your regulatory and governance context.

With the conceptual tools from this section, you can approach this trade-off in a structured way. In the final section of the chapter, we turn to the lifeblood of Monte Carlo engines—random number generation—and show how to manage it on GPUs so that it complements your precision and determinism choices rather than undermining them.

3.6 Random Number Generation with cuRAND

Monte Carlo methods are central to many of the workloads we want to accelerate on GPUs: option pricing, XVA, exposure profiles, stress testing, and scenario-based risk measures. All of these rely on large streams of random (or quasi-random) numbers. Up to now, we have focused on how to organize computation and memory once those numbers exist. In this section, we turn to the source itself.

On CPUs, it is common to have a single pseudorandom generator and draw from it serially. On GPUs, this model breaks down: we need millions of threads, each consuming its own subsequence of a very long random stream, and we must do so in a way that is:

- **Efficient:** generation should not become the bottleneck in the Monte Carlo engine.
- **Well-structured:** streams must be independent enough to avoid bias, yet reproducible for debugging and audit.
- **Statistically sound:** the resulting distributions and correlations should match model assumptions.

NVIDIA's cuRAND library provides GPU-parallel random number generators that are designed for this environment. In this section, we will:

- Introduce the main types of RNGs cuRAND offers and how they relate to quant finance tasks.
- Explain seeding and stream/substream concepts, so you can assign random sequences cleanly across paths and scenarios.

- Discuss practical ways to generate and transform variates on the device.
- Outline simple but effective statistical checks to validate that your random number streams behave as expected.

Types of RNGs in cuRAND

cuRAND gives you several families of random number generators, broadly divided into:

- **Pseudorandom generators:** These produce a deterministic sequence of numbers with very long period and good uniformity properties, given an initial seed. Examples include generators based on XORWOW and counter-based engines.
- **Quasi-random (low-discrepancy) generators:** These produce sequences that fill the unit cube more evenly than pseudorandom numbers, improving Monte Carlo convergence for some integrals. Examples include Sobol sequences.

Each family has its own trade-offs.

Pseudorandom generators.

Pseudorandom generators are usually the default choice for Monte Carlo simulation in finance. They:

- Are easy to understand and reason about.
- Support seeding and stream subdivision.
- Integrate well with variance reduction techniques such as antithetic variates.

For example, if you are pricing barrier options under Black-Scholes dynamics or simulating credit defaults under a factor model, a high-quality pseudorandom engine is often sufficient.

Quasi-random generators.

Quasi-random generators, like Sobol sequences, can accelerate convergence for certain problems, especially when:

- The effective dimensionality of the integrand is moderate.
- The integrand is smooth and well-behaved with respect to the random inputs.

In quant finance, quasi-random methods are common in:

- Pricing high-dimensional but relatively smooth payoffs, such as basket options or some XVA adjustments.
- Estimating sensitivities via pathwise or likelihood ratio methods, where smoother integrands help.

However, quasi-random methods require more care in mapping dimensions to factors and time steps, and in scrambling or randomizing sequences to obtain error estimates.

For the remainder of the section, we will focus on pseudorandom generators, since they are the workhorse for many GPU Monte Carlo engines. The principles of seeding, parallelization, and testing carry over to quasi-random settings with modest adjustments.

Seeding and Parallel Streams: Avoiding Accidental Correlations

On a GPU, you typically have many threads running the same Monte Carlo kernel. Each thread must consume a subsequence of random numbers that:

- Is long enough for the work it must do (for example, one path over many time steps).
- Does not overlap in a problematic way with the subsequences used by other threads.

cuRAND handles this by letting you define:

- A global *seed*, which sets the base for the entire simulation.
- A *sequence* or *substream* index for each thread, which identifies its place in the overall random sequence.

The core design decisions are:

1. How to map your financial notion of "path," "scenario," or "instrument" to RNG streams.
2. How to ensure reproducibility across runs and when changing grid/block configurations.

Mapping paths to RNG streams.

A common pattern is:

- Choose a global seed for the entire simulation (for example, tied to a valuation date).
- For each thread, set its RNG sequence or offset based on its unique path index.

If you have N total paths, you might:

- Assign sequence ID equal to the global path ID.
- Reset each thread's RNG to the beginning of its sequence at the start of the kernel.

This has two important benefits:

- **Stability under re-partitioning:** If you later change the number of threads per block or the number of blocks (for performance tuning), each path still uses the same random stream, because its mapping is based on path ID, not on grid or block indices.
- **Reproducibility across runs:** Given the same seed and path IDs, you will regenerate the same sequences of random numbers, facilitating debugging and regression testing.

Substreams for scenarios or time windows.

Sometimes you want to reuse the same path structure under different macro scenarios, or across different time windows, while maintaining independence. cuRAND's concept of substreams lets you:

- Treat each path ID as a base stream.
- Use a substream index to step to a new non-overlapping segment of that stream for each scenario or time window.

For example:

- Substream 0 corresponds to the baseline scenario.
- Substream 1 corresponds to a stressed volatility scenario.
- Substream 2 corresponds to a rate shock scenario.

By carefully indexing substreams as functions of (path ID, scenario index), you can:

- Guarantee that each (path, scenario) pair sees a unique piece of the global random sequence.
- Reproduce the same random inputs when re-running a specific scenario or path for analysis.

On-the-Fly Generation vs Pre-Generated Buffers

There are two broad approaches to feeding your kernels with random variates:

On-the-fly generation inside the kernel.

Here, each thread:

- Initializes its RNG state (for example, based on its path index).
- Draws uniform or normal variates as needed during path evolution.

Advantages:

- Minimal global memory traffic dedicated to random numbers; variates often live in registers or shared memory only.

- Good cache behavior, since each thread generates and consumes its random numbers locally.
- Simpler pipeline: no need for separate kernels or copies to manage random number arrays.

Disadvantages:

- RNG arithmetic consumes some of the GPU's compute capability; if your path evolution is already compute-bound, RNG operations may become noticeable.
- Care must be taken to ensure proper initialization of RNG state across many threads.

Pre-generated random buffers.

In this approach:

- You run a dedicated kernel (or use cuRAND's host API) to fill large arrays in global memory with random variates.
- Subsequent Monte Carlo kernels read from these arrays as needed.

Advantages:

- Separation of concerns: RNG generation and path evolution are decoupled and can be tuned independently.
- Easier to reuse the same random inputs for different pricing or risk calculations (for example, for variance reduction or sensitivity checks).

Disadvantages:

- Additional global memory consumption for storing random arrays.
- Need to ensure that access patterns to these arrays are coalesced, otherwise you waste bandwidth.

- More complexity in orchestrating pipelines and ensuring that buffers are filled before use.

In practice:

- For many straightforward Monte Carlo pricing tasks, on-the-fly generation inside the main kernel is efficient and simpler.
- For complex multi-stage engines, or where you want to apply the same random samples across multiple models (for example, for scenario consistency across desks), pre-generated buffers can be advantageous.

Generating Uniform and Normal Variates

Most cuRAND generators produce uniform variates on the unit interval. To simulate many financial models, you also need normally distributed variates, sometimes in correlated form.

Uniforms.

Uniform variates in $[0, 1)$ are used for:

- Inverse transform sampling: mapping uniforms through the inverse CDF of the desired distribution.
- Generating discrete events, such as defaults, jumps, or exercise decisions: compare uniforms to model-implied probabilities.

Normals.

Normals are required for:

- Gaussian shocks in diffusion models (for example, geometric Brownian motion).
- Gaussian copulas in credit or exposure models.
- Linear factor models where factors are normally distributed.

cuRAND provides functions to transform uniform variates into normals using standard techniques (such as Box-Muller or other algorithms). On the GPU, these transforms are:

- Applied per-thread, often inside the path simulation kernel.
- Designed to balance numerical quality and performance.

When normals need to be correlated (as in multi-factor models), the typical pattern is:

1. Generate independent standard normal draws for each factor and time step.
2. Multiply them by a Cholesky factor or other square-root decomposition of the covariance matrix.

You have already seen how to tile covariance matrices in shared memory; the same patterns apply here, with the random normals as inputs.

Variance Reduction and RNG Choices

Basic Monte Carlo uses plain pseudorandom draws. In practice, variance reduction techniques can significantly speed convergence and are well-suited to GPUs if designed carefully. Two simple examples are:

Antithetic variates.

For each path using random shocks $\{Z_t\}$, you also simulate a path using $-Z_t$. Many payoffs are approximately symmetric in a way that makes the average of the two paths converge faster.

On the GPU:

- A thread can generate a sequence of normals, simulate the "positive" path, then reuse the negated sequence for the antithetic path.
- Alternatively, two threads can share (or deterministically derive) antithetic streams, as long as the mapping is consistent and reproducible.

Control variates.

You simulate both the payoff of interest and a closely related payoff with known expectation (the control). Their covariance structure can reduce variance.

From an RNG standpoint:

- You must ensure that the same random stream drives both the target and the control payoff for a given path, to maximize correlation.
- This often means grouping both calculations in the same kernel per thread, or at least ensuring consistent stream assignments.

More sophisticated schemes like stratified sampling or quasi-Monte Carlo require more careful mapping between RNG dimensions and model dimensions, but the core principles of stream assignment and reproducibility remain the same.

Reproducibility and Auditable RNG Design

From a governance point of view, your random number generation strategy should be:

- **Documented:** Seeds, stream assignment rules, and any variance reduction techniques should be described clearly.
- **Stable under refactoring:** Changing block sizes, kernel fusion, or other performance tweaks should not silently alter the statistical properties of random sequences in unpredictable ways.
- **Reproducible for specific runs:** Given a valuation date, portfolio snapshot, and configuration, you should be able to regenerate the same random realizations when needed.

A practical design pattern is:

- Derive the global seed from a combination of run metadata (for example, valuation date and a run identifier).
- Define deterministic mapping functions from (path ID, scenario ID, factor ID) to RNG stream and substream indices.
- Log these mappings and seeds as part of run metadata.

Then, if you need to investigate a surprising VaR movement or a stress-test outcome, you can:

- Re-run the engine with the same seed and configuration.
- Drill down to a particular path or scenario knowing it will see the same underlying shocks.

Statistical Sanity Checks

Even when you use well-tested library generators, it is good practice to perform basic statistical checks on the random number streams you rely on. This is especially true when:

- You change GPU models or compiler versions.
- You alter seeding or stream assignment strategies.
- You introduce new variance reduction techniques.

You do not need an exhaustive test suite to gain confidence. A few simple diagnostics go a long way.

Histograms and moments.

Generate a large batch of variates and:

- Plot histograms of uniform and normal variates.
- Compute sample mean, variance, skewness, and kurtosis and compare them to theoretical values.

For example:

- Uniforms on $[0, 1)$ should have mean near 0.5 and variance near $1/12$.
- Standard normals should have mean near 0 and variance near 1.

Small deviations are expected due to finite sample size, but large or systematic deviations indicate problems.

Autocorrelation and cross-correlation.

To ensure independence:

- Check autocorrelation of sequences generated by a single thread or stream; these should be close to zero at non-zero lags for pseudorandom generators.
- Check cross-correlation between sequences from different threads; again, these should bc near zero.

For factor models, you also need to check that:

- After applying the covariance structure, the empirical correlations of factor shocks match the target covariance matrix reasonably well over many paths.

Pathwise diagnostics.

Because the ultimate use of random variates is to drive financial models, diagnostics at the path level can be informative:

- For GBM paths, compare the empirical distribution of log-returns to the theoretical normal distribution implied by your model parameters.
- For default models, compare empirical default frequencies to model-implied probabilities across many simulated entities and time buckets.

These checks combine RNG quality with model implementation correctness.

Putting It Together in a Monte Carlo Engine

To see how these pieces fit together, consider a GPU-based Monte Carlo pricing engine for a portfolio of exotic options:

1. **Choose RNG family and seeding strategy.**

- Select a high-quality pseudorandom generator provided by cuRAND.
- Fix a global seed for the run, derived from run metadata.
- Map path IDs (and possibly scenario IDs) to RNG streams/-substreams in a deterministic way.

2. **Decide on on-the-fly vs buffered generation.**
    - For path simulation, use on-the-fly generation in the main kernel to avoid storing large random arrays.
    - If you need to reuse the same random draws across multiple pricing models (for example, to compute portfolio-level risk under different Greeks), consider a separate pass that fills buffers with random variates.

3. **Generate random variates and simulate paths.**
    - In the simulation kernel, each thread initializes its RNG state based on its path ID and scenario index.
    - Threads draw uniforms or normals step by step, applying drift and diffusion to evolve asset prices or risk factors.
    - If correlations are required, shocks are multiplied by Cholesky factors loaded in shared memory.

4. **Evaluate payoffs and aggregate risk measures.**
    - For each path, compute option payoffs based on the simulated underlying histories.
    - Use appropriate precision and reduction schemes (as discussed in the previous section) to aggregate payoffs into prices, Greeks, and risk measures.

5. **Validate with statistical checks.**
    - Periodically (for example, during development or after significant changes), generate diagnostic samples of the RNG output and path-level outcomes.
    - Confirm that histograms, moments, and correlations align with expectations.

At each step, cuRAND and your seeding strategy form the backbone that ensures:

- Paths are independent where they should be.
- Convergence is as predicted by theory.
- Results are reproducible and auditable.

A Mental Checklist for RNG Design in GPU Monte Carlo

Before wrapping up the chapter, it is useful to consolidate a few key questions you should ask whenever you design a GPU-based Monte Carlo engine:

1. **Which RNG family suits my problem?**
   - Pseudorandom for general-purpose Monte Carlo?
   - Quasi-random (Sobol) for smooth, moderate-dimensional integrals?
2. **How will I map paths, scenarios, and factors to streams and substreams?**
   - Is the mapping deterministic and independent of grid/block configuration?
   - Can I easily reproduce a particular path or scenario?
3. **Will I generate variates on the fly or in buffers?**
   - Does my memory budget allow large random arrays?
   - Do I need to reuse the same random samples across multiple models?
4. **What precision is appropriate for random variates and downstream calculations?**
   - FP32 for draws and path evolution, FP64 for aggregations?

- Are there parts of the pipeline where numerical sensitivity requires higher precision?

5. **How will I validate RNG quality and model behavior?**
    - Do I have simple, repeatable tests for distributions, correlations, and path properties?
    - How often will I rerun these tests, especially after hardware or software changes?

With this checklist and the conceptual tools from earlier sections—architecture, execution model, memory behavior, asynchrony, and precision—you are now equipped to build GPU-accelerated Monte Carlo and risk engines that are not only fast, but also numerically robust and responsible.

Chapter 4

GPU Programming Patterns, Libraries & Numerical Methods

Most GPU tutorials drown you in low-level details; this chapter takes the opposite route. We start from the reusable patterns, math libraries and pricing solvers that actually move the needle in quant research-map/reduce, cuBLAS, CuPy, Monte Carlo, PDE and FFT-based methods-and show how to compose them into high-performance backtests, risk engines and optimizers with minimal custom CUDA. By the end, you'll recognize when a problem is "just" a map, a batched GEMM or a finite-difference stencil-and you'll know exactly which GPU building blocks to reach for first.

4.1 Parallel Patterns: Map, Reduce, Scan & Stencil

In earlier chapters we connected GPU acceleration to the basic CUDA execution model: grids of threads, organized into blocks, all running the same kernel over different pieces of data. In this section we go one level higher and look at the *algorithmic* shapes that sit on top of that model. Most GPU-accelerated pricing, risk, and analytics codes, no matter how complicated they look at first glance, are built from a surprisingly small set of data-parallel patterns. The four most important are:

- **Map**: apply the same operation independently to each element (path, scenario, trade).
- **Reduce**: aggregate many elements down to one or a few summary values.
- **Scan** (prefix sum): compute running cumulative results across an array.
- **Stencil**: update each element based on a small neighborhood of its neighbors.

If you can recognize your financial task as some combination of these, you are already halfway to an efficient GPU implementation. This section develops an intuition for each pattern, shows how it appears in quant finance, and hints at how it is mapped onto CUDA threads, blocks, and memory.

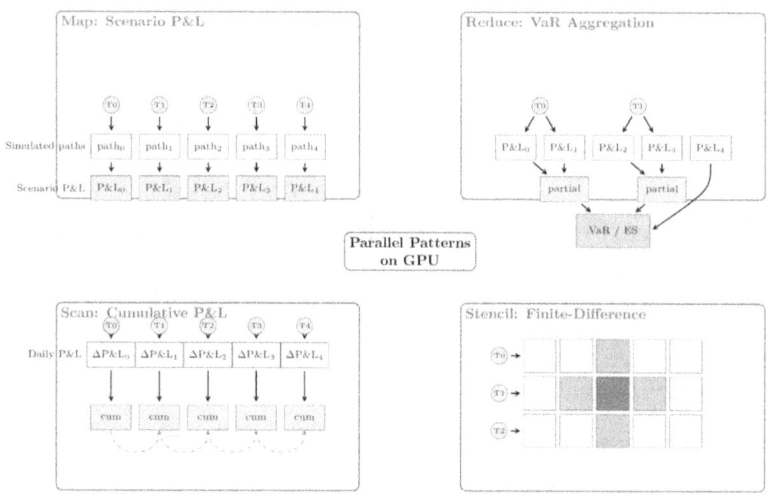

Why Patterns Matter for Quant Workloads

At first sight, a production risk engine or pricing library looks like a jungle of models, payoffs, market data adapters, and reporting code. Yet under the hood, the expensive parts—the parts you want on the GPU—tend to be:

- Evolving millions of Monte Carlo paths.
- Aggregating large scenario sets into risk measures.
- Building cumulative quantities like running exposure or cash balances.
- Sweeping over a grid repeatedly in a finite-difference PDE or similar scheme.

All of these are naturally expressed as map, reduce, scan, or stencil, often in combination. Once expressed in this way, they align neatly with the GPU's strengths: many simple operations in parallel, with predictable memory access patterns and limited cross-thread communication.

From a practical engineering standpoint, these patterns also match what high-level GPU libraries provide. When you call a parallel transform in a C++ template library, or a vectorized operation in a Python GPU array package, you are usually invoking a map. When you call a sum over a large array on the GPU, you are invoking a reduction. Recognizing this helps you write less code, debug less logic, and rely more on tuned building blocks.

Map: One Thread per Path, Trade, or Scenario

The *map* pattern is the simplest: you have a collection of independent items and want to apply the same operation to each of them. There is no dependence between items; what you do to one path or one trade does not affect another.

In quant finance, common map-style tasks include:

- Evaluating a payoff on each simulated path at maturity.

- Revaluing a portfolio under each historical or shock scenario.
- Computing Greeks per scenario once the path has been simulated.
- Applying a transformation to time series data, such as log-returns, on many symbols at once.

Conceptually, you can think "one CUDA thread per item." For example:

- A million Monte Carlo paths to maturity for a simple option: launch a grid so that each thread processes one path, from start to finish.
- Ten thousand risk scenarios for a large portfolio: each thread loops over all positions for a *single* scenario, computing that scenario's P&L.

Two practical considerations make or break the performance of map kernels:

- **Work balance.** Ideally, each thread should do roughly the same amount of work. If some scenarios are much more expensive than others (for example, because they turn on complex path-dependent features), you may end up with some warps idle while others are still busy. At the design stage, try to structure the work so that path or scenario workloads are fairly uniform.
- **Memory access pattern.** Threads in the same warp should read and write to memory locations that are adjacent in address space. If path data are stored as "all time steps of path 0, then all of path 1, and so on," and consecutive threads handle consecutive paths, then at a given time step the warp accesses a nicely contiguous block of memory. This "coalesced" access is central to making a simple map kernel run at high bandwidth.

In terms of correctness, map operations are usually straightforward. There is often no shared state to worry about and no data races, as long as each thread writes only to its own output element. This simplicity makes map an attractive first step when porting legacy CPU loops to the GPU: start by identifying loops over independent items and turn those into maps.

Reduce: From Many Scenarios to a Few Risk Numbers

Where map spreads work out, *reduce* brings it back together. In a reduction, you start with many inputs and repeatedly combine them with an associative operator until you get a smaller set of outputs, often a single value.

Classic reductions in quant finance include:

- Summing P&L across all positions to get total P&L per scenario (a map-reduce: map per position, then reduce across positions).
- Summing portfolio payoffs across all Monte Carlo paths to estimate an expected value.
- Computing risk measures such as Value-at-Risk or Expected Shortfall by aggregating and summarizing a large distribution of scenario P&L.
- Building histograms of realized volatility or order-book events.

On a GPU, reduction is typically done in a tree-like fashion:

- Each thread loads a few elements and computes a *local* partial sum (or partial minimum, maximum, etc.).
- Within each block, threads cooperate using fast on-chip memory to combine their partials down to one per block.
- A small number of remaining partials, one per block, are combined in a second stage, which can be another kernel or a single block.

Two key ideas are worth emphasizing:

- **Associativity and commutativity.** For a parallel reduction to be both correct and efficient, the operation you use to combine elements should be associative, and ideally also commutative. Addition and multiplication are; "take the left operand" is not. For some risk measures, like quantiles, the natural operation is not a simple binary operator. In such cases, you often transform the problem to use a reduction-friendly ingredient; for example, build a histogram in parallel (using atomic updates to bins), then compute the quantile from that histogram.

- **Numerical stability.** Floating-point addition is only approximately associative. Summing millions of scenario P&L values in different orders can lead to slightly different results. Parallel reductions sum parts in a tree order, which may differ from the serial order used by a CPU implementation. Differences are usually tiny, but for sensitive risk reports you should be aware of them. Where necessary, techniques such as pairwise summation, higher-precision accumulation for partials, or compensated summation can reduce discrepancies.

An important pattern in practice is *map-then-reduce*. You might first map each scenario to its portfolio P&L, then reduce those values to compute an expected P&L or a summary risk metric. Structuring the computation in this way helps you separate concerns: the map kernel encodes the financial logic of the payoff or revaluation; the reduction step is a generic, reusable aggregation.

Scan: Cumulative Quantities and Online Views

A *scan*, or prefix sum, is a close cousin of reduction. Instead of collapsing all inputs into a single scalar, scan produces an output array of the same size where each position holds the reduction of all elements up to that point. For a simple sum, this means each output element is a cumulative sum of previous inputs.

Scans show up naturally in finance in several guises:

- Cumulative P&L curves over time for a strategy, given daily or intraday returns.

- Running exposure or inventory, based on a sequence of trades and fills.
- Building indices or offsets into compressed data structures, such as a compact list of active trades or in-the-money paths, where you first mark each element as active or not, then scan to compute the final positions.
- Constructing cumulative distribution functions from histograms for risk reporting.

On a GPU, scan is more subtle than map or reduce because every output depends on all prior inputs. A naive "one thread per element" approach, where each thread loops backward over previous entries, would be entirely serial and defeat the purpose.

Efficient GPU scans use a two-phase strategy:

- **Upsweep** (or reduce phase within blocks): within each block, threads compute partial prefix sums over small chunks of the array, building up local cumulative information.
- **Downsweep** (or distribution phase): the block-level results are combined so that each block knows the sum of all preceding blocks. Threads then adjust their local prefix sums with these offsets to produce the global scan.

From a quant developer's perspective, you rarely need to implement scan by hand. CUDA ecosystem libraries expose scan as a primitive: you provide an input array and an operator (often just addition), and the library returns the prefix results efficiently. The important step is *recognizing* that your problem is a scan, not trying to simulate it with serial loops inside each thread.

One particularly useful GPU pattern is *filtering via scan*. Suppose you have a large array of paths and a Boolean flag indicating whether each path hits a barrier. To efficiently compact only the surviving paths into a new array, you can:

- Map each path to a 0/1 flag (not hit / hit).
- Perform a scan over this flag array to get positions.

- Use the scan result to scatter surviving paths into a compacted output.

This combination of map and scan allows you to manage dynamic sets (such as active paths) efficiently in a data-parallel style.

Stencil: Local Neighborhood Updates on Grids

The first three patterns—map, reduce, scan—operate primarily along one dimension of data (paths, scenarios, time steps) and do so in ways that are mostly "embarrassingly parallel." The *stencil* pattern is different: each output element depends on a small neighborhood of input elements, often on a spatial or state grid.

The most direct appearance of stencil computations in quant finance is in finite-difference solutions of pricing partial differential equations (PDEs). For example:

- A one-dimensional grid of underlying prices where each node's new value depends on itself and its two nearest neighbors.
- A two-dimensional grid over underlying and variance in a stochastic volatility model, where each node depends on several neighbors in both dimensions.

In each time step of an explicit finite-difference scheme, you sweep over the grid and update each node based on its neighbors according to a fixed pattern. That pattern—which neighbors, with which weights—is the stencil.

Other stencil-like operations include:

- Smoothing or filtering a volatility surface with local averaging.
- Applying spatial filters to limit-order-book features in microstructure analysis when represented on a price-time grid.

On the GPU, stencil computations are natural because:

- You can assign one thread per grid point.

- Neighboring grid points are usually stored in neighboring memory addresses, so adjacent threads can access them efficiently.

However, two implementation aspects deserve attention:

- **Boundary conditions.** Grid edges (for example, very low or very high underlying prices) require special treatment. Threads operating on boundary points may need to apply Dirichlet, Neumann, or other conditions, which can introduce conditional logic. If not handled carefully, this can cause divergence within warps. A common strategy is to separate interior updates from boundary updates, or to handle boundaries in small dedicated kernels.

- **Shared memory tiling.** Each stencil update reads multiple nearby values. If every thread fetches its neighbors directly from global memory, you will waste bandwidth re-reading the same values. A standard GPU optimization is to load tiles of the grid into shared (on-chip) memory, including a small halo of neighboring cells, then perform several stencil updates using this fast local copy before moving on.

Stencil computations often involve a time-stepping loop: at each time step you apply the same stencil kernel to update the grid. Although the outer time loop is serial, every step is rich in parallel work across the entire grid. This fits the GPU model well: the kernel performs a wide, uniform sweep over the grid at each step.

Composing Patterns in Real Workloads

Real GPU-accelerated finance applications rarely use just one pattern. Instead, they compose them into pipelines. A typical Monte Carlo pricing pipeline illustrates this:

- **Map**: evolve each path independently over time steps using random draws, producing final underlying values per path.

- **Map**: compute payoff and perhaps pathwise Greeks on each path.

- **Reduce**: aggregate path payoffs into an expected present value and risk measures.

In risk engines that apply full-revaluation under many scenarios, you might see:

- **Map**: for each scenario, revalue each trade or netting set.
- **Reduce**: for each scenario, sum across trades to get portfolio P&L.
- **Reduce / histogram**: aggregate the scenario P&L distribution to get VaR or Expected Shortfall.

A PDE-based pricing pipeline combines stencil and reduction:

- **Stencil**: repeatedly update the grid under a finite-difference scheme for each time step.
- **Reduce**: after convergence, perhaps integrate over the grid or reduce along one dimension to obtain marginal prices or sensitivities.

Scan often appears as a supporting actor:

- Build cumulative cash flows or cumulative exposure curves after a map-based simulation.
- Construct indices and offsets for sparse data structures before a stencil or map operation.

Thinking in patterns helps you separate numerical finance logic from parallel programming mechanics. When facing a complex legacy CPU implementation, you can:

- Identify loops over independent items (map candidates).
- Identify places where you sum or otherwise aggregate (reduce candidates).
- Look for running totals or cumulative structures (scan candidates).

- Look for grid or lattice sweeps with neighbor dependencies (stencil candidates).

Once identified, these pieces can often be delegated to standard GPU building blocks, whether hand-written kernels using established recipes or library calls that encapsulate the details.

Patterns and the CUDA Execution Model

Finally, it is helpful to connect these patterns explicitly back to the CUDA execution and memory model:

- **Map** aligns with assigning independent elements to threads, using coalesced global memory accesses. Blocks are formed simply by partitioning the element range.
- **Reduce** typically uses shared memory within blocks and synchronization primitives inside the block, followed by a second-stage kernel or atomic operations to finish the aggregation.
- **Scan** requires more structured cooperation across threads and blocks, often relying on library implementations that are carefully tuned to the hardware.
- **Stencil** is about arranging threads in one or two dimensions to match grid topology, exploiting shared memory tiling and paying attention to boundary handling.

In subsequent sections, when we turn to concrete libraries and numerical methods, these patterns will keep reappearing. cuBLAS implements dense linear algebra that is, at its core, large map and reduction operations over matrix elements. cuSPARSE encapsulates sparse-structured map and reduce patterns. cuFFT realizes a highly optimized sequence of structured maps and small stencils in the Fourier domain. PDE solvers, Monte Carlo engines, and optimization routines will all largely consist of these patterns chained together.

By building an instinct for map, reduce, scan, and stencil, you equip yourself with a mental toolkit that cuts through surface complexity. When a new model or risk requirement arrives, your first question should be: "Which parts of this are maps, which are reductions, which are scans, and where is there a stencil-like grid structure?" The answer will guide both your choice of GPU libraries and your custom CUDA kernels.

4.2 High-Performance Math Libraries: cuBLAS, cuSPARSE, cuFFT

In the previous section we looked at four fundamental parallel patterns: map, reduce, scan, and stencil. Those patterns describe *how* work is organized across thousands of GPU threads. In this section we move one level closer to what a quant developer actually writes on a daily basis. Rather than designing every kernel from scratch, we ask a more pragmatic question:

> Which parts of my pricing, risk, or analytics code are really just linear algebra or transforms, and can therefore be handed off to tuned GPU libraries?

NVIDIA's math libraries—cuBLAS for dense linear algebra, cuSPARSE for sparse operations, and cuFFT for fast Fourier transforms—exist precisely to answer that question. They hide the low-level CUDA details and present a compact interface: a function call that takes arrays on the GPU and returns the result. Internally, those calls are elaborate compositions of the parallel patterns you have already seen, carefully tuned for memory hierarchies and specific GPU architectures.

The core message of this section is simple but powerful: for a large class of quant workloads, you can obtain most of the available GPU speedup by:

- Identifying which parts of the algorithm are dense linear algebra, sparse linear algebra, or transforms.
- Reshaping your data into the layouts those libraries expect.
- Replacing loops with a handful of library calls.

We will explore each library in turn, emphasizing finance-flavored examples and practical trade-offs that matter in research and production code.

cuBLAS: Dense Linear Algebra as a Workhorse

Dense linear algebra is everywhere in quant finance. Whenever you see vectors and matrices without a special sparsity pattern, cuBLAS is a natural candidate.

Common examples include:

- Covariance and correlation estimation from returns.
- Factor model projections, such as mapping returns into factor space or reconstructing returns from factors.
- Portfolio risk calculations that multiply exposure vectors by covariance matrices.
- Batched transformations of many scenarios, curves, or surfaces at once.

At a high level, cuBLAS implements standard BLAS levels:

- Level 1: vector-vector operations (such as dot products and scaling).
- Level 2: matrix-vector operations.
- Level 3: matrix-matrix operations, the most important for performance.

Thinking in matrices rather than loops

On the CPU it is common to write nested loops: for each scenario, loop over assets, then loop over factors. On the GPU, you should instead aim to express this as a small number of matrix operations.

For example, suppose you have:

- A matrix of factor loadings: rows correspond to assets, columns to factors.

- A matrix of factor realizations across scenarios: rows correspond to factors, columns to scenarios.

The asset return under each scenario is then simply the product of these two matrices. Rather than launching a custom kernel that does triple nested loops, you move the matrices to the GPU and call the cuBLAS matrix-matrix multiply. Internally, cuBLAS will apply a sophisticated combination of map and reduce across tiles of the matrices, using shared memory and registers much more effectively than most hand-written kernels.

The same idea extends to covariance estimation. If you organize your return data as a matrix where each row is an asset and each column is a time observation, you can express the covariance matrix as a matrix product plus some vector operations, all of which are readily handled by cuBLAS.

Data layout: row-major vs column-major

One practical hurdle when starting with cuBLAS is memory layout. Most C and C++ code, and many CPU-based numerical libraries, store matrices in row-major order: consecutive elements of a row are adjacent in memory. In contrast, BLAS libraries traditionally expect column-major order, where columns are stored contiguously.

You do not need to become an expert in storage formats, but you do need a consistent mental picture:

- Decide whether you will store your matrices in row-major or column-major form on the device.
- Understand how to tell cuBLAS which orientation it is looking at, for example by treating a row-major matrix as the transpose of a column-major one.
- Aim to avoid unnecessary data rearrangements, which can eat into the speed gains from offloading to the GPU.

A pragmatic approach is:

- For new GPU-native code, follow the BLAS convention and store matrices in column-major order from the start.

- For existing CPU code, consider whether it is cheaper to transpose once when moving data to the GPU than to refactor large parts of your code base. Often a single transpose at the boundary is entirely acceptable.

Batched operations: many small problems at once

Quant workloads often involve many small to medium-size matrices rather than one huge matrix. Examples include:

- Per-issuer or per-sector risk blocks in a large portfolio.
- Many Monte Carlo scenarios where you apply the same linear transformation independently to each scenario.
- Calibration tasks where you fit models to many time series or cross sections in parallel.

Launching a separate kernel for each small matrix multiply is inefficient. The overhead of each launch becomes a bottleneck. cuBLAS addresses this with batched APIs: you provide pointers or strides describing a collection of matrices, and the library processes them together in a single call. Internally, the batched routines look very different from the unbatched ones, but at the interface level you still think in terms of matrices.

For a risk engine, batched operations are particularly attractive when you have to apply the same covariance or factor model to many scenario sets or portfolios. Instead of writing custom kernels that juggle multiple indices and risk making off-by-one errors, you define a batch of matrices and delegate the work.

Precision and performance trade-offs

Modern GPUs support multiple numeric precisions, including single precision, double precision, and in some cases lower-precision formats. cuBLAS exposes operations for each. In pricing and risk, you typically care about:

- Sufficient accuracy for decisions and regulatory reporting.
- Throughput and latency for intraday or real-time analytics.

Single precision is usually faster and uses less memory, which means more data can fit on the GPU and bandwidth is used more efficiently. Double precision is more accurate but may run significantly slower on some hardware generations. A common pattern is:

- Use single precision for large-scale exploratory or intraday calculations where small numerical differences are acceptable.
- Use double precision for end-of-day risk reports, official valuations, or calibration routines that are sensitive to tiny discrepancies.

cuBLAS also provides mixed-precision capabilities, which can be useful when the core multiplications can tolerate lower precision but accumulations or final reductions require higher precision. The details depend on hardware support, but the conceptual idea is straightforward: you separate where you can afford to be approximate from where you must be accurate.

Integrating cuBLAS into C++ and Python

From a distance, using cuBLAS is simply:

- Allocate memory on the GPU.
- Copy input matrices and vectors from the host (CPU) to the device (GPU).
- Call cuBLAS routines to perform the operations.
- Copy results back to the host when needed.

In a C++ code base, this typically means managing device pointers explicitly and using a cuBLAS `handle` that represents a context for library calls. In Python, higher-level libraries such as CuPy or PyTorch hide most of this plumbing. You operate on array objects that already live on the GPU, and their methods internally call cuBLAS.

In either language, the key design discipline is: try to move data to the GPU once, perform as many chained operations as possible there, and only transfer reduced or final results back. Extra transfers can easily offset the gains from fast GPU math.

cuSPARSE: Exploiting Structure in Large Problems

Not all matrices in finance are dense. Many important problems produce matrices where most entries are zero:

- Discretized PDE operators in finite-difference grids.
- Constraint matrices in large portfolios, where each asset appears in only a few constraints.
- Factor loading matrices with a block or band structure.

Storing such matrices as dense arrays wastes memory and compute. cuSPARSE targets these structured cases, providing data formats and routines that operate only on the non-zero entries.

Sparse formats: CSR, CSC, and COO

The intuition behind sparse formats is simple: rather than keep all entries, you store:

- The values of non-zero elements.
- Their row and column positions.
- Some indexing information to find quickly which entries live in each row or column.

The most common cuSPARSE formats are:

- **CSR (Compressed Sparse Row).** Non-zero entries are grouped row by row. This is natural when you often multiply the matrix by a dense vector on the right, which is exactly what happens in many iterative solvers and PDE time steps.
- **CSC (Compressed Sparse Column).** Similar concept but grouped by columns. More convenient if your algorithm naturally moves along columns.
- **COO (Coordinate Format).** A simple triplet form: one array of row indices, one of column indices, and one of values. Easy to construct but less efficient for repeated operations, so it is often used as an intermediate representation.

For a quant developer, the main design choice is which sparse pattern arises in the model. A tridiagonal PDE operator fits naturally into CSR with exactly three non-zero entries per row. A more complex two-dimensional grid might have a band structure still well-suited to CSR. Once you settle on a format, you can reuse it across many time steps or iterations.

Sparse matvec and iterative methods

The fundamental operation in cuSPARSE is sparse matrix-vector multiplication. In a PDE solver, each time step may involve repeatedly applying the operator to a vector of grid values. In an optimization context, iterative solvers such as conjugate gradient or GMRES repeatedly call sparse matvec as part of their loops.

Internally, sparse matvec is a carefully orchestrated combination of map and reduction:

- Each non-zero entry contributes to one element of the result.
- Contributions to the same output element must be combined.

cuSPARSE handles this efficiently, taking into account the sparsity pattern and using shared memory where helpful.

For you as a user, the main task is to:

- Build the sparse representation once, usually from model parameters or grid definitions.
- Pass it, along with input vectors, to cuSPARSE routines inside your time-stepping or optimization loops.

This is particularly valuable in finite-difference PDE solvers. The same sparse operator is applied at every time step. Building it once and then reusing it through cuSPARSE allows your GPU code to focus on evolving the solution, rather than repeatedly re-deriving the structure.

Triangular solves and preconditioners

Beyond matvec, cuSPARSE includes routines for triangular solves and related operations. These appear in:

- Implicit PDE schemes, where each time step requires solving a banded or otherwise structured linear system.
- Preconditioners for iterative solvers in calibration and optimization tasks.

A triangular solve is more sequential than a matvec, because each variable can depend on previously solved ones. Nonetheless, cuSPARSE exploits whatever parallelism is available, for example across independent rows or blocks. On the user side, you still think in terms of solving linear systems with known sparsity, not in terms of how to coordinate threads.

cuFFT: Transforms for Pricing and Signal Processing

The fast Fourier transform (FFT) is another workhorse algorithm with deep connections to quant finance. At a high level, FFTs allow you to:

- Turn convolutions into multiplications, which is central to certain pricing methods.
- Move between time and frequency domains for signal processing tasks on high-frequency data.
- Implement pricing frameworks based on characteristic functions.

cuFFT provides highly optimized implementations of one-dimensional and multi-dimensional FFTs, including batched transforms.

FFT-based option pricing

In several option pricing frameworks, notably those based on characteristic functions, you can express option prices as integrals that look like Fourier transforms. By discretizing these integrals on a grid and using FFTs, you can compute prices across many strikes and maturities in one go.

From a GPU perspective, an FFT-based pricer often looks like:

- Prepare an input array on a grid of transformed variables (for example, log-strikes or frequency variables).
- Apply the FFT using cuFFT, obtaining values in the complementary domain.
- Apply a simple pointwise transformation (a map) to scale or adjust these values.
- Optionally apply an inverse FFT to return to the original domain.

All the heavy lifting is in the cuFFT calls. Your custom kernel work is limited to preparing inputs and applying simple per-point operations, which align perfectly with the map pattern.

Signal processing for high-frequency data

In market microstructure research or high-frequency trading analytics, you may want to:

- Estimate spectral densities of returns.
- Apply filters to remove certain frequency components.
- Detect periodicities or structural breaks in order-book events.

These tasks generally involve applying FFTs to many overlapping windows of time series data across multiple instruments. This is an ideal setting for cuFFT's batched interface:

- You lay out your windows as rows or columns of a large array on the GPU.
- You call a batched FFT, which processes all these windows in parallel.

Just as with cuBLAS, batching is crucial. A single small FFT does not provide enough work to saturate a modern GPU. Hundreds or thousands of small FFTs processed together can.

Practical issues: sizing and padding

FFT algorithms are efficient when the transform length has small prime factors, especially powers of two. In practice:

- You may pad your input arrays to the next convenient length for performance, even if the extra entries are logically zero.
- You need to be aware of how this padding interacts with your numerical model, ensuring that it does not introduce unintended effects such as aliasing.

For pricing, this often shows up as a compromise between grid resolution and computational cost. For signal processing, it shapes window sizes and overlaps.

cuFFT allows you to specify strides and distances between transforms in batched mode, which is useful when your data for each asset or window are not laid out contiguously. As with cuBLAS and cuSPARSE, some up-front attention to data layout pays off repeatedly.

An Engineering Mindset: Identify, Reshape, Delegate

Across cuBLAS, cuSPARSE, and cuFFT, a common engineering mindset emerges:

- **Profile first.** Find where your CPU code spends most of its time. In quant applications this is often in linear algebra or transforms.
- **Recognize structure.** Ask whether that hotspot is dense linear algebra, sparse linear algebra, or a convolution/transform.
- **Reshape the problem.** Organize your data so it can be fed to the corresponding GPU library: matrices in suitable layouts, sparse operators in CSR or another format, time series in batched FFT-friendly form.
- **Delegate to the library.** Replace hand-written loops or custom kernels with calls to cuBLAS, cuSPARSE, or cuFFT. Adjust batching and precision as needed.

This approach has several advantages:

- **Performance.** NVIDIA invests heavily in optimizing these libraries for each hardware generation. Your code benefits automatically as GPUs evolve.
- **Robustness.** Library routines are heavily tested and widely used, reducing the risk of subtle bugs in low-level parallel logic.
- **Maintainability.** Your own code remains focused on financial logic—which payoff, which model, which risk measure—instead of the details of synchronization or memory tiling.

It also aligns neatly with the parallel patterns from the previous section. Internally, cuBLAS, cuSPARSE, and cuFFT combine map, reduce, scan, and stencil in finely tuned ways. By working at the library level, you leverage those patterns without having to reimplement them.

Connecting Back to Quant Workflows

To make these ideas concrete, consider a few end-to-end examples:

- **Factor-based risk engine.** Use cuBLAS to project returns onto factors and to build covariance matrices; use additional cuBLAS calls to propagate factor shocks through portfolios. If your factor structure is block-diagonal, batched operations can process many blocks in parallel.
- **PDE-based pricing.** Use cuSPARSE to store the finite-difference operator and to apply it at each time step, possibly combined with cuSPARSE triangular solves for implicit schemes. The stencil pattern from the previous section is realized here via sparse matvec calls.
- **Characteristic-function-based pricing.** Use cuFFT to compute prices on a grid of strikes and maturities via Fourier transforms, applying simple map-style adjustments before or after the transform. Batched FFTs allow you to handle many parameter sets simultaneously.
- **Intraday analytics dashboard.** Use cuFFT's batched transforms to analyze high-frequency returns streams; use cuBLAS to

run small regression or factor models on top of those features across many instruments in parallel.

In each case, you are not writing kernels that directly manipulate thread indices or shared memory. Instead, you design the computation at a higher level of abstraction, in terms of matrices, sparse operators, and transforms. The GPU libraries provide the bridge from that level to efficient execution on the hardware.

As we move into later sections on Python-based GPU workflows and specific numerical methods such as Monte Carlo and PDE solvers, these libraries will reappear. Python libraries like CuPy and RAPIDS wrap cuBLAS, cuSPARSE, and cuFFT, making them accessible in interactive research environments. Monte Carlo codes often call cuBLAS to perform correlated draws via Cholesky factors. PDE solvers build their operators with cuSPARSE. FFT-based pricers rest directly on cuFFT.

The overarching theme is that you do not have to be a CUDA specialist to benefit from GPU acceleration. By learning to recognize where dense linear algebra, sparse structure, and transforms live inside your models, and by trusting well-engineered libraries where appropriate, you can move the bulk of your computational effort onto the GPU with only a modest increase in code complexity.

4.3 Python on GPU: CuPy, Numba & RAPIDS

In the last two sections we reasoned from the bottom up and the top down. From the bottom, we saw how GPU workloads decompose into patterns such as map, reduce, scan, and stencil. From the top, we saw how vendor libraries like cuBLAS, cuSPARSE, and cuFFT package those patterns into dense linear algebra and transform routines.

Most quant researchers, however, do not spend their day writing C++ or CUDA. They live in Python notebooks, wiring together NumPy, pandas, and SciPy, experimenting with models, running backtests, and pulling data from internal databases. The central question for this section is therefore:

> How can we keep using Python for research while still taking advantage of GPU acceleration, without rewriting everything in CUDA C++?

The modern answer revolves around three main tools:

- **CuPy** for GPU-accelerated array computing with a NumPy-like interface.
- **Numba** for writing custom CUDA kernels directly in Python syntax.
- **RAPIDS** (cuDF, cuML, cuGraph, and others) for higher-level data science operations on the GPU.

Together, these form a stack that allows you to:

- Prototype in familiar Python abstractions.
- Gradually move bottlenecks onto the GPU.
- Only drop down to custom kernels when library calls are not enough.

In this section we will build an intuition for how each of these tools works, where it fits in a quant workflow, and what to watch out for in practice.

CuPy: NumPy, but on the GPU

CuPy is best thought of as "NumPy for CUDA-enabled GPUs." It provides an array object whose interface is intentionally very close to that of NumPy. If you know how to work with NumPy arrays, you already understand most of CuPy's surface area.

Conceptually, you should picture:

- A *NumPy array* as a block of memory in main RAM, manipulated by CPU instructions and linked to libraries such as BLAS, LAPACK, or FFTW.

- A *CuPy array* as a block of memory on the GPU device, manipulated by CUDA kernels and calling into cuBLAS, cuSPARSE, and cuFFT under the hood.

The differences are mostly about where the data lives and which libraries are called to perform the heavy computations. The syntax for indexing, slicing, broadcasting, and many ufunc-style operations is intentionally similar.

Why CuPy is attractive for quants

CuPy is particularly appealing in a quant setting for several reasons:

- **Low friction.** Many array-based research scripts can be gradually migrated by changing array creation and a few function imports, rather than rewriting entire models.
- **Library interop.** CuPy acts as a bridge to cuBLAS, cuSPARSE, and cuFFT, meaning that vector and matrix operations, decompositions, and FFTs can be mapped directly onto optimized GPU routines.
- **Familiar idioms.** Broadcasting over axes, stacking and concatenating arrays, computing statistics along a dimension: all of this looks much like NumPy, which shortens the learning curve.

Common CuPy-friendly tasks in quant finance include:

- Large Monte Carlo simulations where each path or scenario is an element in a CuPy array.
- Factor model calculations, including matrix-matrix and matrix-vector operations on returns and loadings.
- Covariance and correlation estimations across many assets or factors.
- Spectral analysis or convolution-based pricing using CuPy's FFT wrappers.

Mental model: data movement is the real cost

The main conceptual shift when moving from NumPy to CuPy is to think carefully about *data movement*:

- When you create an array with CuPy, it resides on the GPU.
- When you convert a CuPy array back to a NumPy array, its contents must be copied from the GPU device to the CPU host.
- Similarly, converting a NumPy array to CuPy triggers a transfer from host to device.

Each of these transfers incurs latency and uses finite bandwidth over the PCIe bus (or NVLink on some systems). If you repeatedly move arrays back and forth for small operations, you can easily negate the performance benefit of GPU computation.

Therefore, a good design heuristic when using CuPy is:

- Bring data to the GPU once (for example, at the beginning of a simulation or a large analytics calculation).
- Perform as many chained operations as possible in CuPy space.
- Only convert back to NumPy at the end, when you truly need data on the CPU for logging, plotting, or integration with legacy systems.

CuPy and the patterns from earlier

Under the hood, many CuPy operations are direct realizations of the parallel patterns:

- Elementwise expressions (for example, computing option payoffs on arrays of terminal prices) are map operations.
- Aggregations such as sums, means, or variances across axes are reductions.
- Cumulative sums or products are scans.
- Convolutions or finite-difference style operations can be expressed either as stencils or via FFT-based transforms.

Because CuPy dispatches these operations to tuned CUDA kernels and math libraries, you rarely need to think about thread blocks or shared memory. You instead think at the level of array operations and linear algebra, letting CuPy manage the mapping onto parallel patterns.

Numba: Custom Kernels in Python Syntax

CuPy shines when your algorithm fits well into elementwise operations, reductions, and library routines. But in real trading and risk systems, you will occasionally face logic that does not map cleanly to existing primitives. You might need:

- A bespoke path-dependent payoff with state machines or triggers.
- Custom simulation steps that do not align with standard random processes.
- A specialized aggregation across paths or scenarios that mixes conditions and arithmetic in a domain-specific way.

In these cases, writing a CUDA C++ kernel from scratch is an option, but it increases the cognitive and maintenance burden. Numba offers a middle ground: you write functions in a restricted subset of Python, decorate them to indicate they should run on the GPU, and let Numba compile them into CUDA kernels.

The Numba CUDA mental model

Numba's CUDA support gives you explicit control over:

- The function body, which describes what each thread does.
- The grid and block configuration, which describes how many threads run and how they are grouped.
- Access to special variables such as the thread's index within the grid.

Conceptually, you think:

- "This Numba function will execute on the GPU; each call of its body corresponds to one CUDA thread."
- "I will launch it with a grid size that covers all my paths, timesteps, or scenarios."

Inside the function, you can write loops, conditionals, and arithmetic similar to standard Python, but you must avoid features that cannot be easily translated to GPU instructions (for example, arbitrary Python objects or dynamic list operations).

When to reach for Numba

Numba is most useful when:

- You have identified a bottleneck in a Python loop that operates elementwise or over a structured grid, but the logic is too irregular for clean expression with CuPy's vectorized operations.
- You want to control the parallelization strategy—for example, mapping threads across two dimensions (paths and timesteps) or over a two-dimensional PDE grid.
- You want to gradually move performance-critical sections of a Python backtest or risk engine to the GPU without rewriting everything in another language.

A typical workflow is:

- Start with a pure Python implementation using NumPy and idiomatic loops.
- Profile to find hotspots.
- For the most expensive loops, attempt to "vectorize" with CuPy.
- If vectorization becomes unwieldy or leads to obscure code, rewrite those loops as clear Numba CUDA kernels.

This allows you to balance clarity and performance. CuPy covers common operations; Numba fills the gaps where custom logic is unavoidable.

Interoperability with CuPy and libraries

Numba kernels can operate on device arrays that originate from CuPy. In practice this means:

- You can use CuPy for high-level linear algebra, random number generation, and FFTs.

- Then, when necessary, pass CuPy arrays into Numba kernels for bespoke operations.

Internally, this works because both tools agree on how device memory is represented. From your point of view, you are composing two layers:

- A library layer (CuPy) that is close to cuBLAS, cuSPARSE, and cuFFT.
- A custom layer (Numba) that encodes your model-specific logic.

This composition matches our earlier pattern-based view. Library calls implement well-known patterns; custom kernels implement the "special cases" that differentiate your model or strategy from everyone else's.

RAPIDS: DataFrames, ML, and Graphs on the GPU

While CuPy and Numba focus on array and kernel-level computation, many modern quant workflows also rely heavily on higher-level tools:

- DataFrames (pandas) for ingesting, cleaning, and joining time series and cross-sectional data.
- Machine learning libraries (such as scikit-learn) for building predictive models or analyzing factor structures.
- Graph analytics for network-based risk, such as counterparty exposures or liquidity networks.

The RAPIDS ecosystem aims to provide GPU-accelerated counterparts to these tools, with APIs that feel familiar to Python data scientists:

- **cuDF** for DataFrame-like operations on the GPU.
- **cuML** for machine learning algorithms implemented on the GPU.
- **cuGraph** for graph analytics.

For a quant researcher, RAPIDS offers a way to keep the entire pipeline—from raw data to backtest output—on the GPU as much as possible, even when the operations are not obviously linear algebra.

cuDF: GPU DataFrames

cuDF is a columnar DataFrame library whose interface is deliberately close to pandas. Typical operations include:

- Reading and writing tabular data (for example, CSVs or Parquet files).
- Filtering rows based on conditions.
- Group-by aggregations (for example, by symbol or sector).
- Windowed operations over time, such as rolling means or volatilities.

In a factor research setting, you might:

- Load daily or intraday price and fundamental data into cuDF.
- Compute features such as moving averages, momentum scores, or valuation ratios entirely on the GPU.
- Join these features with future returns to create a training set for a model.

Because cuDF operates on device memory, subsequent steps—such as feeding the data into cuML models or converting selected columns to CuPy arrays for custom analysis—can often be done without copying back to the CPU. This keeps the whole feature engineering stage GPU-resident.

cuML: Machine learning on the GPU

cuML implements many supervised and unsupervised learning algorithms with APIs inspired by scikit-learn. Examples include:

- Linear and logistic regression.
- Principal component analysis (PCA).

- Clustering algorithms like k-means.
- Gradient-boosted trees and random forests (in some submodules).

Common quant use cases include:

- Running PCA or other dimensionality reduction on large factor or return matrices.
- Training cross-sectional return models with thousands of features across many assets.
- Building risk factor models where exposures are learned from data rather than specified analytically.

Because cuML is built on the same lower-level libraries, its algorithms internally call cuBLAS, cuSPARSE, and related primitives. From your perspective, you call high-level methods such as "fit" and "predict" on cuML estimators, passing cuDF columns or CuPy arrays as inputs.

cuGraph: Networks of exposure and liquidity

Graph analytics is less central to many shops than time series and cross-sectional analysis, but when it appears, it is often performance-sensitive and structurally irregular:

- Networks of counterparty exposures.
- Limit-order-book connectivity between venues and instruments.
- Correlation or co-movement networks among assets or factors.

cuGraph provides GPU-accelerated implementations of algorithms such as PageRank, shortest paths, community detection, and centrality measures. In a risk context, this could support:

- Identifying key counterparties in a web of exposures.
- Simulating contagion or shock propagation across a network.

Although cuGraph is more specialized, it rounds out the picture: you can now treat tables, arrays, and graphs as first-class GPU data structures in Python.

Putting It Together: A Pythonic GPU Workflow

Let us now piece together how CuPy, Numba, and RAPIDS might work in a realistic research or backtesting pipeline.

Example: Factor backtest at scale

Imagine you want to backtest a cross-sectional equity strategy across thousands of stocks and many years of data, with dozens or hundreds of candidate factors.

A GPU-friendly workflow could look like this:

- **Data loading and cleaning with cuDF.** Read historical price and fundamental data into cuDF DataFrames, perform joins and filters on the GPU, and align data across symbols and dates.

- **Feature engineering with cuDF and CuPy.** Use cuDF for windowed operations such as rolling returns, volatilities, and volume averages. Convert selected columns to CuPy arrays for vectorized transformations, such as nonlinear rescaling, ranking within cross sections, or normalization.

- **Risk model and covariance estimation with CuPy (and cuBLAS).** Assemble large return matrices as CuPy arrays and compute covariance or correlation matrices using CuPy's linear algebra interface, which dispatches to cuBLAS. Use these matrices to estimate risk or to build factor portfolios.

- **Custom backtest logic with Numba.** For the parts of the backtest that require complex logic—such as trade scheduling, position capping, or transaction cost modeling—write Numba CUDA kernels that operate over time and instruments, using device arrays produced earlier. These kernels implement your bespoke map and reduce operations at scale.

- **Modeling with cuML.** If your strategy includes a predictive component, such as forecasting relative returns from a feature set, use cuML to train models on GPU-resident features and labels. Predictions remain on the GPU, ready to feed into the backtest logic.

- **Aggregation and reporting.** Use CuPy reductions and scans to compute P&L curves, risk statistics, and drawdown profiles on the GPU. Only for the final summaries and plots do you move small arrays back to the CPU for integration into reports or dashboards.

This pipeline illustrates the key advantages:

- Data moves across GPU-native abstractions (cuDF, CuPy, Numba, cuML) without repeated host-device transfers.
- You use high-level operations where possible, dropping down to custom kernels only for idiosyncratic logic.
- You remain in Python throughout, which preserves the speed of iteration and the accessibility important in research teams.

Example: Monte Carlo risk engine prototype

As another example, consider prototyping a Monte Carlo risk engine in Python:

- Use CuPy to generate large arrays of random numbers on the GPU, possibly drawing correlated shocks via Cholesky factors using CuPy's linear algebra interface.
- Use CuPy elementwise operations and broadcasting to evolve paths under chosen models.
- Implement complex path-dependent payoffs in Numba kernels, operating on GPU arrays of paths and parameters.
- Aggregate scenario results with CuPy reductions to obtain risk measures such as expected loss or tail quantiles.

This mirrors the patterns from earlier chapters: map for path evolution and payoff evaluation, reduce for aggregation, with the workload expressed and executed entirely within Python.

Practical Considerations and Pitfalls

As with any powerful toolset, there are trade-offs and practical details to manage.

Environment management

GPU-enabled Python stacks can be sensitive to versions of:

- The CUDA toolkit and driver.
- cuBLAS, cuSPARSE, and cuFFT.
- CuPy, Numba, and RAPIDS libraries.

It is usually best to:

- Use environment managers such as conda to create isolated environments.
- Align versions according to tested combinations from distribution channels or your infrastructure team.
- Keep a record of environment configurations that are known to work in production settings.

Debugging and observability

Debugging GPU code, even when written in Python, is less straightforward than debugging pure CPU code. Some guidelines:

- Start with small problem sizes where you can compare GPU outputs to trusted CPU reference implementations.
- Use assertions and sanity checks frequently, especially around device-host transfers and shape assumptions.
- Where possible, build your Numba kernels incrementally, validating each additional piece of logic against a simpler Python version.

Logging from inside GPU kernels is limited, so most diagnosis happens by inspecting inputs and outputs. That reinforces the importance of clean, well-structured kernels.

When GPUs do not help

Not every Python workload benefits from moving to the GPU. Situations where CPU may be preferable include:

- Very small problem sizes, where kernel launch overhead dominates.
- Highly irregular control flow, with heavy branching on a per-element basis.
- Work that is I/O-bound rather than compute-bound, such as reading from slow storage or remote APIs.

In these cases, sticking to optimized CPU libraries, possibly with multithreading, may be simpler and more efficient. The decision should be driven by profiling and an understanding of where time is truly spent.

Summary: Staying in Python, Thinking in GPUs

CuPy, Numba, and RAPIDS collectively answer a crucial organizational and technical requirement: they let quant teams stay in a productive, high-level Python environment while still reaping the performance benefits of GPUs.

Conceptually:

- CuPy connects your array-based thinking to GPU-accelerated linear algebra and transforms.
- Numba lets you encode custom parallel patterns in Python syntax, targeting the GPU without leaving the language.
- RAPIDS brings DataFrames, machine learning, and graph analytics into the GPU realm, integrating naturally with both CuPy and Numba.

This stack builds directly on the foundations laid in earlier sections:

- The parallel patterns you learned—map, reduce, scan, and stencil—are the invisible backbone of the kernels that CuPy, Numba, and RAPIDS rely on.

- The math libraries you just saw—cuBLAS, cuSPARSE, cuFFT—sit underneath many of the operations in these Python tools.

As you move into later chapters on Monte Carlo, PDE/FFT solvers, and optimization, remember that you rarely need to choose between "clean Python" and "fast CUDA." With careful design and an awareness of data movement, you can prototype and run sophisticated GPU-accelerated quant analytics entirely in Python, reserving low-level CUDA work for the rare cases where you need absolute control.

4.4 Monte Carlo Techniques on GPU

In earlier sections we saw that many quant workloads can be described in terms of simple parallel patterns (map, reduce, scan, stencil) and then delegated to high-performance libraries through Python tools like CuPy and Numba. Monte Carlo simulation sits at the intersection of these themes. It is numerically straightforward, highly parallel, and crucial for pricing complex derivatives and computing risk measures.

This makes Monte Carlo a natural candidate for GPU acceleration. The high-level idea is simple:

> Assign each path or scenario to one or more GPU threads, evolve all paths in parallel, and then aggregate the resulting payoffs into prices and risk statistics.

In this section we develop that idea into a complete workflow. We will:

- Map each stage of a Monte Carlo pricer onto the GPU.
- Discuss random number generation and how to obtain many independent streams in parallel.
- Show how common variance-reduction techniques can be implemented without destroying parallel efficiency.
- Introduce quasi-Monte Carlo (low-discrepancy) sequences and their GPU-specific pitfalls.

Throughout, we keep a tight connection to the patterns you have already seen: map for path evolution and payoff evaluation, reduce for aggregating across paths, and scan-style ideas where running quantities are needed.

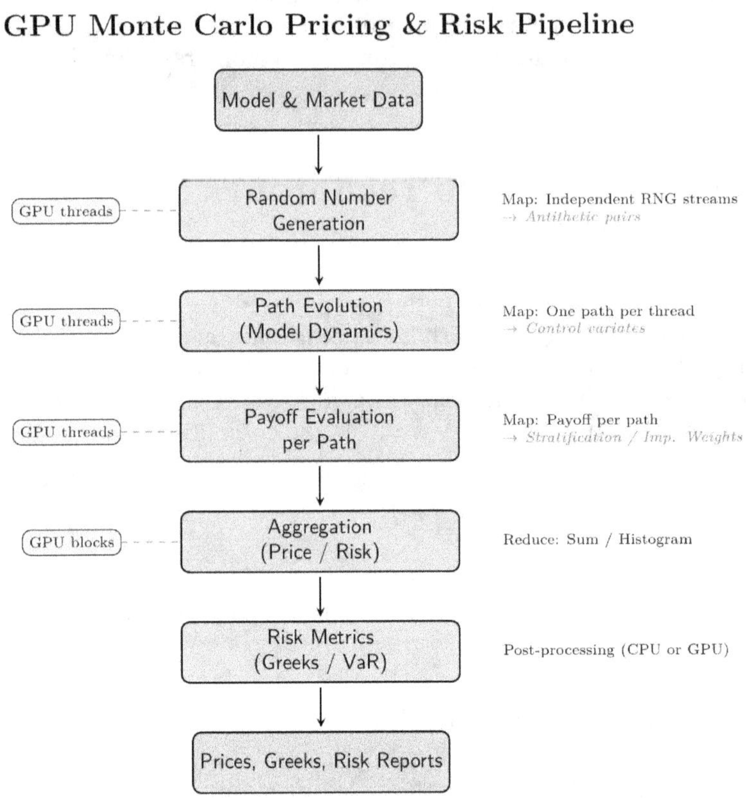

Decomposing Monte Carlo into GPU-Friendly Stages

A generic Monte Carlo pricer for a derivative or portfolio can be described in five conceptual stages:

1. Generate random numbers or low-discrepancy points.
2. Map those random inputs into paths of underlying risk factors.
3. Evaluate payoffs or P&L for each path or scenario.
4. Aggregate across paths to obtain prices or risk measures.
5. Optionally post-process results into Greeks or further risk analytics.

Each stage offers an opportunity for parallelism:

- Stages 1–3 are naturally *map*-like: each path or scenario can be handled mostly independently.
- Stage 4 is *reduce*-like: you collapse per-path values down to a few summary numbers.

The power of the GPU lies in always keeping these stages as vectorized and independent as possible. The central design principle is:

> Give each thread a well-defined, self-contained piece of work (for example, one path), and avoid cross-thread dependencies until the final aggregation step.

We now go through these stages in more detail.

Random Number Generation on GPU

The starting point for Monte Carlo is a large supply of random variates. In a GPU context, you need:

- Many independent random sequences, one for each path or thread.
- Efficient generation of standard distributions (uniform, normal, lognormal).
- Reproducibility for debugging and backtesting.

Vendor libraries such as cuRAND, and their Python wrappers via CuPy or other frameworks, address these needs. Conceptually, you can think of two approaches.

Pre-generate random numbers in bulk

In this pattern:

- You call a library routine to fill a large array on the GPU with random values, for example, standard normals arranged as a two-dimensional array (paths by timesteps).
- Path-evolution kernels read from this pre-populated array.

This is attractive because:

- It separates concerns: the RNG is one kernel, the path evolution is another.
- You can reuse the same random draws for multiple models or payoffs in what-if analyses.

However, pre-generating all random numbers may require large amounts of device memory if paths are long or very numerous. In those cases, you may instead generate random numbers on the fly.

Generate random numbers inside the path kernel

Here, each thread maintains its own random number generator (RNG) state. The workflow is:

- Initialize an RNG state per thread, using a global seed and a per-thread sequence identifier (such as the path index).
- Within the path evolution loop, each thread draws random variates from its RNG state as needed.

This design:

- Supports arbitrarily long paths without pre-storing all variates.
- Keeps RNG state local to threads, which is good for parallelism.

The challenge is to ensure that different threads' random streams do not overlap or exhibit unwanted correlations. Modern GPU RNG libraries provide counter-based or parameterized generators designed for this purpose. As a user, you mainly need to:

- Use recommended seeding and sequence-indexing schemes from the RNG documentation.
- Avoid "naively" seeding each thread with consecutive integers without understanding how the generator uses seeds and subsequences.

Reproducibility and debugging

For risk and backtesting, reproducibility matters. You want:

- A fixed mapping from a combination of *global seed* and *path index* to the stream of random numbers for that path.
- Stability of results across runs on the same hardware and software configuration.

In practice, you should:

- Use explicit seeds in RNG calls, not default seeds.
- Log seeds as part of your experiment or backtest metadata.
- Keep an option to run on a single thread or on the CPU for small test cases, so you can cross-check the logic against a reference implementation.

Path Evolution: One Thread per Path

Once you have random drivers, you need to evolve underlying variables according to a model. For example:

- Equity prices under a geometric Brownian motion or stochastic volatility model.
- Interest rate term structures under a short-rate or HJM model.

- A portfolio value driven by multiple correlated risk factors.

On the GPU, the simplest and often best approach is *one thread per path*. Each thread:

- Starts from initial conditions (spot, rates, volatilities, etc.).
- Steps through time, using random draws to update the state according to the discretized model.
- Optionally records path-dependent information (for example, running maximum for barricr options or accumulated exposure for CVA calculations).

This design is a classic *map* over paths:

- Paths are independent given the random draws.
- Each thread's work is similar in structure, which reduces warp divergence.

Grid design: paths versus timesteps

You must decide how to map two dimensions—number of paths and length of each path—onto the one-dimensional thread index. There are two common strategies:

- **Path-major.** Each thread handles one full path across all timesteps. Timesteps form an inner loop within the thread. This is easy to reason about and well-suited when each path has the same length.
- **Time-slice-based.** You launch kernels timestep by timestep. At each step, many threads update the state for many paths in parallel. This can be useful if your model requires communication or normalization across paths at each time (for example, resampling in certain particle filters).

For most standard derivative pricing tasks, the path-major layout is simpler and effective. It also aligns well with memory layouts where you store state variables for all paths at a given time contiguously, enabling coalesced memory access.

Memory layout for efficiency

To achieve high throughput, you want:

- Coalesced reads of random numbers: threads in a warp should read from adjacent memory locations when they fetch shocks for the next timestep.
- Coalesced writes of state variables or payoffs: when threads store final values or intermediate states, their writes should also be to adjacent locations.

One practical pattern is to:

- Store random numbers as a two-dimensional array indexed by timestep and path, with paths as the fastest-changing index.
- Have each thread walk through that second index for its path, which leads to coalesced accesses across warps at each timestep.

Even when using higher-level tools like CuPy and Numba, it is worth verifying that your array shapes and index orders support contiguous slices along the dimension your threads are parallelizing over.

Payoff Evaluation and Pathwise Greeks

After evolving paths, you evaluate payoffs. This is again a map: each thread, responsible for one path, computes:

- The discounted payoff of a derivative.
- Per-path contributions to Greeks (sensitivities) if you use pathwise or likelihood-ratio methods.
- Path-level P&L or exposure for portfolios, possibly per time bucket.

For simple European options, payoff evaluation is a direct transformation of the final underlying value. For path-dependent options (barriers, Asians, lookbacks), you may need information accumulated along the path, which the evolution phase can record.

Pathwise Greeks on GPU

For many models and payoffs, you can compute Greeks directly from the same random paths, without resorting to "bump-and-revalue" approaches that require rerunning the entire simulation. Pathwise estimators do this by:

- Propagating additional sensitivity variables alongside the main state during path evolution.
- Combining these with payoff derivatives at the end of each path.

On the GPU, this simply adds more fields to each thread's local state and a bit more arithmetic per timestep. As long as you avoid expensive per-path branching, this is an ideal use of the GPU's arithmetic throughput: each thread does more work, which can improve overall utilization, while still keeping paths independent.

Aggregation: From Millions of Paths to a Few Numbers

Once you have per-path payoffs (and maybe per-path Greeks), you must aggregate them into:

- Estimated prices (for example, the mean discounted payoff).
- Risk measures (for example, value-at-risk or expected shortfall).
- Confidence intervals or error estimates.

These are all *reductions* over the array of path results. On a GPU, reductions are typically implemented in two phases:

1. Each thread block computes partial sums or partial statistics over its subset of paths, using shared memory for speed.

2. A second pass combines these partials into final results.

If you are using a high-level library such as CuPy, this is hidden behind calls like "mean", "sum", or "percentile" executed on device arrays. Under the hood, the library uses well-tested reduction kernels.

Computing risk measures

Beyond simple averages, risk measures involve:

- Estimating quantiles of the loss distribution, for example, for value-at-risk.
- Estimating tail expectations, for expected shortfall.

Two common GPU strategies are:

- **Sort or partial sort paths on the GPU.** Sorting millions of values is feasible on modern GPUs using parallel sort algorithms. Once sorted, quantiles and tail means are easy to read off. GPU sorting libraries encapsulate the complex parallel pattern.
- **Histogram-based approximations.** For some tasks you can bin P&L into a histogram in parallel (using atomic updates on bin counts), then approximate quantiles and tail means from the histogram. This trades some accuracy for speed and lower memory.

Both approaches are compatible with the map-reduce picture: you map each path to its P&L, then reduce through sorting or histogramming.

Variance Reduction Techniques on GPU

Raw Monte Carlo can be slow to converge. Variance-reduction methods improve accuracy for a given number of paths—or, equivalently, reduce the number of paths needed for a target error. The key question for GPU implementations is:

> Can we apply variance-reduction without destroying the data parallelism that makes GPUs effective?

The answer is usually yes, with careful design. We focus on three widely used methods.

Antithetic variates

Antithetic variates use pairs of negatively correlated paths to reduce variance. For example, in a model driven by standard normals, for each random vector Z you also use $-Z$ as a driver for a companion path. Their payoffs are then averaged.

On the GPU, antithetic variates can be implemented by:

- Either having each thread simulate a pair of paths (one with Z, one with $-Z$) and average their payoffs.
- Or assigning Z to thread i and $-Z$ to thread $i+N$, then combining their results in a later reduction.

The first approach keeps everything local to the thread, which is simple and avoids cross-thread communication. It doubles the per-thread computation but maintains the same number of random draws. The second approach is more involved but can sometimes exploit additional parallelism.

Control variates

Control variates exploit correlation with a payoff that has a known or easily computed expectation. A classic example is:

- Using the analytic price of a simple vanilla option as a control for a more complex payoff driven by the same underlying.

In Monte Carlo terms, each path produces:

- The target payoff.
- The control payoff.

You then adjust the estimator by subtracting a multiple of the difference between the control's sample mean and its known expectation.

On the GPU, this is almost free:

- During payoff evaluation, each thread computes both payoffs.

- Reductions compute sample means of both.
- A final CPU or GPU post-processing step combines them into a control-variate-adjusted estimator.

Because both payoffs are pathwise functions of the same random drivers, the extra cost per path is small compared to the variance reduction gained.

Stratification and importance sampling

Stratification divides the sample space into regions (strata) and draws a controlled number of samples within each, while importance sampling draws more frequently from important regions. Both can be used to focus effort on tail behavior or other regions of interest.

On GPUs, the main implementation concerns are:

- Making sure that each stratum can be simulated independently and mapped to a contiguous group of threads, which helps with coalesced memory and avoids warp divergence.
- Keeping per-path weights (for example, likelihood ratios in importance sampling) as simple scalar multipliers applied after payoff evaluation.

For example, you might:

- Partition the range of a key random driver into strata.
- Pre-assign thread ranges to strata and adjust how random numbers are generated for those threads.
- Apply weights when aggregating payoffs across all paths.

The overall structure remains map-reduce; stratification is mainly about how you generate random inputs and how you interpret outputs.

Quasi-Monte Carlo on GPU

Quasi-Monte Carlo (QMC) replaces pseudo-random numbers with low-discrepancy sequences such as Sobol or Halton. These sequences aim to fill the unit hypercube more evenly than uncorrelated random points, which can accelerate convergence for well-behaved integrands.

On a GPU, QMC is attractive because:

- Each point in the low-discrepancy sequence is independent of the others in terms of computation; you can map one point to one thread.
- Libraries exist to generate Sobol and related sequences efficiently on GPUs.

However, there are also pitfalls.

Dimensionality and effective dimension

QMC works best when the integral's "effective dimension" is not too large—roughly, when most of the variance comes from the first few coordinates of the input. In Monte Carlo path simulation, each time step may correspond to one or more dimensions in the sequence. For long time horizons or fine time discretizations, this can lead to very high apparent dimension.

On the implementation side, you can:

- Use techniques such as Brownian bridge or principal component construction to reduce effective dimension by making early coordinates in the sequence capture more of the path variability.
- Carefully assign QMC coordinates to timesteps, ensuring that your mapping preserves the low-discrepancy structure as much as possible.

Both strategies can be implemented in GPU kernels that transform unit hypercube points into Brownian paths or factor shocks.

Scrambling and parallelization

To obtain error estimates and reduce certain artifacts, QMC sequences are often used with scrambling: randomization that preserves low-discrepancy properties. On GPUs, you may want to:

- Generate multiple scrambled versions of the low-discrepancy sequence, assigning different scrambles to different batches of threads.

- Treat each scramble as analogous to a different random seed in standard Monte Carlo.

This again fits GPU strengths: many independent scrambled blocks of QMC points, each processed in parallel. Care must be taken to:

- Use library-provided scrambling functions appropriately.
- Avoid manual hacks (like arbitrary permutations) that can destroy the low-discrepancy structure.

Performance and Practicalities

Designing a fast GPU Monte Carlo engine is not only about mapping paths to threads. Several practical considerations can significantly affect performance.

Balancing work per thread

If each thread performs only a tiny amount of work (for example, one timestep and one payoff operation), kernel launch overhead and memory latency will dominate. Conversely, if each thread does a lot of work (for example, a very long path with many expensive operations per step), you may reduce the number of concurrently active threads and underutilize the GPU.

A good rule of thumb is:

- Ensure that each thread does enough arithmetic to hide memory and RNG latencies, but not so much that the device runs out of threads to schedule.

In practice, this usually means simulating an entire path per thread, with tens to hundreds of timesteps, and moderate per-step arithmetic.

Batching across strikes or parameters

Many pricing and risk tasks require evaluating the same model for many strikes, maturities, or parameter sets. Rather than re-running the entire Monte Carlo simulation from scratch for each configuration, you can:

- Simulate underlying paths once.
- Evaluate multiple payoffs or parameterized payoffs per path in a batched fashion.

On the GPU, this can be done by:

- Assigning additional dimensions to represent different strikes or parameters.
- Having each thread compute a vector of payoffs for its path.

This approach increases arithmetic intensity and amortizes the cost of path generation over more outputs, which often yields better overall throughput.

Interfacing with Python and libraries

As discussed in previous sections, Python stacks like CuPy and Numba make GPU Monte Carlo more accessible:

- Use CuPy to allocate large arrays of paths and payoffs on the GPU, invoke random number generation, and perform reductions.
- Use Numba to write custom kernels for path evolution and payoff evaluation.

The same design principles still apply:

- Move data to the GPU once; keep the entire simulation on-device until final results are ready.
- Validate kernels against small CPU reference implementations.
- Profile to check that time is spent in arithmetic, not memory transfers.

Summary and Outlook

Monte Carlo is perhaps the clearest example of how GPU computing, parallel patterns, and high-level libraries come together for quant finance:

- Path evolution and payoff evaluation are pure map operations over paths.
- Aggregation into prices and risk measures is a reduce.
- Variance reduction and quasi-Monte Carlo adjust how random inputs are generated and interpreted, but they fit naturally into the same parallel framework.

By designing your Monte Carlo code around these patterns, and by using GPU-aware tools for random numbers and reductions, you can scale from thousands to millions or even billions of paths within realistic time budgets.

In later sections on PDE and FFT-based solvers, and on GPU-accelerated optimization, we will contrast Monte Carlo's strengths and weaknesses with alternative numerical methods. The techniques described here will remain valuable even then: Monte Carlo remains a flexible and often indispensable tool for pricing and risk, and GPUs are now a practical way to push its brute-force nature into production-scale performance.

4.5 PDE & FFT Solvers for Option Pricing

In the previous section we treated Monte Carlo as the archetypal "map and reduce" workload: each path evolved independently on the GPU, then path-level results were aggregated into prices and risk measures. Monte Carlo is flexible and conceptually simple, but sometimes it is not the most efficient tool. For many options, especially vanillas and moderately exotic structures, deterministic grid- and transform-based methods can converge faster and yield richer outputs such as full price surfaces and sensitivities in one shot.

This section focuses on two such approaches:

- **Finite-difference PDE solvers**, which discretize the pricing partial differential equation on a grid and repeatedly apply *stencil* updates.

- **FFT-based methods**, which express prices in terms of Fourier transforms of characteristic functions or convolutions and evaluate them via fast Fourier transforms (FFTs).

Both approaches are highly amenable to GPU acceleration:

- PDE solvers map naturally to stencil kernels over one- or two-dimensional grids, often backed by sparse linear algebra via cuSPARSE.

- FFT-based methods rely on cuFFT to perform large batches of transforms across strikes or maturities.

We will first build an intuitive picture of each method, connect it to the GPU patterns introduced earlier, and then discuss practical implementation details for vanilla and selected exotic options.

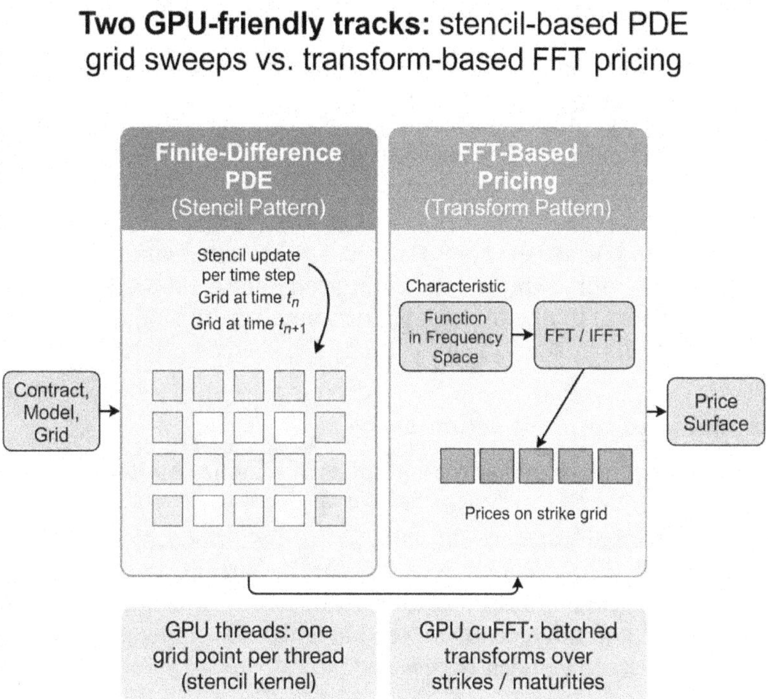

Finite-Difference PDE Solvers as Stencil Computations

Under standard no-arbitrage assumptions, many option prices satisfy a partial differential equation. For example, in a simple equity model the value of a European option as a function of underlying price and time solves a parabolic PDE with boundary and terminal conditions given by the payoff and contractual features.

Finite-difference methods approximate this continuous PDE on a discrete grid:

- You choose a grid over the underlying price (and possibly other state variables) and over time.
- Derivatives in the PDE are replaced by finite differences that involve neighboring grid points.
- Time is marched backward from maturity to the valuation date, updating the grid at each step.

Each such update at a grid point involves only a *small neighborhood* of nearby points: for example, "the point itself plus its immediate left and right neighbors" in one dimension, or a small cross-shaped neighborhood in two dimensions. This is exactly the *stencil* pattern introduced earlier.

Explicit and implicit schemes

At a conceptual level, two broad families of schemes matter:

- **Explicit schemes.** The value at the next time step is expressed directly in terms of known values at the current step. The update at each grid point is a weighted average of a few neighbors. This is simple and fully local: you read neighbors at time t_{n+1} and write the updated value at time t_n.
- **Implicit and Crank-Nicolson schemes.** The value at the next time step appears implicitly in the finite-difference equations, leading to a linear system that must be solved at each step. In one dimension, this often means solving a tridiagonal system; in higher dimensions, the system is larger and more complex.

From a GPU perspective:

- **Explicit schemes** are almost perfectly parallel: each thread updates one grid point using a fixed stencil of neighbors.
- **Implicit schemes** require solving structured linear systems; here, cuSPARSE and specialized tridiagonal solvers come into play.

Mapping a one-dimensional grid to CUDA

Consider a one-dimensional underlying grid, as in vanilla equity options with price as the only spatial variable. The grid is a one-dimensional array of values at each time level. A typical explicit step:

- Reads the value at a grid point and its immediate neighbors at time t_{n+1}.
- Combines them with model coefficients (which depend on volatility, interest rate, and grid spacing).
- Writes the new value at time t_n for that grid point.

On the GPU, you can:

- Assign one thread to each interior grid point.
- Load a tile of the grid into shared memory, including a small halo of neighbor points at each block boundary, to reduce repeated global memory reads.
- Apply the stencil update in parallel, writing the new values to a separate array to avoid overwriting data still needed by other threads.

Boundary points (for example, very low or very high underlying prices) are handled with known boundary conditions, which might be processed:

- In the same kernel with simple conditional logic, if that does not cause severe warp divergence.
- Or in a small separate kernel focused solely on the boundaries, leaving the main kernel to handle the interior uniformly.

Extending to two dimensions

For models with two state variables, such as stochastic volatility or two-asset options, the grid becomes two-dimensional. Each grid point now depends on a small neighborhood in both dimensions. The ideas remain similar:

- Threads are organized in a two-dimensional block and grid structure, matching the layout of the PDE grid.
- Each thread updates one grid point, reading neighbor values from a shared-memory tile of the grid.
- Tiles include halos in both dimensions to cover the stencil.

As dimension grows, explicit schemes can become unstable or require very small time steps. In such cases, implicit or alternating-direction implicit (ADI) schemes, which split multi-dimensional updates into sequences of one-dimensional implicit steps, can be more effective. On the GPU, ADI maps well to batched tridiagonal solves, again aligning with cuSPARSE and specialized solvers.

Implicit steps and sparse linear algebra

In implicit or Crank-Nicolson schemes, each time step requires solving a linear system whose matrix is sparse and structured (for example, tridiagonal in one dimension, banded or block-structured in higher dimensions). On the GPU:

- You represent this matrix once in a sparse format such as CSR (compressed sparse row), suitable for cuSPARSE.
- You use cuSPARSE routines for sparse matrix-vector multiplies within iterative solvers, or dedicated tridiagonal solvers for banded one-dimensional systems.

Because the operator typically does not change with time (or changes slowly), you can amortize the cost of setting up the sparse structure across many time steps or parameter configurations.

Handling early exercise and simple exotics

American options and some exotics (such as certain barrier options) introduce early exercise or path-dependence features. In a PDE framework, these often appear as:

- An inequality constraint: at each time step, the option's value must be at least as large as its intrinsic value.

- Modified boundary conditions or payoff adjustments when certain regions of the grid correspond to knocked-out or knocked-in states.

On the GPU, this means that after each time step (explicit or implicit), you may:

- Apply a simple map-style operation to each grid point, taking the maximum of the computed PDE value and the intrinsic value for early-exercise features.
- Adjust values at or beyond barrier levels according to the product specification.

These operations are embarrassingly parallel and well-suited to CUDA threads. The main challenge is designing a grid that adequately resolves important features such as barrier locations or strike levels without becoming prohibitively large.

FFT-Based Pricing as Transform Computation

FFT-based methods attack the pricing problem from a different angle. Instead of solving a PDE in the time-price domain, they:

- Express option prices as integrals involving the characteristic function of the underlying's return distribution.
- Evaluate these integrals efficiently by discretizing them and using FFTs to compute values across many strikes in one pass.

The most widely known families include:

- Carr-Madan-style methods that apply FFTs to a damped version of the option price or payoff function.
- Convolution-based approaches that recognize pricing formulas as convolutions in log-price space.

Mathematically, these methods require some care (choice of damping parameters, integration limits, and discretization), but their computational structure is regular and GPU-friendly.

High-level computational structure

A typical FFT-based pricer proceeds as follows:

1. Choose a grid of frequency-domain points (for example, Fourier transform variables) and a corresponding grid of log-strike or log-price points.
2. For each frequency, evaluate the characteristic function of the log-return, adjusted by any damping or weighting needed to make the integral converge.
3. Arrange these values into an array and apply an FFT (or inverse FFT) to obtain a vector of prices across the log-strike grid.
4. Extract prices at the desired strikes by interpolating or selecting appropriate entries.

From a GPU pattern standpoint:

- Evaluating the characteristic function on the frequency grid is a map: one thread per frequency point.
- The FFT itself is a highly structured transform, efficiently implemented by cuFFT.
- Adjustments and scaling before and after the FFT are again map-style operations.

Batching across strikes, maturities, or parameters

One of the main attractions of FFT-based methods is that they produce a *whole slice* of the price surface in one run (for example, many strikes for a single maturity). On the GPU you can go further:

- Use cuFFT's batched interface to compute transforms for many maturities or parameter sets simultaneously.
- Arrange your input arrays so that each batch corresponds to a different maturity or model calibration point.

This aligns perfectly with GPU hardware:

- Each batch is large enough to give cuFFT substantial work.
- Multiple batches in parallel keep the GPU fully occupied.

For example, if you have to price options at ten maturities under a given model, you can:

- Stack ten characteristic-function grids into a three-dimensional array (frequency by maturity by parameter set).
- Call a batched FFT to transform all ten at once.

Numerical considerations: aliasing, truncation, damping

While GPUs handle the computation, numerical design still requires care:

- **Truncation.** You must choose a finite integration range in the frequency domain. Too small, and you lose important contributions; too large, and you waste grid points and computational effort.
- **Aliasing.** Discretized Fourier transforms implicitly assume periodicity. If you do not choose grid spacings and damping correctly, the periodic copies of your function can overlap and contaminate results.
- **Damping.** Weighting the payoff or price function with an exponential factor before transforming can improve convergence and control oscillations.

These choices are mostly model- and product-specific. Once set, they translate into fixed parameters in your GPU code: grid sizes, spacing, and scaling factors. The actual FFT calls remain the same.

FFT-based pricing of exotic features

Although FFT methods were popularized for vanilla options, variations can handle certain exotic structures:

- Barrier options under models where the joint distribution of the underlying and its extrema is tractable in transform space.
- Options on realized variance or volatility, where the characteristic function of the relevant quantity is known.

The GPU implications are largely unchanged:

- The per-frequency evaluation of more complex characteristic functions is still a map.
- The FFT remains the core transform step, now with possibly different weighting and post-processing.

Compared with PDEs, FFT-based methods often give more direct access to entire slices of the implied volatility surface but may be less convenient for complicated path-dependent features or high-dimensional underlyings.

GPU Implementation Themes and Trade-offs

Having sketched both PDE and FFT approaches, it is helpful to step back and compare them along axes relevant for GPU-based quant work.

Dimensionality and scalability

- PDE methods scale poorly with dimension: a grid with N points in each of d dimensions has N^d total points. In practice, one or two spatial dimensions are common; three is challenging.
- FFT methods on log-price can handle one or two dimensions, but complexity also grows rapidly with dimension of the transform. Many practical implementations focus on one-dimensional underlyings.
- Monte Carlo, discussed earlier, scales more linearly with dimension and can be preferable for genuinely high-dimensional problems.

On the GPU:

- One- and two-dimensional grids fit nicely into thread blocks for stencil kernels; beyond that, memory and bandwidth become limiting.
- Large batches of one-dimensional FFTs are particularly efficient on GPUs, and often the most attractive use case for FFT-based pricing.

Calibration and repeated pricing

For calibration and scenario analysis, you often:

- Recompute prices many times with varying parameters (volatility, jump intensity, correlation).
- Need fast responses for near-real-time calibration loops.

PDE and FFT methods fit differently:

- PDE solvers require re-running time-stepping for each parameter set, though sparse operator structures can sometimes be reused.
- FFT pricers can precompute certain grids and reuse them across parameter sets, especially if only some model ingredients change.

On GPUs, both benefit from batching:

- For PDEs, you can solve multiple right-hand sides or parameter sets in parallel if they share grid structure.
- For FFTs, you can batch transforms across strikes, maturities, or parameter sets using cuFFT.

Greeks and sensitivity analysis

PDE methods have a natural advantage for some sensitivities:

- Delta, gamma, and sometimes vega can be approximated directly by finite differences of the grid along the relevant dimension, which is already discretized.

- Computing these on the GPU is just another stencil-like operation on the final grid.

In FFT methods:

- Greeks may be obtained either by differentiating pricing formulas analytically in the transform domain or by finite differences of output prices.
- In both cases, GPU implementations are straightforward: either adjust map-style pre-/post-processing or apply additional FFTs with modified inputs.

Case Studies: Vanilla and Barrier Options

To connect the ideas, let us briefly sketch how one might implement two representative products.

Vanilla European option via PDE

1. Build a one-dimensional grid over underlying price, with sufficient range to cover plausible moves to maturity.
2. At maturity, initialize the grid with the payoff function (for example, $\max(S - K, 0)$), which is a simple map.
3. Step backward in time using an explicit, implicit, or Crank-Nicolson scheme:
    - For an explicit scheme, launch a stencil kernel at each time step: one thread per grid point reads neighbors and writes the updated value.
    - For an implicit scheme, use cuSPARSE-based solvers for the tridiagonal system at each step.
4. At each step, enforce boundary conditions with small map-style kernels.
5. At valuation time, interpolate the price at the current underlying level from the grid.

This pipeline is a sequence of stencil and linear-algebra operations, all well-suited to GPUs.

Vanilla European option via FFT

1. Choose a grid of frequency-domain points and corresponding log-strike points.

2. Map each frequency to a value of the damped characteristic-function-based integrand; launch a map kernel or use a vectorized CuPy expression for this stage.

3. Apply a cuFFT transform to obtain values on the log-strike grid.

4. Post-process and scale the transformed values to obtain prices, again via map-style operations.

5. Interpolate to strikes of interest.

Here, the heavy lifting is in cuFFT, with small custom kernels around it.

Barrier option via PDE

For a simple barrier option (for example, an up-and-out call), a PDE solver might:

- Use a one-dimensional grid over underlying price, ensuring the barrier lies exactly on a grid node if possible.

- Apply standard finite-difference updates in the interior.

- At each time step, apply barrier conditions:

  - For a knock-out barrier, set grid values on or beyond the barrier to zero where appropriate.

Because barrier enforcement is a local condition applied at grid points, it is a pure map operation and easy to embed in GPU kernels, with care taken to avoid excessive divergence.

Summary: Stencils and Transforms as GPU Building Blocks

Finite-difference PDE methods and FFT-based pricing illustrate how seemingly sophisticated numerical schemes boil down to a few structured patterns:

- Repeated stencil applications over grids.
- Sparse linear algebra for implicit steps.
- Structured transforms via FFT.

On GPUs, these patterns align with:

- One thread per grid point for stencil kernels, possibly organized into two-dimensional thread blocks.
- cuSPARSE primitives for sparse matrix-vector products and tridiagonal solves.
- cuFFT for batched forward and inverse transforms across many strikes, maturities, or parameters.

The practical art lies in:

- Choosing discretizations and grids that are numerically sound for the model and product.
- Laying out data to exploit coalesced memory access and shared-memory tiling.
- Batching across contracts and parameters to keep the GPU fully utilized.

Monte Carlo, PDE, and FFT methods each occupy a different region of the pricing and risk toolbox. GPUs do not change their fundamental mathematical properties, but they do shift the performance trade-offs. Once you recognize PDE schemes as stencil computations and FFT-based pricers as transform pipelines, you can bring the full machinery of CUDA patterns and libraries to bear on them, achieving substantial speedups without sacrificing numerical rigor.

4.6 GPU-Accelerated Optimization Solvers

The previous sections of this chapter focused on speeding up the "forward" side of quant finance: pricing paths with Monte Carlo, solving PDEs on grids, and evaluating Fourier transforms. In practice, however, much of a quant's day is spent on *inverse* problems: calibrating models to market data, allocating portfolios under constraints, or fitting large cross-sectional regressions. All of these are optimization problems at their core.

This section explains how to:

- Recognize common calibration and portfolio tasks as structured optimization problems.
- Cast them into forms suitable for GPU acceleration, typically least-squares or quadratic programs.
- Use batched formulations, iterative solvers, and ADMM-style decompositions to exploit the parallelism we have already learned to harness.

We will not derive optimization theory from scratch. Instead, we assume you are comfortable with least-squares, quadratic objectives, and basic constrained optimization. Our goal is to connect those familiar ideas to GPU patterns and libraries.

From Financial Problems to Structured Optimization

Many quant tasks, once written down carefully, share a small set of algebraic shapes:

- **Linear least-squares:** fit parameters so that a linear combination of factors matches observed returns or prices as closely as possible.

- **Quadratic programs (QPs):** minimize a quadratic objective (often risk) subject to linear constraints (such as budget, position limits, or regulatory rules).
- **Regularized problems:** add penalties to encourage sparsity or control overfitting, such as Lasso or ridge-type terms.

Concrete examples include:

- **Mean-variance portfolio optimization:** choose portfolio weights to minimize variance for a given expected return, subject to budget and box constraints.
- **Factor-based risk budgeting:** find weights so that contributions to variance from each factor meet target budgets.
- **Constrained regression:** fit factor loadings to return data with sign, sector, or exposure constraints.
- **Model calibration:** choose model parameters to minimize the difference between model and market prices across a set of instruments, possibly with regularization.

These problems are typically expressed in terms of matrices and vectors:

- Covariance or correlation matrices.
- Design matrices of factor exposures or Greeks.
- Constraint matrices linking decision variables to risk and regulatory constraints.

This is exactly the realm where the GPU libraries from earlier sections (cuBLAS, cuSPARSE, cuFFT) shine. Optimization solvers are, in essence, sophisticated wrappers around repeated linear algebra operations. On the GPU, we care less about which solver is used philosophically and more about:

> Does the solver reduce to repeated matrix-vector and matrix-matrix operations that we can batch and offload?

Why Batched Optimization Matters

GPU acceleration is most compelling when you have:

- **Many similar problems** to solve, each of moderate size, such as one mean-variance optimization per client or per scenario set.
- **Repeated solves** with varying parameters, as in calibration loops where you recompute risk or pricing quantities for many candidate parameter vectors.

In both cases, each individual optimization problem might be too small to fully utilize a modern GPU. But if you treat them as a batch:

- You can store the underlying matrices or their factorizations in GPU memory.
- You can solve hundreds or thousands of optimization problems in parallel, each mapped to different thread blocks or batched linear algebra calls.

Thinking in batches is analogous to:

- Monte Carlo: many independent paths.
- FFT pricing: many strikes or maturities.
- Machine learning: many samples in a mini-batch.

Here, the batch dimension is either *clients*, *scenarios*, or *calibration iterations*.

Quadratic Programs on the GPU

Quadratic programs (QPs) are central to quant optimization. A typical QP in finance has:

- A quadratic term representing risk (for example, portfolio variance via a covariance matrix).

- A linear term representing return or tracking error.
- Linear equality and inequality constraints: budgets, exposure limits, regulatory requirements, and so on.

Two broad strategies map QPs onto GPUs:

- **Direct methods:** Factorize the KKT (Karush-Kuhn-Tucker) system or related normal equations and solve them with dense or sparse linear algebra.
- **Iterative methods:** Use gradient-based or operator-splitting algorithms such as projected gradient, conjugate gradient, or ADMM, each step involving matrix-vector operations and simple projections.

Direct methods are often used for one-off large problems, but building robust GPU implementations of generic direct QP solvers is non-trivial and beyond our scope. Iterative methods, on the other hand, fit the GPU mindset very naturally because they rely on the repeated application of the same linear operators.

Many small QPs: batched solves

Consider a scenario where:

- You manage portfolios for 500 clients.
- Each client's investable universe has a few hundred assets.
- You solve a mean-variance QP for each client daily, with client-specific risk aversion and constraints.

Each QP is modest in size, but there are many of them. On the GPU, you can:

- Store all client covariance matrices and constraint matrices in batched arrays (for example, a three-dimensional array: clients by asset by asset).
- Use batched cuBLAS routines for operations shared across QPs, such as multiplying covariance matrices by candidate weight vectors.

- Implement an iterative method where each iteration:
  - Applies the covariance matrix to the current weights (batched matrix-vector products).
  - Applies simple elementwise projections (such as clipping weights to box constraints, which is a map).

This way, each client's optimization trajectory is independent and mapped to a slice of the GPU's work, much like independent paths in Monte Carlo. Over dozens of iterations, the GPU can converge all client portfolios simultaneously.

Iterative Solvers and Matrix-Vector Patterns

Many optimization algorithms boil down to repeated steps of the form:

- Compute residuals or gradients via matrix-vector multiplies.
- Apply simple non-linear operations, such as projections onto constraint sets or soft-thresholding for regularization.
- Update the iterate (the current guess of the solution) using a combination of the current and previous iterates.

Examples include:

- **Conjugate gradient (CG):** often used to solve large symmetric positive definite systems arising from least-squares or simple QPs.
- **Projected gradient descent:** gradient steps followed by projections onto feasible sets (for example, non-negativity or box constraints).
- **Proximal gradient methods:** gradient steps followed by proximal operators that encode regularization such as Lasso.

On the GPU, each of these steps is composed of:

- Dense or sparse matrix-vector multiplies (cuBLAS or cuSPARSE).
- Elementwise operations (map) for projections or proximal steps.
- Reductions for inner products and norms used in step-size and convergence checks.

The finicky algebra of each particular iterative scheme is handled in host code (C++ or Python), while the heavy lifting happens in batched linear algebra kernels.

Example: Factor regression and risk decomposition

Suppose you are fitting a factor model by regressing asset returns onto factor returns with regularization:

- Rows correspond to time observations.
- Columns correspond to factors.

You might:

- Formulate a regularized least-squares problem per asset.
- Use a proximal gradient method with GPU-accelerated matrix-vector multiplies and simple elementwise shrinkage.

Because there can be thousands of assets, you can treat each asset's regression as a small independent problem:

- Use batched operations across assets for common design matrices (factors).
- Update loadings in parallel using map-style operations and reductions for each asset.

The structure is identical to the batched QP setting-many small, similar problems solved in parallel.

ADMM and Operator-Splitting on the GPU

Alternating Direction Method of Multipliers (ADMM) and related operator-splitting methods are attractive in finance because:

- They handle complex constraints and regularization terms by splitting the problem into simpler subproblems.
- Each subproblem often has a closed-form solution or reduces to a standard linear algebra operation.
- They are inherently parallel when the objective or constraints separate across components or groups.

Conceptually, ADMM:

- Introduces auxiliary variables so that different parts of the objective or constraints can be handled separately.
- Alternates between updating these variables and Lagrange multipliers, with simple updates at each step.

In quant applications, you may encounter ADMM in:

- **Sparse or structured portfolios:** encourage sparsity or group sparsity in weights while controlling risk and return.
- **Large-scale calibration:** split parameters into blocks (for example, per maturity or asset class) with coupling constraints.

On the GPU, ADMM is particularly friendly when:

- The problem decomposes into many similar subproblems (for example, per client, per scenario, or per group of assets).
- Each subproblem update is a simple map or small linear solve that can be batched.

ADMM structure mapped to patterns

A typical ADMM iteration includes:

- **x-update:** Solve a least-squares-type problem, often via a linear system. This is where cuBLAS or cuSPARSE-powered solvers appear.
- **z-update:** Apply a proximal operator-often a simple elementwise or groupwise operation such as clipping, shrinkage, or projection. This is pure map.
- **Dual update:** Adjust Lagrange multipliers, which is a simple vector addition-again a map.

Convergence checks require norms and residuals, implemented as reductions. Thus, each ADMM step is a composition of:

- Matrix-vector multiplies (map+reduce).
- Elementwise transformations (map).
- Norm computations (reduce).

If you batch multiple independent problems or subproblems, the GPU can perform all of these in parallel. The outer ADMM loop, which may require tens or hundreds of iterations, runs on the host and orchestrates data movement and convergence criteria.

Sparse Structure and cuSPARSE

Many real optimization problems in finance involve sparse and structured matrices:

- Constraint matrices where each decision variable participates in only a few constraints.
- Block-diagonal or banded covariance matrices reflecting sector or factor structures.
- Calibration sensitivities (Jacobian or Hessian approximations) with local coupling in time or strike dimensions.

On the GPU, exploiting sparsity is crucial when:

- The problem size is large enough that dense storage is prohibitive.
- You iterate many times and cannot afford to multiply by dense matrices at each step.

cuSPARSE provides:

- Formats such as CSR and CSC for storing sparse matrices compactly.
- Routines for sparse matrix-vector multiplies used in iterative solvers.
- Some support for sparse triangular solves, useful when preconditioners or partial factorizations are available.

In an optimization context:

- The sparse Hessian or constraint Jacobian is represented once in GPU memory.
- Each iteration of CG, projected gradient, or ADMM calls cuSPARSE routines to apply these operators, without reconstructing them.
- Preconditioners (if used) are also stored in sparse form and applied in each iteration.

This fits the earlier picture of PDE and FFT solvers: the optimization algorithm becomes a driver that repeatedly invokes well-tuned sparse and dense operations.

Warm-Starting and Repeated Solves

Financial optimization problems are rarely solved in isolation. Instead, you:

- Rebalance portfolios at regular intervals, with changes in inputs (covariances, expected returns) that are modest from one period to the next.

- Update calibration parameters daily or intraday as new market quotes arrive.

A powerful technique in this setting is *warm-starting*: using the previous solution (or parameter estimate) as the initial iterate for the new optimization run. On the GPU:

- You keep previous weights or parameters in device memory.
- For each rebalance or calibration step, you update input arrays (for example, covariances, target returns) in place.
- You run a small number of additional iterations of your iterative solver, often enough to converge given the modest change in inputs.

Warm-starting reduces:

- The number of iterations per optimization run.
- The need for expensive factorizations, since the structure of the problem does not change much between runs.

This is especially valuable in intraday applications, where solutions need to be updated quickly in response to market moves, and in calibration loops, where you may evaluate small perturbations around a current parameter guess.

Integration into Research Pipelines

So far we have spoken mostly in conceptual terms. In practice, integrating GPU-accelerated optimization into a research or production pipeline involves:

- Choosing a host language (C++ or Python) and a GPU array representation (raw CUDA device pointers, CuPy arrays, or similar).
- Implementing or reusing iterative solvers that call cuBLAS and cuSPARSE for their core linear algebra.

- Designing data structures so that batched problems are packed contiguously in device memory.

In a Python-centric environment:

- You might represent decision variables, gradients, and residuals as CuPy arrays.
- Use custom Numba kernels or CuPy raw kernels for projection steps.
- Call into cuBLAS and cuSPARSE via CuPy's linear algebra interface for matrix-vector multiplies.

In a C++ environment:

- You manage device pointers explicitly.
- Wrap cuBLAS and cuSPARSE routines in small abstractions that represent operations like "apply covariance" or "apply constraint matrix".
- Implement iterative schemes that operate on these abstractions rather than on raw arrays, improving modularity.

In both cases, the design goal is the same: keep as much of the iterative loop as possible on the GPU, moving only summary diagnostics and final solutions back to the CPU.

Choosing Between Methods and Recognizing Patterns

Optimization algorithms are a rich field, and choosing the right one for a given problem is a discipline in itself. From a GPU engineering perspective, a few guidelines help:

- Favor methods where each iteration is dominated by matrix-vector multiplies and simple elementwise operations; these map best to GPUs.

- Use batching whenever you have many similar problems; avoid launching separate kernels for each tiny instance.
- Exploit sparsity via cuSPARSE for genuinely large and structured problems.
- Warm-start whenever the problem sequence is slowly varying over time.

Crucially, all of the algorithms we have discussed can be viewed in terms of the same parallel patterns introduced at the beginning of the chapter:

- Matrix-vector multiplies are large compositions of map and reduce operations over entries.
- Elementwise projections and proximal operators are maps.
- Norm computations and convergence checks are reductions.
- Preconditioner applications or local constraint adjustments can be treated as structured stencils or sparse maps.

Recognizing this helps you apply a unified mental model across pricing, risk, and optimization. Whether you are solving a PDE on a grid, computing FFT-based prices, running Monte Carlo, or optimizing portfolios and model parameters, the GPU is doing the same few things again and again: applying maps, reductions, and structured linear operators to large arrays of numbers.

Optimization is the final piece of this chapter's story:

- We began with basic GPU patterns: map, reduce, scan, and stencil.
- We then moved to math libraries that pack these patterns into high-performance linear algebra and transforms.
- We added Python tooling to access all of this from familiar research workflows.
- We applied the ideas to Monte Carlo, PDEs, and FFTs to accelerate pricing and risk.

- Now we have extended them to calibration and portfolio problems via batched QPs, iterative solvers, and ADMM-style decompositions.

Across all of these domains, the theme is the same: express financial problems in terms of structured numerical operations, then map those operations onto GPU-friendly patterns and libraries. When you do this successfully for optimization tasks, you gain not only speed but also the ability to scale to more clients, more scenarios, richer constraints, and more ambitious models—all while staying within the same conceptual and software framework developed throughout this chapter.

Chapter 5

Accelerated Financial Models & Analytics

This chapter is about turning theoretical edge into computational leverage. We take the financial models you already trust-Monte Carlo engines, factor regressions, portfolio optimizers, option pricers, risk aggregators, and learning-based trading signals-and rebuild their heaviest components to run natively on the GPU. Along the way, you'll see not only where the big speedups come from, but also how to preserve numerical stability, ensure reproducibility, and keep risk controls front and center as your research loop accelerates by an order of magnitude or more.

5.1 Monte Carlo Simulation for Derivatives & Risk

In the previous chapters we have focused on two pillars:

- financial models that describe asset dynamics and derivative payoffs,
- and the basic GPU and CUDA building blocks that let us move

large, regular computations from the CPU to the GPU.

We now combine these threads into one of the most useful workhorses in quantitative finance: a fully GPU-accelerated Monte Carlo engine for derivatives pricing and portfolio risk.

The goal of this section is practical: by the end you should understand how to design a Monte Carlo stack that lives largely on the GPU and can generate millions of paths, evaluate payoffs (including early exercise and barriers), and compute Greeks, all while staying reproducible and statistically efficient.

What a Monte Carlo Engine Actually Does

At a high level, a Monte Carlo pricer is just an averaging machine:

- Draw many random scenarios (paths) for the underlying risk factors (prices, rates, volatility, etc.).
- For each path, compute the discounted payoff of the derivative or the revalued P&L of the portfolio.
- Average across paths to estimate the expected value; from the distribution of outcomes you can also extract risk measures such as Value-at-Risk and Expected Shortfall.

In concrete implementation terms, a modern Monte Carlo engine for derivatives contains four main components:

- **Random number generation** (uniform or normal draws, pseudo- or quasi-random).
- **Path construction** under a stochastic model: for example, geometric Brownian motion, stochastic volatility, or multi-factor interest rate models.
- **Payoff evaluation** per path, including any path-dependent features such as barriers or early exercise checks.

- **Aggregation** of results: averaging discounted payoffs, computing standard errors, and, in a risk context, extracting quantiles or tail averages.

Each of these stages can be parallelized. The natural unit of work is a *path*: one possible future trajectory of the underlying variables. Monte Carlo is therefore an almost perfect match to GPU architectures, which excel at running the same instructions over many independent data items.

Mapping Monte Carlo to the GPU

A Monte Carlo kernel on the GPU typically assigns:

- one thread to one path, or
- one warp (a group of threads) to a small bundle of paths.

The exact mapping depends on the amount of work per path and the dimensionality of the model, but the conceptual picture is simple: each GPU thread is responsible for evolving a path from time zero to maturity and then computing the associated payoff.

To structure our thinking, it is helpful to view the engine as a pipeline that crosses the CPU–GPU boundary in a few well-defined places.

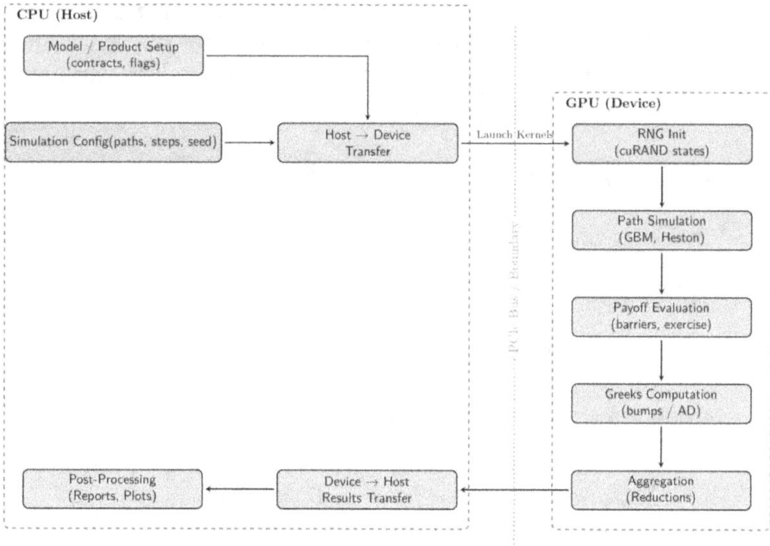

The CPU's role is to define the contracts, models, and simulation settings; the GPU's role is to carry out the heavy numerical work. Minimizing data transfer between host and device is critical for performance: once the GPU has the parameters and seeds, it should do as much of the work as possible in-device, including random number generation, path evolution, payoff and Greeks evaluation, and aggregation of results.

Random Number Generation on the GPU

Randomness is the raw material of Monte Carlo. The quality and efficiency of your random number generator (RNG) matter for both accuracy and speed.

On the GPU, you have two broad options:

- **Pseudo-random generators**, which produce sequences that mimic independent draws from a distribution. These include well-known families such as Mersenne Twister or counter-based generators.

- **Quasi-random (low-discrepancy) sequences**, such as Sobol sequences, which are designed to fill space more uniformly than pure random draws and often reduce variance in high-dimensional integration problems.

In a GPU Monte Carlo engine you normally:

- Choose a generator type and parameters (for example, pseudo-random for path-dependent exotics, quasi-random for large portfolios under smooth payoffs).
- Allocate and initialize RNG state on the device. Typically, each GPU thread gets its own RNG state, so that it can independently produce a stream of draws for its path.
- Transform these base uniform draws into normal or other distributions as needed for your stochastic model.

Two design points are especially important.

Parallel independence. Because each thread evolves its own path, you must ensure that different threads do not inadvertently reuse overlapping segments of the same random sequence. Good GPU RNG libraries are explicitly designed to handle this: they provide ways to *skip ahead* or to parameterize each state so that streams are independent. At a high level, you provide a global seed and a per-thread index, and the generator sets up a separate, reproducible stream for each path.

Reproducibility. In risk and pricing environments you often need to rerun a calculation and obtain the same answer bit-for-bit, for example to validate a model or investigate a discrepancy. On GPUs, reproducibility involves:

- using a fixed global seed and a stable mapping from path index to RNG stream;
- avoiding race conditions or non-deterministic reductions when aggregating results;
- controlling the order of operations when summing payoffs or Greeks (floating-point addition is not associative; changing the order can change the final bits).

Within those constraints, you can still enjoy large-scale parallelism: over paths, factors, and scenarios.

Path Generation and Memory Layout

Once you can draw random numbers on the device, the next step is to transform them into price paths. Suppose you are simulating a simple equity under a model where the next price increment depends on the current price and a random shock. This basic structure generalizes to more complex models: the state of the system at the next time step is a function of the current state and one or more random variables.

On the GPU, you want each thread to perform the following loop conceptually:

- Initialize local variables for the state (for example, the starting asset price).
- For each time step:
  - draw the required number of random variables (for example, one standard normal for a single-factor model, or a vector of correlated normals for a multi-asset model);
  - update the state using the model dynamics;
  - optionally store the state at this time step if the payoff depends on the full path (as in an Asian option).
- After the last time step, compute any summary statistics needed for the payoff (such as the running maximum for a lookback option).

The principal GPU-specific challenges here are:

Memory coalescing. GPUs prefer when consecutive threads access consecutive memory locations. If thread 0 writes its path to one chunk of memory, thread 1 writes to the next chunk, and so on, the GPU can combine these into a small number of wide memory transactions. If, instead, threads write in a scattered pattern, you pay a heavy performance penalty.

This affects how you lay out path data. A common pattern is to store paths in a "time-major" layout: for a given time step, you store the state of all paths contiguously. That way, when a kernel needs to process all paths at a certain time (for example, to apply a barrier condition), accessing those values is coalesced. Alternatively, for some products you may not need to store the full path; you can update in-place and track only the statistics necessary for the payoff. This reduces memory pressure and bandwidth.

Branching and warp divergence. GPUs execute threads in groups that prefer to follow the same control flow. If some threads in a group take one branch (for example, a barrier is hit) and others take another branch (barrier not hit), the GPU may end up serializing these paths, cutting effective parallelism.

You cannot eliminate divergence entirely in path-dependent products, but you can design kernels to reduce it. For example:

- avoid early *break* statements that cause different threads to exit loops at different iterations; instead, you can keep looping for the full number of steps but mark paths that have already knocked out with a flag, and then skip work cheaply inside the loop;

- group products with similar payoff logic into the same kernel launch, so that threads within a warp see comparable branching patterns.

Payoff Evaluation and Early Exercise

Once each thread has evolved its path to maturity or beyond, it must compute the payoff. For vanilla European options this is straightforward: the payoff depends only on the terminal state. For path-dependent exotics, the payoff depends on some functional of the path (for example, the average price, the maximum, or whether a barrier was crossed).

From a GPU design perspective, payoff evaluation is usually lightweight compared with path generation, but it can become non-trivial in two cases:

- **Early exercise** products, such as American options, where the holder can choose the exercise time optimally.
- **Complex path-dependence**, such as multiple barriers, coupons, or callable features.

For early exercise, the classic Monte Carlo technique is to work backwards in time and approximate the continuation value of the option using regression on simulated paths. In a GPU setting, this breaks the "one thread per path" simplicity because you must repeatedly fit regressions on cross-sections of simulated states. A common design is:

- Simulate and store paths to all exercise dates on the GPU.
- For each exercise date, moving backwards:
  - collect the states of all paths that are in-the-money and still alive;
  - perform a regression of realized future payoffs on basis functions of the current state to estimate the continuation value;
  - compare, per path, the immediate exercise payoff with the estimated continuation value and decide whether to exercise;
  - update a pathwise exercise indicator and discounted payoff variable.

The heavy numerical steps here—forming the regression inputs and solving the regression problems—are well-suited to GPUs, as they involve either large matrix operations or many small, independent regressions. The control flow, however, can be complex. Good implementations keep as much of the work on the device as possible, batching regressions and using GPU linear algebra libraries.

For other path-dependent payoffs, we can often maintain a small set of per-path state variables as we simulate (for example, running sums, maxima, knock-in flags), and then compute the payoff in a simple, branch-light kernel at the end.

Variance Reduction at Scale

Monte Carlo estimates converge slowly: the error shrinks roughly like one over the square root of the number of paths. Doubling accuracy can require four times as many paths, which is expensive even with a GPU. Variance reduction techniques aim to get more accuracy from the same number of paths.

The challenge is to implement them in a GPU-friendly way, without introducing too much branching or synchronization. Three widely used techniques are:

Antithetic variates. For each path driven by a sequence of random numbers, you also simulate a "mirror" path driven by the negation of those random numbers. For many payoffs, the average of the two payoffs has lower variance than a single path. On a GPU, this is nearly free to implement: you can either have each thread simulate a pair of paths (one with the original shocks, one with their negatives) or treat antithetic pairing as an indexing pattern across threads.

Control variates. You identify a related random variable whose expectation is known in closed form and that is strongly correlated with your payoff. You then adjust your Monte Carlo estimator using the difference between the simulated and known expectation of this control. On the GPU, the main work is computing the control variate value per path and then estimating the optimal adjustment coefficient, usually via a simple regression. Both are highly parallel operations.

Stratification and quasi-random sequences. Instead of using independent random draws, you deliberately cover the input space more uniformly. Quasi-random sequences are often provided directly by GPU RNG libraries. Using them mostly means choosing the right generator and dimension, and making sure that your mapping from draws to paths preserves the uniformity properties.

In all cases, you need to balance statistical benefit against implementation complexity and branchiness. A practical approach is to start with antithetic variates (cheap and robust), then add control variates for products where you have good analytic surrogates.

Greeks: Sensitivities on the GPU

Pricing alone is rarely sufficient; risk management requires *Greeks*: sensitivities of the price to underlying inputs such as spot, volatility, and interest rates. Monte Carlo offers several ways to compute Greeks.

Bump-and-revalue. The simplest method is to rerun the entire Monte Carlo simulation with a slightly perturbed input (for example, spot plus a small increment) and approximate the sensitivity by the change in the price divided by the bump. On a GPU this is more practical than on a CPU because you can:

- run multiple bumped scenarios in parallel, either on separate GPUs or as separate kernels on the same GPU;
- reuse the same random number streams across bumps to reduce variance in the finite-difference estimate.

However, naive bump-and-revalue multiplies runtime by the number of Greeks, which can be large in practice.

Pathwise derivatives. For many payoffs and models, you can propagate derivatives of the payoff with respect to inputs along each path. Intuitively, as you simulate the path state, you also simulate how that state changes when you nudge an input slightly. At the end, each thread outputs not only a payoff but also derivative estimates for, say, delta and vega. Averaging across paths gives you the corresponding Greeks.

Pathwise methods are well-suited to GPUs:

- they add a modest amount of arithmetic per thread but avoid repeated simulations;
- the calculations follow the same control flow as the underlying path, so you do not introduce extra divergence.

They do, however, require differentiability of the payoff with respect to the input and can be tricky around discontinuities (for example, digital payoffs or sharp barriers). In such cases you may combine pathwise derivatives where valid with bump-and-revalue elsewhere.

Likelihood ratio and mixed methods. Other techniques, such as the likelihood ratio method, express Greeks as expectations of alternative random variables under the same paths. They can be implemented as additional per-path accumulators, again fitting naturally into the GPU thread model. In practice, production engines often use a mix: pathwise where possible, likelihood ratio for certain parameters, and bump-and-revalue as a fallback.

Aggregation, Error Estimates, and Risk Metrics

After each thread has produced its payoff (and possibly a vector of Greeks), you must aggregate these over all paths. This stage involves:

- summing payoffs to compute averages (prices);
- computing sample variances and confidence intervals;
- in a risk context, computing quantiles (for VaR) and tail means (for Expected Shortfall).

On the GPU, these are handled using parallel reduction and selection primitives:

- **Reductions** combine many values into a single result (for example, sum or mean). They are typically implemented in a tree-like fashion, where each block of threads reduces its local subset of values, and then higher-level kernels combine these partial results.
- **Sorting or selection** can be used to find quantiles: you can either fully sort the array of path outcomes or use a selection algorithm that finds, for example, the 1% worst loss without sorting everything. Because sorting is relatively expensive, risk engines often use selection for quantiles and a second pass to average the tail for Expected Shortfall.

Keeping this aggregation on the GPU is critical. Transferring millions of per-path payoffs back to the CPU solely for averaging or quantile computation would waste bandwidth and time. Instead, you let the

GPU reduce the results to a compact set of statistics and only then copy those to the host.

Precision, Stability, and Reproducibility

Financial Monte Carlo is numerically sensitive. Very small differences in inputs can lead to visible differences in prices or Greeks, especially for long-dated or highly leveraged products. On the GPU, you must balance precision and performance:

- **Single precision** arithmetic is faster and uses less memory, allowing more threads to run concurrently.
- **Double precision** is more accurate but slower and sometimes limited in peak throughput on consumer-grade GPUs.

A practical compromise is mixed precision:

- perform most per-step calculations in single precision, where errors are small relative to model noise;
- accumulate sums and perform final reductions in double precision, where rounding errors can otherwise build up across millions of paths;
- selectively switch to double precision for especially sensitive quantities, such as discount factors over long horizons or small spreads.

For reproducibility, you should:

- control seeds and the path-to-thread mapping, as discussed earlier;
- use deterministic reductions (for example, fixed parallel reduction patterns rather than opportunistic atomics) when exact bit-level reproducibility across runs is required;

- document and fix configuration options that affect results, such as whether antithetic variates are enabled, the type of RNG, and the precision mode.

In production risk systems, it is common to maintain a strict separation between *research mode*, where you can freely change variance reduction or precision to explore trade-offs, and *production mode*, where these are locked down to ensure consistency across days and systems.

Integrating the GPU Monte Carlo Engine into Pricing and Risk Pipelines

A GPU Monte Carlo engine is only as useful as its integration with the rest of your stack. Typical usage patterns include:

- **Intraday derivatives pricing**, where the GPU engine is called repeatedly as market data updates to refresh prices and Greeks for a large book.
- **Overnight risk runs**, where the engine is used inside a broader scenario framework: for each scenario of underlying curves and vol surfaces, you revalue derivatives via Monte Carlo.
- **Stress testing and model validation**, where the engine is run under extreme market configurations or alternative model assumptions.

In all cases, the same design principles apply:

- keep parameter and state data resident on the GPU as long as possible;
- batch work to amortize kernel launch and data transfer overheads;
- design your API so that the CPU side passes compact descriptors of contracts and models, while the GPU handles the repetitive, per-path operations.

Once you have a robust GPU Monte Carlo core, many higher-level features become natural extensions: portfolio-level risk metrics, calibration loops that iterate model parameters to match market prices, and even hybrid engines that combine Monte Carlo with analytic or PDE methods for different parts of the book. The core ideas—random number generation, path simulation, payoff evaluation, variance reduction, Greeks, and aggregation—remain the same; the GPU simply lets you execute them at a scale that is impractical on CPUs alone.

5.2 Factor Models & Cross-Sectional Alphas

In the Monte Carlo section we treated one complex derivative or portfolio at a time and used the GPU to explore many random future paths. In this section, we shift perspective. Instead of simulating forward paths for a given instrument, we analyze the *historical cross-section*: thousands of assets observed over many dates, with the goal of extracting common risk factors and testing candidate alpha signals.

From a computational viewpoint, this is a different but equally GPU-friendly workload. Most factor and alpha research reduces to repeated applications of linear algebra: regressions, matrix multiplications, and decompositions. When you design your workflow to respect the GPU's strengths, you can estimate factor models and test huge libraries of alphas on large universes in minutes rather than hours.

Our objectives in this section are:

- to show how standard factor models and alpha tests can be expressed as matrix operations;
- to demonstrate how to organize panel data so that you can run thousands of regressions as a small number of batched GPU calls;
- to discuss practical issues such as missing data, changing universes, and numerical precision.

From Time Series to Panels: How Factor Models Look in Practice

Most readers will already have seen the basic idea of a factor model: instead of treating each asset's return as completely idiosyncratic, you represent it as the sum of a common component driven by a small number of factors and an idiosyncratic residual.

There are two common perspectives:

- **Time-series factor models.** For each asset in your universe, you regress its returns over time on a set of factor returns. For example, you might regress each stock's daily excess return on the daily returns of a market factor, a size factor, and a value factor to obtain that stock's factor loadings.
- **Cross-sectional factor models.** At each point in time, you regress the cross-section of asset returns on asset characteristics or factor exposures at that date. For example, on a particular day you might regress all stocks' returns on their current value, quality, and momentum scores to estimate factor risk premia.

In both setups, the core numerical problem is the same: solve a large number of least-squares regressions. In the time-series case you have many regressions, one per asset. In the cross-sectional case you have many regressions, one per date. In alpha testing you often combine both views:

- you may use time-series regressions to construct pure factor returns and exposures;
- then you may run cross-sectional regressions of returns on candidate alpha signals, controlling for those factors, to see whether the alpha adds incremental explanatory power.

The key observation is that these regressions are embarrassingly parallel across assets, dates, and alphas. Each one has the same small structure but uses different slices of the data. This is exactly the pattern GPUs are built for.

Panel Data as Matrices: Designing the Layout

To leverage GPU linear algebra, it is helpful to view your data as large matrices and tensors:

- A returns matrix where rows correspond to time and columns to assets.
- A factor returns matrix where rows are time and columns are factors.
- A matrix (or tensor) of signals or characteristics where each entry is the value of a particular alpha candidate, for a given asset and time.

Conceptually, the workflow is:

- Load historical prices and factors, compute returns and standardize inputs on the CPU or GPU.
- Arrange these into dense or sparse arrays on the GPU with an ordering that allows coalesced reads along the dimensions you use most often.
- Define regression problems in terms of slicing and combining these arrays.

For example, suppose you want to perform daily cross-sectional regressions of returns on factors and alpha candidates. For each date, you select the vector of returns across assets and the corresponding matrix of factor exposures (including alpha signals as extra columns). Across all dates, this becomes a *batch* of regressions, one per day.

From a layout perspective, you typically have to choose which dimension of your panel is "fastest changing" in memory (time-major versus asset-major storage). There is no single optimal choice; it depends on what kind of regressions you need most often:

- If you frequently run time-series regressions asset by asset, it is convenient to store returns in a contiguous block per asset.

- If you frequently run cross-sectional regressions date by date, it is convenient to store returns in a contiguous block per date.

For very large datasets, you may keep multiple views or precomputed transposes on the GPU if memory allows, trading storage for speed.

Time-Series Factor Models as Batched Regressions

Consider the time-series view first. For each asset, you have a historical return series and a common set of factor returns. You want factor loadings and idiosyncratic risk estimates for every asset.

Numerically, this means:

- Many small regressions: one per asset.
- Each regression has the same design matrix of factor returns (or very similar, if some assets list later or delist earlier).
- Only the dependent variable (the asset's return series) changes from regression to regression.

On the GPU, this is a textbook use case for *batched linear algebra*. Instead of launching thousands of independent small regressions from the CPU, you assemble them into a batch and call a batched least-squares solver once. Under the hood, the GPU processes these small problems in parallel, using its many cores efficiently.

There are two main cost drivers here:

- Forming any required cross-products or transformations of the factor returns.
- Solving many small linear systems to obtain the regression coefficients and residual variances.

The first cost can often be amortized: if all assets share the same factor design matrix, you can compute its key products once and reuse them for all assets. The second cost is where batching shines: even if each regression is small, collectively they can saturate the GPU.

The outputs of these time-series regressions are:

- a matrix of factor loadings (assets by factors), which you can think of as exposures;
- a vector of idiosyncratic variances for each asset, useful for risk modeling;
- residual time series that you can feed into further analysis.

These become building blocks for cross-sectional models and alpha testing.

Cross-Sectional Factor and Alpha Regressions

The cross-sectional perspective reverses the roles of time and assets. At each date, you consider the vector of asset returns and regress it on a set of explanatory variables measured at that date. These can include:

- factor exposures estimated from the time-series stage;
- simple characteristics like size, value, and momentum;
- more exotic alpha candidates, such as intraday order flow imbalances or machine-learned signals.

If you have T dates and want to run one regression per date, you now have T regressions to solve. In many equity universes, T can be several thousand. More importantly, for alpha research you often repeat this entire exercise for thousands of candidate signals.

The computational challenge is therefore two-dimensional:

- Many dates (one regression per date).
- Many alphas (each alpha adds columns to the design matrix, or you may run separate regressions with different sets of regressors).

The basic idea remains the same: express these regressions as a batched operation and push them to the GPU. One practical pattern is:

- For a given alpha candidate, build the design matrices for all dates, with columns for baseline factors plus the alpha.
- Transfer this block of data to the GPU if it is not already resident.
- Use a batched regression routine to fit all dates in one or a few GPU calls.
- Record, for each date, the estimated coefficient on the alpha, its t-statistic, and any residual diagnostics you care about.
- Reduce these per-date statistics to a summary measure of the alpha's strength and stability, such as an overall t-statistic or information ratio.

You then repeat this for the next alpha, ideally keeping as much of the shared data (returns, baseline factors, masks for missing assets) on the GPU as possible. The only changing piece across alphas is the column or columns that encode the signal values.

Handling Missing Data and Dynamic Universes

Real datasets seldom look like clean rectangles of numbers. Assets enter and leave the universe. Some observations are missing or unreliable. Corporate actions can create large jumps. If you ignore these issues, your GPU regressions will be fast but misleading.

In cross-sectional regressions, the usual solution is to *mask* unavailable observations: for a specific date and asset, if you consider the return or signal invalid, you simply exclude that asset from that date's regression. On the GPU, this raises two questions:

- How do you represent the masks without destroying the regular structure that the GPU likes?
- How do you avoid wasting time processing assets that are mostly missing?

A practical approach consists of:

- Maintaining a dense representation for the main arrays (returns, factors, signals) to keep memory access predictable.
- Using a companion mask array of the same shape that indicates whether each entry is valid.
- Before launching the regression, compressing each date's data into a compact list of valid assets on the GPU, using parallel scan and compaction primitives.

Conceptually, for each date:

- you scan the mask to count how many assets are valid;
- you write out the indices or rows that correspond to valid assets into a temporary buffer;
- you run the regression on this compressed buffer, which now looks like a dense regression problem with fewer observations.

This adds some overhead but preserves both correctness and GPU efficiency. Dynamic universes (where the set of tradable assets changes over time) are handled naturally because at each date the set of valid assets is whatever passes your filters and liquidity thresholds.

Scaling to Thousands of Alphas

In many research teams, alpha discovery has become a combinatorial challenge: researchers generate feature after feature, and the bottleneck is no longer creativity but evaluation. A well-designed GPU pipeline changes this dynamic: you can test more ideas more quickly, which in turn encourages more systematic exploration and more rigorous validation.

The scaling challenge arises from two directions:

- **Width:** the number of alphas you wish to test.

- **Depth:** the length of the historical sample and the number of assets.

A naive CPU workflow might loop over alphas, then over dates, then over assets. A GPU-centric workflow inverts this:

- You treat the number of alphas as an additional batch dimension, just like time or assets.
- For example, you might organize your data as a three-dimensional array: alphas by dates by assets.
- You then call a batched regression routine that processes many alphas and many dates in one or a few launches.

This requires some care in memory layout so that the dimensions along which you parallelize fastest correspond to contiguous memory regions, enabling coalesced access. It also requires careful attention to GPU memory limits: storing thousands of alphas, each across thousands of dates and assets, can quickly consume tens of gigabytes.

Common strategies to stay within resource constraints include:

- Processing alphas in tiles: load a subset of alphas onto the GPU, run all required regressions, write out summary statistics, then move on to the next subset.
- Aggressively compressing and standardizing data: for example, storing signals in single precision or even more compact formats if the loss of precision is acceptable for ranking and regression.
- Precomputing and caching intermediate results that are shared across many alphas, such as baseline factor regressions or per-date masks.

The payoff is substantial. Instead of waiting hours for a serial backtest loop, you can evaluate hundreds or thousands of alphas in the time it previously took to test a handful.

Precision, Stability, and Regularization

As in the Monte Carlo context, numerical precision matters. Regressions over large panels with highly correlated regressors can be ill-conditioned, meaning small perturbations in the data can lead to large swings in coefficient estimates.

On GPUs, you face the trade-off between speed and precision:

- Single precision is often sufficient for raw regressions and can significantly increase throughput.
- Double precision may be desirable when computing diagnostics, inverting ill-conditioned matrices, or aggregating statistics over many dates and alphas.

A sensible mixed-precision strategy is:

- Perform the core regression steps in single precision to exploit GPU speed.
- Use double precision for accumulating sums over long time horizons, computing standardized t-statistics, or handling particularly sensitive calculations.

Beyond precision, there is the more statistical question of *regularization*. Penalized regression methods, such as ridge and lasso, add penalties to the objective to stabilize coefficient estimates and encourage simpler models. From a computational perspective, many of these methods are still driven by matrix multiplications and small linear algebra problems, and therefore map well onto GPUs.

For example, ridge regression can often be implemented as a standard least-squares problem on a slightly modified system, while coordinate descent methods for lasso can be parallelized across features and batches. If you design your GPU pipeline with a modular view of "solve regression problem with this loss and regularization," you can swap in different solvers as needed without changing how data moves between CPU and GPU.

Workflow Integration and Intraday Use

So far we have treated factor and alpha estimation as an offline research activity. In practice, factor models and alpha signals often feed into intraday trading and risk systems. A GPU-accelerated pipeline makes it feasible to:

- Recompute factor exposures and risk premia daily or even intraday as new returns and fundamentals arrive.
- Monitor the decay of alpha performance in near real time by updating regressions with the latest data.
- Run "what-if" analyses on the fly, such as asking how portfolio exposures or predicted returns would change if you include or exclude a certain alpha.

The design principles mirror those in the Monte Carlo engine:

- Keep core data (returns, factors, validated alpha signals) resident on the GPU.
- Stream in only incremental updates, such as the latest prices or revised accounting figures.
- Batch operations wherever possible instead of issuing many small, scattered computations.

By integrating factor and alpha estimation with GPU-based backtesting and risk engines, you can create a loop where:

- New alphas are proposed and quickly evaluated with historical regressions and simulated trading.
- Promising alphas are promoted to live monitoring, where their realized performance is tracked and compared with modeled expectations.
- Live exposures and risk are computed with the same factor model infrastructure that powered backtests, ensuring consistency between research and production.

In this section we recast classic factor modeling and alpha testing problems in a GPU-friendly language: matrices, batches, and parallel regressions. The key ideas are simple but powerful:

- Many of the most time-consuming steps in equity and multi-asset research are just large collections of small, similar linear algebra problems.
- GPUs excel at handling such collections when you present them in the right batched form and organize data to respect their memory hierarchy.
- With care over missing data, dynamic universes, numerical precision, and regularization, you can scale these methods to universes of tens of thousands of assets and libraries of thousands of alpha candidates.

This GPU-centric view of factor models and cross-sectional alphas not only accelerates existing workflows but also enables new ones: more frequent recomputation of factors, richer stress tests, and broader exploration of the alpha space. In the next section, we will take these estimated factors and alphas and feed them into GPU-accelerated portfolio construction engines, closing the loop from data to decisions.

5.3 Portfolio Optimization & Risk Parity

In the previous sections we used GPUs to accelerate two core pieces of a quant research stack:

- Monte Carlo engines for derivatives and portfolio risk, where the basic unit of work was a simulated path.
- Factor and alpha estimation, where the basic unit of work was a regression on large panels of returns and characteristics.

We now turn to the third pillar: *portfolio construction*. Here the basic unit of work is a vector of portfolio weights, chosen to trade off expected return against risk, subject to many real-world constraints.

Almost all practical portfolio optimizers, whether they use classical mean-variance logic or more modern risk-based criteria, are driven by the same numerical ingredients:

- estimates of expected returns for many assets or factors;
- large covariance and correlation matrices describing joint risk;
- solvers for quadratic or related optimization problems under constraints.

These are exactly the kinds of tasks that GPU linear algebra excels at: they involve big matrix operations, repeated solves with similar structure, and many independent scenarios that can be batched.

Our goal in this section is to show how to:

- compute and update large covariance matrices on the GPU;
- solve mean-variance and related quadratic programs efficiently, taking constraints into account;
- construct risk-parity and related portfolios using GPU-friendly iterative schemes;
- use mixed-precision methods to gain speed while preserving numerical stability.

Throughout, we build on the factor models and Monte Carlo components you have already seen, reusing them where possible.

From Factor Models to Optimization Inputs

The factor and alpha section provided us with two key objects that are natural inputs for portfolio optimization:

- A vector of *expected returns* for each asset or factor, obtained from historical averages, cross-sectional regressions, or alpha models.

- A *covariance matrix* of asset or factor returns, capturing the joint variability and correlations.

Conceptually, the covariance matrix answers the question: if I hold these assets together, how volatile will the combined portfolio be, and how will shocks propagate across names and sectors?

On the GPU, you often maintain these inputs in factor space rather than asset space:

- You estimate factor covariances and asset factor loadings (as in the previous section).
- You map from factor risk to asset risk by multiplying through with the loading matrix, possibly adding an idiosyncratic risk term.

This factor representation is more compact (because the number of factors is usually much smaller than the number of assets) and often leads to better-conditioned optimization problems. However, even in factor space you are still dealing with dense matrices that must be updated frequently and inverted or factorized repeatedly. This is where GPU acceleration becomes crucial.

Covariance and Correlation Estimation on the GPU

Let us start with the mechanics of covariance estimation. Suppose you have a matrix of returns for N assets (or factors) across T time periods, stored on the GPU. The covariance matrix is essentially a scaled version of the product of this matrix with its transpose, after subtracting means.

In words:

- Compute the average return for each asset over the sample period.
- For each observation, subtract the corresponding asset mean to obtain demeaned returns.

- Compute the covariance matrix as the average of all outer products of these demeaned return vectors.

Each step is a large but simple linear algebra operation:

- Averaging across time is a reduction over one dimension.
- Demeaning is a pointwise operation.
- Forming the covariance is a matrix multiplication of a tall, skinny matrix (time by assets) with its transpose (assets by time).

All of these map naturally to GPU primitives. A typical design might be:

- Keep the returns matrix in device memory, with time steps as rows and assets or factors as columns.
- Use a GPU reduction to compute per-column means and subtract them in-place.
- Call a high-performance GPU matrix multiplication routine to compute the covariance matrix.

If you maintain the returns in factor space, you perform exactly the same operations, just on a smaller matrix.

In practice, you rarely rely on raw sample covariances. You may:

- apply exponential weighting, which gives recent observations more influence than older ones (implemented as elementwise scaling before multiplication);
- shrink the sample covariance toward a structured target, such as a diagonal matrix or a factor-based model;
- blend information across different subsamples or frequencies.

All of these operations involve combinations of:

- elementwise transformations of matrices;

- linear combinations of multiple covariance estimates;
- occasional eigenvalue or Cholesky decompositions to ensure the result is positive-definite and well-conditioned.

Again, each of these steps has a standard GPU implementation. The key is to design your workflow so that once the return data reach the device, you can carry out the entire covariance pipeline there, returning only the finished covariance or factor-risk objects to the host when required.

Mean-Variance Optimization as a Quadratic Program

With expected returns and a covariance matrix in hand, the classical mean-variance problem takes the following form conceptually:

- Choose portfolio weights to maximize expected return minus a penalty for risk, or equivalently,
- Minimize portfolio variance subject to a target return and other constraints.

Mathematically, this leads to a *quadratic program* (QP):

- The objective contains a quadratic term in the weights (due to variance) and a linear term (due to expected return).
- The constraints are linear: budget constraints, box constraints, sector caps, leverage limits, and so on.

Solving such problems repeatedly is the heart of many portfolio construction workflows: you might solve once per rebalance, or thousands of times within a scenario or stress-testing engine.

On the GPU, the computational bottlenecks of a QP solver are almost always linear algebra operations:

- Factorizing the covariance or related matrices (for example, via Cholesky decomposition) to make solving linear systems fast.

- Solving many linear systems with the same factorized matrix but different right-hand sides (for different targets or constraints).
- Applying iterative updates to enforce inequality constraints and complementary slackness conditions, often via interior-point or projected-gradient methods.

A GPU-backed QP solver exploits this structure by:

- Pushing the large, dense parts of the problem—covariance factorization and linear solves—onto the device.
- Keeping the higher-level control logic on the CPU, which orchestrates iterations, checks convergence, and updates dual variables.

A typical workflow in a mean-variance optimizer might look like this:

- On the GPU, factorize the covariance matrix once (for example, with a Cholesky decomposition).
- For each trial solution or scenario, use the factorization to quickly compute the implied risk and gradient information.
- Use an iterative solver (such as an interior-point method) guided by the CPU, where each iteration calls GPU routines to evaluate necessary matrix-vector operations.

The advantage is that the expensive part—working with large matrices—is handled by hardware specialized for such tasks. Once the factorization is done, you can re-use it across many optimizations, provided the covariance does not change.

Constraints and Structure: Making QPs GPU-Friendly

Real-world portfolios are not unconstrained. You may need to respect:

- lower and upper bounds on individual asset weights;

- sector and country limits;
- turnover constraints between successive portfolios;
- cardinality or minimum lot sizes (which introduce non-convexities).

Some of these constraints fit neatly within the standard QP framework (linear equality and inequality constraints), while others are more challenging.

From a GPU perspective, the key design questions are:

- Can we keep the core linear algebra operations dense and well-structured?
- Can we batch multiple related optimization problems so that they share factorized matrices?

For many practical constraints:

- Budget and box constraints can be encoded directly in the QP and handled by standard solvers whose inner loops are GPU-accelerated.
- Soft constraints (such as preferences for low turnover or low sector concentration) can often be translated into additional penalty terms in the objective, which keep the problem convex and maintain a simple structure.

Hard combinatorial constraints (such as exact cardinality) are more difficult. In many institutional contexts, these are either relaxed into soft penalties or handled by heuristic layers on top of a core convex optimizer. In either case, the heavy numerical work still consists of repeated linear algebra on similar matrices, which the GPU can accelerate.

Another structural trick is to operate in factor space rather than asset space wherever possible. Instead of optimizing over all assets directly, you:

- optimize weights in factor space, where the covariance matrix is smaller and often better conditioned;
- then map back to asset weights via precomputed loadings, perhaps with a secondary optimization that enforces asset-level constraints.

This approach reduces problem size and can make both CPU and GPU solvers far more efficient.

Risk-Parity Portfolios and Iterative Schemes

While mean-variance optimization focuses on an explicit trade-off between expected return and risk, many practitioners prefer *risk-based* allocations. One popular example is the risk-parity portfolio, in which the contribution of each asset or asset class to total portfolio risk is equalized (or at least balanced).

Intuitively, in a risk-parity portfolio:

- assets with higher volatility or higher correlation with others receive smaller weights;
- more stable or diversifying assets receive larger weights;
- the portfolio is designed so that no single component dominates the risk budget.

There are different formalizations of risk parity, but most lead to a set of nonlinear equations relating weights and the covariance matrix. Directly solving these equations is rarely practical; instead, you use iterative algorithms that converge to a risk-parity solution.

Common iterative schemes include:

- fixed-point iterations where you repeatedly adjust weights in the direction that equalizes risk contributions;
- projected gradient methods where you minimize a loss function that measures deviation from equal risk contributions;

- coordinate-update methods where you update one weight (or one group) at a time while keeping others fixed.

From a numerical standpoint, each iteration requires:

- computing portfolio volatility and risk contributions, which involves matrix-vector products with the covariance matrix;
- normalizing or projecting weights back into the feasible set (for example, enforcing that they sum to one and respect bounds);
- occasionally solving small linear or quadratic subproblems if you use more sophisticated algorithms.

These steps are again dominated by linear algebra operations: matrix-vector multiplications and simple vector transformations. On the GPU, you can implement a risk-parity solver by:

- Keeping the covariance matrix and current weights on the device.
- Using GPU kernels to compute risk contributions and propose weight updates each iteration.
- Using either GPU or CPU to check convergence and manage stopping criteria.

Because each iteration is relatively cheap and many iterations are required, moving as much as possible onto the GPU pays off. This is especially true when you run many risk-parity optimizations in parallel, for example, across different client accounts, strategy variants, or macro scenarios. In that case, you treat each optimization problem as a separate "batch element" and let the GPU update all portfolios simultaneously.

Mixed Precision: Speed without Losing Stability

Portfolio optimization is sensitive to numerical issues. Small changes in the covariance matrix or expected returns can cause large swings in weights, especially when assets are highly correlated or when the risk budget is tightly constrained. Purely single-precision arithmetic may not be adequate in such cases.

At the same time, GPUs deliver their highest performance when they can rely heavily on single precision (or even lower precision). Mixed-precision strategies aim to combine these advantages:

- Use single precision wherever errors are small relative to the inherent noise in the data and model.
- Reserve double precision for steps where rounding errors can accumulate or where very small differences are critical.

In a covariance-estimation and optimization pipeline, sensible mixed-precision choices include:

- Storing raw returns and intermediate products in single precision, as daily returns are themselves noisy and small rounding errors are negligible at that level.
- Performing covariance matrix multiplications and most matrix-vector operations in single precision, then casting to double precision for final factorization or inversion steps.
- Accumulating sums and inner products related to volatility and risk contributions in double precision, particularly when these involve long histories or near-cancelling terms.
- Running the most sensitive parts of the QP solver (such as the final factorization or the last few refinement iterations) in double precision to reduce the risk of instability in the solution.

Mixed precision often also requires algorithmic safeguards, such as:

- regularizing the covariance matrix with small diagonal additions (shrinkage) to improve conditioning;
- monitoring condition numbers and pivot sizes during factorization, and falling back to higher precision or alternative decompositions if problems are detected;

- enforcing constraints softly when necessary to avoid ill-posed problems.

By combining these techniques, you can obtain performance that is close to a pure single-precision implementation while preserving the stability expected from double-precision solvers.

Parallel Optimizations across Scenarios and Strategies

One of the most powerful aspects of GPU-backed optimization is the ability to run many portfolio problems in parallel. Typical use cases include:

- **Scenario analysis:** Given a base covariance matrix and expected returns, you explore hundreds of what-if scenarios where specific sectors are stressed, correlations shift, or volatilities spike.
- **Parameter sweeps:** You vary regularization strengths, risk aversion parameters, or turnover penalties to understand their impact on portfolio characteristics.
- **Client customization:** You solve nearly identical optimization problems for many accounts that share a core strategy but differ by constraints and preferences.

Instead of solving each optimization sequentially on the CPU, you:

- Organize scenario or strategy-specific data (for example, modified covariances, constraint sets, targets) into batches.
- Call GPU-accelerated linear algebra routines that treat each scenario as one element of a batch, using the same kernels for all.
- Reuse base factorizations wherever possible, applying scenario adjustments as perturbations rather than recomputing from scratch.

This approach is conceptually similar to batched regressions in the factor-model section: each optimization problem has the same structure but different data. The GPU is particularly efficient at processing such homogenous collections of tasks.

Integration with Backtesting and Risk Engines

Ultimately, portfolio optimization is not an isolated activity. It sits in the middle of a loop that runs from research to live trading:

- Factor and alpha models produce expected returns and risk estimates.
- Portfolio optimizers transform these into implementable weight vectors, subject to constraints.
- Backtesting engines evaluate how these weights would have performed historically.
- Risk engines assess the distribution of future portfolio outcomes, often using Monte Carlo or scenario generation.

A GPU-centric design lets you keep most of this loop on the device:

- Factor and covariance estimation: GPU linear algebra, as discussed.
- Optimization: GPU-backed QP and risk-parity solvers.
- Risk analysis: GPU Monte Carlo and scenario engines that revalue portfolios under simulated shocks using the same covariance and factor models.

Because all these components share core data structures—returns, factors, covariances, and weights—it is natural to store them on the GPU and move only small summaries (such as final weights, key risk numbers, or diagnostics) back to the CPU.

This integrated view also improves consistency. If you recompute factors, covariances, and optimal weights daily using the same GPU pipeline, you reduce the risk of subtle discrepancies that can arise when research and production rely on different implementations.

In this section we have built on earlier GPU-accelerated components to construct portfolio optimization engines that are both fast and robust:

- Covariance and correlation estimation can be expressed as straightforward combinations of reductions, elementwise operations, and matrix multiplications, all of which are natural GPU workloads.
- Mean-variance optimization leads to quadratic programs whose main computational burden is linear algebra. By moving factorization and related operations to the GPU, you can solve many such problems quickly, even under realistic constraints.
- Risk-parity and related risk-based allocations can be implemented as iterative schemes dominated by matrix-vector operations, again highly suitable for GPU acceleration.
- Mixed-precision methods allow you to exploit the GPU's speed while maintaining the numerical stability required in sensitive optimization problems.
- By batching across scenarios, parameter sets, and client variants, you can fully utilize modern GPUs and perform rich scenario and sensitivity analyses that would be prohibitively slow on CPUs.

With portfolio construction now GPU-accelerated alongside pricing, factor modeling, and risk estimation, you have the core ingredients for a truly end-to-end GPU-native quant research and trading platform. In the next section, we will extend this toolkit to alternative option-pricing engines based on partial differential equations and transform methods, and compare their strengths with the Monte Carlo approaches already in place.

5.4 Option Pricing via PDE/FFT Methods

So far, this chapter has leaned heavily on Monte Carlo. We used paths and random numbers to price derivatives, compute portfolio risk, and propagate factor models through time. Monte Carlo is flexible and maps beautifully to GPUs, but it is not always the best tool:

- For large books of vanilla options, you often want prices and Greeks for many strikes and maturities at very low latency.
- For calibration, you may need to evaluate model-implied prices thousands of times inside an optimization loop.
- For certain products, you care deeply about accuracy near the money or around specific barriers.

In these settings, *deterministic* methods—finite-difference solvers for pricing partial differential equations (PDEs) and transform/FFT-based pricers—can be faster and more accurate than Monte Carlo, especially when the underlying model has well-understood structure.

In this section, we will:

- place Monte Carlo, PDE, and FFT pricing engines side by side conceptually;
- show how finite-difference PDE solvers map to GPU kernels and sparse linear algebra;
- explain how FFT-based methods use characteristic functions and batched transforms on the GPU;
- highlight numerical and practical trade-offs between these approaches, and when each one shines.

Three Engines, One Goal

All three engines share the same high-level task: map model parameters and contract specifications to option prices and Greeks. They differ in how they explore the underlying mathematical structure.

- **Monte Carlo** estimates the expected payoff by simulating random paths and averaging.

- **PDE finite-difference** methods discretize the evolution equation for the option price across an underlying grid of states and time, then solve this grid-based system backward from maturity to today.
- **FFT-based** methods use the fact that many models have known characteristic functions. They transform pricing integrals into operations in the frequency domain, which can be evaluated very efficiently via FFTs.

To frame PDE and FFT methods in relation to Monte Carlo, it is helpful to visualize the pipeline.

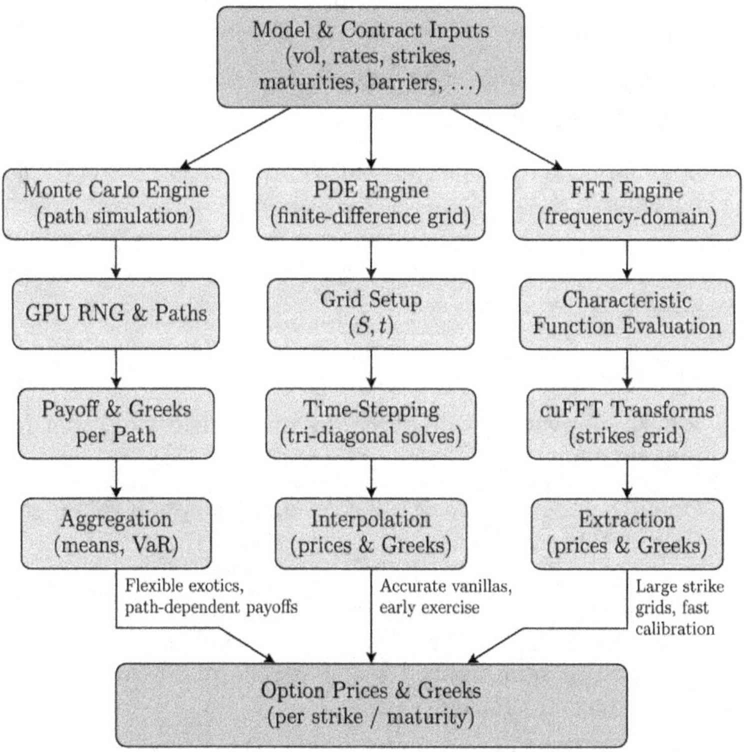

This figure emphasizes a recurring theme: the same conceptual pricing problem can be attacked with very different numerical tools, each with its own strengths on the GPU.

Finite-Difference PDE Pricing on the GPU

Many diffusion-based option pricing models imply a PDE for the option value as a function of underlying price and time. For a single underlying under a standard diffusion, that PDE is one-dimensional in space (the price axis) and one-dimensional in time. In more complex models you may have additional state dimensions (for example, volatility or interest rates), but the core idea is the same:

- the option price evolves smoothly as time moves backward from maturity to today;
- the PDE encodes how local movements in the underlying affect the option value;
- boundary and terminal conditions encode payoff and asymptotic behavior.

A finite-difference method approximates this continuous PDE on a discrete grid:

1. Choose a grid of underlying prices and time steps.
2. Replace derivatives with difference quotients between neighboring grid points.
3. Obtain a system of linear equations linking option values at one time level to those at the next.

For one-dimensional problems, this system is typically tri-diagonal: each grid point in price is linked only to its immediate neighbors. The classic implicit or semi-implicit schemes require, at each time step, solving a tri-diagonal linear system.

Mapping to GPU kernels. At first glance, a one-dimensional tri-diagonal system does not look like a natural GPU target: the direct solve along a single tridiagonal system is mostly sequential. The key to GPU efficiency lies in batching and parallelism across:

- many independent options under the same model;
- many independent models or scenarios;
- multiple spatial dimensions, if present (for example, two-asset options).

A practical GPU PDE engine works as follows:

- For a given model and time grid, you precompute the coefficient matrices that define the tri-diagonal system at each time step, or exploit the fact that they may be time-homogeneous.
- You arrange option contracts into groups that can share the same grid or at least the same model parameters; for instance, many European and American options on the same underlying but with different strikes and maturities.
- For each time step, you launch a batched tri-diagonal solver on the GPU: each system in the batch corresponds to one contract or one slice of the state grid.

GPU libraries typically provide specialized routines for solving many tri-diagonal systems in parallel. Internally, they use parallel algorithms (such as cyclic reduction) that trade extra arithmetic for more parallelism.

Grid layout and boundary conditions. To keep memory access efficient, you store grid values in contiguous blocks that match the solver's expectations. A common layout is:

- a two-dimensional array where one axis indexes the price grid and the other indexes the batched systems (options or scenarios);
- tri-diagonal coefficients stored in similar batched arrays, aligned for coalesced access.

Boundary conditions—what happens at very low or very high underlying prices—are usually simple functions of time and can be encoded by modifying the first and last equations in each linear system. On the GPU, you can treat these boundary updates as small, independent kernels that update the right-hand side before each solve.

Early exercise and American options. American-style contracts, which can be exercised any time before maturity, satisfy a *free-boundary problem*: at each grid point and time, the option value must be at least as large as the immediate exercise value. In finite-difference terms, after each time step you:

- compute the continuation value from the PDE solve;
- compare it with the payoff of immediate exercise at each grid point;
- replace the value by the maximum of the two.

This max operation is an elementwise, massively parallel GPU kernel: each grid point can be updated independently. The resulting procedure alternating between linear solves and pointwise max operations maps very naturally to a GPU: tri-diagonal solves are batched, and the exercise check is a simple vectorized step.

Numerical Characteristics of PDE Solvers

Finite-difference methods have a number of attractive properties in options contexts:

- **Smoothness and stability.** Well-chosen schemes converge smoothly as you refine the grid. You can often achieve high accuracy with far fewer degrees of freedom than an equivalent Monte Carlo simulation.
- **Structured Greeks.** Once you have the grid of option values, sensitivities like delta and gamma can be approximated by simple differences across grid points. This yields very smooth Greeks, which are valuable for hedging and risk management.

- **Determinism.** There is no sampling noise. For a given grid and scheme, you get the same answer every time.

The main limitations are:

- **Dimensionality.** Grids in more than two or three dimensions become extremely expensive; PDE methods are best for one or two state variables.
- **Model constraints.** Not every model has a convenient PDE formulation, especially if it includes jumps or other nonlocal features.

On GPUs, PDE solvers are especially compelling for:

- large batches of vanilla or early-exercise options under diffusion-like models;
- calibration loops where you repeatedly solve under slightly different parameters;
- risk systems that need reliable delta-gamma approximations across a grid of market states.

FFT-Based Pricing on the GPU

FFT-based methods take a very different route. Many asset price models, especially those with jumps or stochastic volatility, have known characteristic functions: functions that encode the distribution of log-returns in the frequency domain. Under mild conditions, European option prices can be expressed as integrals whose integrands involve these characteristic functions.

The FFT method exploits three facts:

1. Numerical integration can be accelerated by evaluating integrands on regular grids and applying FFTs.
2. Each point in frequency space can be treated independently, making it highly parallel.

3. You often want prices for many strikes at one maturity under the same model parameters, or for many maturities and strikes in a reusable grid.

The typical workflow for an FFT pricer is:

1. Fix a maturity and a grid of frequencies and log-strikes.
2. Evaluate the model's characteristic function at each frequency.
3. Multiply by a known kernel that incorporates discounting and payoff structure.
4. Apply an inverse FFT (or similar transform) to obtain prices at the chosen log-strike grid.

GPU implementation. This pipeline is a natural fit for GPUs:

- Evaluating the characteristic function at many frequency points is an embarrassingly parallel task; each GPU thread can handle one or more frequencies.
- The FFT itself is performed by highly tuned GPU libraries that exploit the hardware's parallelism and memory hierarchy.
- Batching across maturities or model parameter sets allows you to reuse the same transform structure.

On the device, you maintain arrays of complex numbers representing the characteristic function on your frequency grid. For each maturity or parameter vector in a batch, you:

- launch a kernel to evaluate the characteristic function at all required frequencies;
- call the FFT library with appropriate parameters to carry out the transform;
- apply simple scaling and extract real parts to obtain option prices on the strike grid.

If you need Greeks, you can either:

- differentiate the pricing formula analytically and implement additional FFT-based integrals, or
- approximate sensitivities numerically by perturbing inputs (such as volatility or spot) and reusing the same FFT grids where possible.

Complex-valued data and memory layout. FFT methods introduce complex numbers as first-class citizens. On the GPU, this means:

- using complex-valued array types provided by your FFT library and ensuring they are laid out contiguously in memory;
- being mindful of alignment and stride when batching transforms;
- handling conjugate symmetry and similar properties, which can halve storage needs in some cases.

The good news is that once you commit to the FFT library's data structures, much of this complexity is encapsulated. Your kernels focus on evaluating characteristic functions and applying payoff-related weightings, both of which are elementwise operations well-suited to GPUs.

Numerical Characteristics of FFT Methods

FFT-based pricers have their own distinct profile:

- **Speed on grids.** For a fixed model and maturity, you can obtain prices for hundreds or thousands of strikes in a single transform. This is ideal for building or refreshing implied volatility surfaces.
- **Model flexibility.** Characteristic functions exist for many jump and stochastic-volatility models where PDEs are more awkward. FFT-based pricers therefore extend well beyond diffusions.

- **Suitability for calibration.** Calibration often requires matching model prices to a dense set of market option quotes. FFT-based methods can evaluate the entire grid at once, enabling fast objective-function evaluations.

However, there are trade-offs:

- **Oscillatory integrals and damping.** Accurate numerical inversion requires careful choice of damping parameters and grids. Poor choices can produce oscillations or slow convergence.
- **Boundary artifacts.** Since FFTs implicitly assume periodicity on the chosen grid, you must ensure that the function decays appropriately at boundaries or accept some wrap-around error.
- **European limitation.** FFT methods work best for European-style payoffs; path-dependence and early exercise usually push you back toward PDEs or Monte Carlo.

On GPUs, these issues are less about performance and more about correct parameterization and numerical analysis. Once the grid and damping choices are made, the engine runs extremely fast and predictably.

Contrasting Monte Carlo, PDE, and FFT on GPUs

We can now summarize the practical trade-offs among the three engines from a GPU practitioner's point of view:

Monte Carlo.

- **Strengths:**
  - handles complex path-dependent and exotic payoffs with relative ease;
  - easily extended to high-dimensional problems and portfolios;
  - maps almost perfectly to the GPU's path-parallel model.
- **Weaknesses:**

  - relatively slow convergence; variance reduction can help but not eliminate this;
  - statistical noise in prices and Greeks, especially for deep out-of-the-money or near-discontinuous payoffs;
  - less suited to sub-millisecond pricing for vanilla surfaces.

Finite-difference PDE.

- **Strengths:**
  - highly accurate and smooth prices and Greeks for low-dimensional problems;
  - very fast for large batches of vanilla and American options on the same underlying;
  - deterministic, with clear control over discretization error.
- **Weaknesses:**
  - scales poorly with dimensionality; becomes impractical for many state variables;
  - requires careful grid design and boundary conditions;
  - implementation is model-specific; each new PDE structure may require new kernels and grids.

FFT-based.

- **Strengths:**
  - extremely fast generation of price grids across strikes and sometimes maturities;
  - well-suited to calibration and implied surface construction;
  - handles many models with jumps and stochastic volatility naturally.
- **Weaknesses:**
  - mainly limited to European-style payoffs;
  - requires careful tuning of damping and grid parameters;

  - can exhibit subtle numerical artifacts if misconfigured.

On GPUs, both PDE and FFT methods complement Monte Carlo:

- Use **FFT** pricers to build and refresh vanilla surfaces and to calibrate model parameters quickly.
- Use **PDE** for high-accuracy pricing and Greeks of vanilla and early-exercise options in low dimensions, especially when those options form a large book.
- Use **Monte Carlo** for exotic and path-dependent products, portfolio-level risk measures, and high-dimensional problems where grids or transforms become unwieldy.

Integrating PDE/FFT Engines into a GPU Pricing Stack

In practice, you rarely run just one pricing engine. A production GPU stack often looks like this:

- A central model-parameter layer, where you calibrate volatility or jump parameters using FFT pricers on vanillas.
- A vanilla pricer layer, where PDE or FFT engines price and re-hedge large books of European and American options.
- An exotic pricer and risk layer, where Monte Carlo handles complex path-dependent derivatives and portfolio scenarios.

From an implementation angle, you aim for:

- shared data structures for model parameters and contract descriptors across engines;
- GPU-resident grids and transforms that can be reused across many calls;
- thin CPU orchestration that routes each trade to the appropriate GPU engine and aggregates portfolio-level results.

For example, when market data update:

1. You recalibrate the model using FFT-based methods, running multiple calibrations in parallel on the GPU.

2. You refresh PDE grids and FFT price surfaces under the new parameters, again in batched fashion.

3. You update Monte Carlo-based risk numbers for the exotic book using the updated model parameters, reusing random number streams where appropriate for stability.

This integrated, GPU-accelerated approach gives you the best of all worlds: the flexibility of Monte Carlo, the precision of PDE solvers, and the speed of FFT-based pricers, all working from a consistent model foundation.

In this section, we extended our GPU pricing toolkit beyond Monte Carlo to include two powerful deterministic methods:

- **Finite-difference PDE solvers**, which discretize the option pricing PDE on a grid and use batched tri-diagonal solves and pointwise operations on the GPU. They excel for vanilla and early-exercise options in low dimensions.

- **FFT-based pricers**, which exploit known characteristic functions and GPU FFT libraries to compute prices for many strikes and maturities in one go. They are particularly effective for calibration and surface construction under a broad class of models.

By contrasting their numerical profiles and mapping them onto GPU primitives, we can choose the right engine for each task and combine them into a cohesive, GPU-native pricing stack. In the following section, we will see how these pricing components feed into risk measures such as Value-at-Risk and Expected Shortfall, where high-throughput scenario generation and tail aggregation become the next performance-critical steps.

5.5 Risk Modeling: VaR & Expected Shortfall

In the previous sections we focused on *pricing*: using Monte Carlo, factor models, optimization, and PDE/FFT methods to assign values and sensitivities to instruments and portfolios. Risk modeling asks a different but tightly related question:

> Given today's portfolio and a model of how markets can move, how bad could my loss be over a specified horizon?

Two of the most widely used answers to this question are *Value-at-Risk* (VaR) and *Expected Shortfall* (ES), also known as Conditional VaR:

- VaR at a given confidence level is a threshold loss that you exceed only rarely (for example, on 1% or 5% of days).
- ES is the *average* loss on those worst days, providing a more tail-focused measure.

Computationally, both metrics follow the same basic pattern:

1. Generate a large number of plausible future *scenarios* for market risk factors.
2. Revalue the portfolio under each scenario to obtain a distribution of profit and loss (P&L).
3. Extract tail statistics from this distribution: quantiles for VaR, tail averages for ES.

Each step can be extremely heavy for large portfolios and realistic models. Fortunately, each step also maps naturally onto GPU primitives:

- scenario generation maps to Monte Carlo or resampling kernels;
- portfolio revaluation maps to parallel pricing calls (Monte Carlo, PDE, FFT, analytic where available);

- tail extraction maps to parallel sort, select, and reduction operations.

In this section we will build a coherent GPU pipeline for VaR and ES that reuses many components you have already seen, and we will highlight design choices that keep the system both fast and auditable.

Three Flavors of VaR/ES

Before diving into GPUs, it is useful to recall the three main VaR/ES paradigms:

- **Historical VaR/ES.** Use actual past market moves as scenarios. For example, you might look at the last 1,000 daily return vectors, apply each to today's portfolio, and use the resulting P&L distribution.
- **Parametric VaR/ES.** Assume a distribution (often, but not always, multivariate normal) for risk-factor changes. Then VaR and ES can sometimes be computed analytically from means, variances, and correlations. This is fastest but least flexible.
- **Monte Carlo VaR/ES.** Simulate risk-factor paths or shocks from a specified stochastic model, then revalue the portfolio under each simulated scenario. This is the most flexible and often the most computationally demanding.

GPU acceleration is most impactful in historical and Monte Carlo VaR/ES, where you need to handle:

- large numbers of scenarios (from tens of thousands to millions);
- complex portfolios with derivatives requiring non-trivial pricing;
- repeated runs (intraday updates, overnight full revaluations, stress-test sweeps).

Parametric VaR/ES can benefit from GPU-accelerated covariance and factor computations (as in earlier sections), but once you have a covariance matrix, the remaining analytics are relatively light.

A GPU-Centric VaR/ES Pipeline

At a conceptual level, a high-throughput VaR/ES engine consists of three main blocks:

1. **Scenario generation.** Build a large set of risk-factor shocks or paths (historical or simulated).

2. **Portfolio revaluation.** Apply these scenarios to today's portfolio to get scenario-specific P&Ls.

3. **Tail extraction.** From the resulting P&L distribution, compute VaR and ES.

On a GPU, we aim to:

- keep as much of this pipeline on the device as possible;

- use batched operations to fully utilize the hardware;

- minimize host-device data transfers by copying only compact results back to the CPU.

Figure shows the overall architecture.

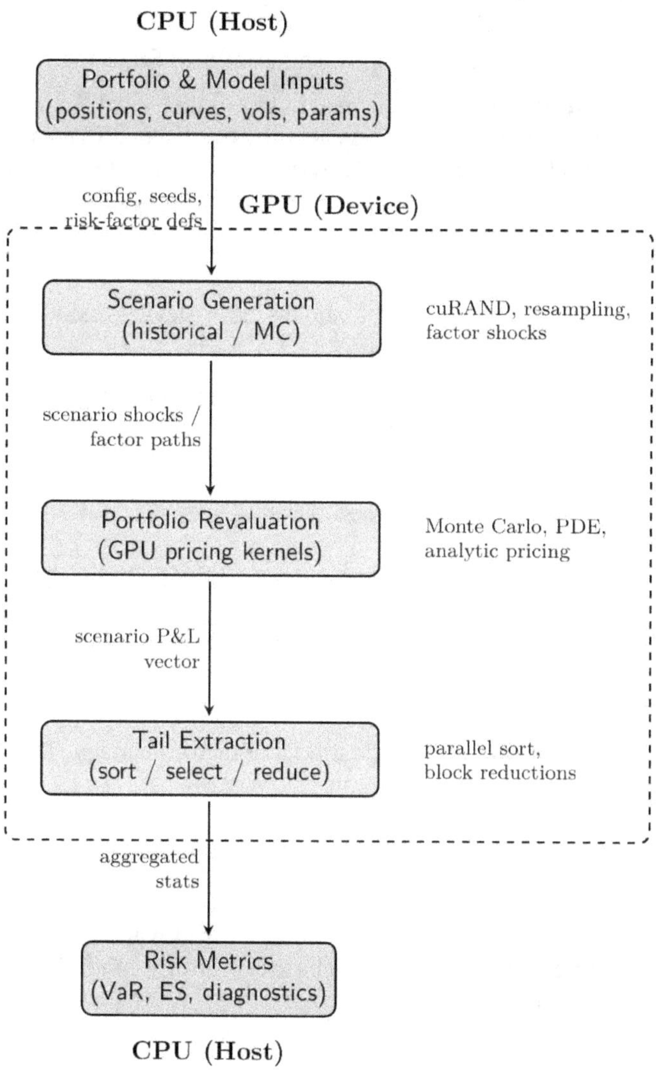

We now examine each stage in more detail.

Scenario Generation on the GPU

Scenario generation depends on the chosen VaR/ES flavor.

Historical scenarios. You have a matrix of historical factor returns, such as daily changes in yield curves, equity indices, FX rates, and implied volatilities. For each historical date, you construct a scenario by applying that day's factor changes to today's market state.

On the GPU, you can:

- store the historical factor shocks as a device-resident matrix (dates by factors);
- optionally reweight or resample these shocks to emphasize recent periods or specific regimes;
- map factor shocks into full risk-factor curves or surfaces using GPU vector and matrix operations.

If your risk factors are already defined in a reduced-dimensional factor model (for example, principal components of yield curves), you simply apply historical factor moves and reconstruct curves on the device with matrix multiplications.

Parametric and Monte Carlo scenarios. For Monte Carlo VaR/ES, you rely on a stochastic model of factor changes. This reuses the GPU Monte Carlo infrastructure from earlier:

- Use GPU random number generators to sample shocks or short paths for each scenario.
- Apply model dynamics (for example, multivariate normal with a given covariance, or a stochastic-volatility model) in parallel across scenarios.
- Produce a large matrix of factor shocks or end-of-horizon factor values on the device.

Depending on horizon, you may:

- simulate a single-step shock (for short horizons like one day);

- simulate multi-step paths (for longer horizons where path-dependence in risk factors matters).

The key GPU design principle is to represent scenarios as large, contiguous arrays in device memory. For example, you might use:

- one dimension for scenarios;
- another dimension for factors or curve points.

This layout ensures that when pricing kernels read scenario-specific risk factors, memory access is coalesced.

Portfolio Revaluation in Parallel

Once you have scenarios, the next step is to revalue the portfolio under each of them. This step is conceptually simple but numerically demanding:

- You have a list of positions (trades) with their terms: notionals, strikes, maturities, underlying instruments, and so on.
- For each scenario, you need to compute the price of each trade under scenario-specific market inputs.
- Aggregating prices across trades and subtracting the base portfolio value yields scenario-specific P&L.

On the GPU, you can exploit two levels of parallelism:

- across *scenarios* (for each scenario, the same pricing logic runs with different inputs);
- across *trades* (for each trade, the same set of scenarios must be evaluated).

There are two common approaches:

Scenario-major kernels. You assign one GPU thread block or warp to each scenario, and within that scenario you:

- loop over trades, pricing each under the scenario's curves and vol surfaces;
- accumulate P&L contributions into a scenario-level sum.

This layout is natural when you have many scenarios and a moderate number of trades, and when pricing a single portfolio under many scenarios.

Trade-major kernels. You assign work per trade and process all scenarios for that trade in parallel. This is convenient when:

- the number of trades is large;
- each trade uses a specialized pricing routine that benefits from focusing on its own inputs.

In practice, mixed designs are common: simple trades are grouped together and priced in a scenario-major fashion, complex exotics may be priced trade-major with their own Monte Carlo or PDE kernels, and then contributions are combined.

Reusing earlier GPU pricing engines. The portfolio revaluation stage reuses the GPU pricing components already introduced:

- For vanillas, you may use analytic, PDE, or FFT-based GPU pricers depending on your model and latency constraints.
- For exotics, you may invoke the Monte Carlo engine, possibly with fewer paths than for front-office pricing if you can tolerate more noise in risk runs.
- For simple linear instruments (bonds, swaps, futures), you use vectorized formulae that apply across all scenarios.

A key design goal is to maintain a uniform interface: given a scenario's risk factors and a trade's static terms, a pricing kernel returns a scenario-specific price or P&L contribution. This modularity allows you to plug in new product types without changing the overall VaR/ES pipeline.

Aggregation to scenario P&L. To compute total P&L per scenario, you:

- run pricing kernels to produce trade-level prices or P&Ls per scenario;
- sum across trades for each scenario using parallel reduction on the GPU.

If trade pricing outputs are organized as a two-dimensional array (scenarios by trades), you can perform scenario-wise reductions efficiently:

- each block or warp sums contributions for one scenario;
- or you use batched reduction primitives that operate across one axis.

The result is a single device vector of P&L values, one per scenario. This vector is the raw input for VaR and ES.

Tail Extraction with Sort, Select, and Reduction

Once you have the P&L distribution across scenarios, VaR and ES become pure data-analysis tasks:

- VaR at a given confidence level is the appropriate loss quantile.
- ES is the average loss beyond that quantile.

On the GPU, extracting these statistics efficiently involves:

- **Parallel sort.** Fully sort the P&L vector once and then read off quantiles and tail averages as needed.
- **Selection algorithms.** Find the element at the desired quantile without fully sorting all values; then optionally average all elements beyond that threshold.
- **Reductions.** Compute sums and counts in the tail to obtain ES.

Full sort. A full sort is straightforward conceptually:

1. Use a GPU sorting library to sort the P&L vector in ascending order (losses at one end, gains at the other).
2. For a confidence level like 99%, take the element at the appropriate index as the VaR estimate.
3. Sum the worst 1% of losses and divide by their number to obtain ES.

Sorting is relatively expensive, but modern GPU sort implementations are still very fast even for millions of elements. The advantage of full sort is simplicity and flexibility: once sorted, you can compute VaR and ES at many confidence levels without extra cost.

Partial selection. If you only need VaR and ES at one or a few levels, you can avoid full sorting:

1. Use a selection algorithm (for example, a GPU implementation of quickselect-like methods) to find the quantile element. This partitions the array into values below and above the threshold, but does not fully order them.
2. In the partition containing the tail (for example, the worst 1% of losses), perform a reduction to sum those elements.
3. Divide by the count to get ES.

This approach can be faster than full sort, especially when you have very large numbers of scenarios and relatively simple tail requirements.

Streaming vs in-core. For extremely large scenario sets, storing all P&L values in device memory at once may be infeasible. In that case, you can use streaming approaches:

- Process scenarios in chunks (for example, 100,000 at a time).
- Maintain running summaries of the tail, such as approximate quantiles or tail sums, using sketching and reservoir sampling techniques.
- Combine chunk-level results into a global VaR/ES estimate.

These methods are more complex and introduce approximation error, but they allow you to scale VaR/ES to portfolios and scenario counts beyond a single GPU's memory.

Intraday vs Overnight: Two Operating Modes

Risk engines often run in two distinct regimes, with different performance and design constraints.

Intraday incremental VaR/ES. During the trading day, you may want to update VaR/ES as markets and positions change:

- Input changes are incremental: a subset of prices or positions has changed.
- Turnaround time requirements are strict: you may have only seconds to respond.

In this regime, you can:

- reuse the existing scenario set and risk-factor mappings on the GPU;
- update only the pricing of trades whose values are sensitive to recent changes (for example, impacted by a specific curve or volatility surface);
- reuse previously computed P&L contributions for unaffected trades;
- recompute VaR/ES using updated scenario P&Ls.

Because the heavy scenario-generation stage is reused, intraday updates focus on selective revaluation and fast tail extraction, both of which are well within GPU capabilities.

Overnight full revaluation. Once per day (or overnight), you may run a *full* VaR/ES computation:

- update models and calibrations (as in the PDE/FFT section);

- regenerate or extend scenarios to incorporate the latest data or new stress periods;
- fully revalue the entire portfolio under all scenarios.

Here, throughput is more important than latency. You can:

- use multiple GPUs, splitting scenarios or portfolio segments across devices;
- run Monte Carlo and historical engines side by side (for different model variants or risk views);
- batch complex exotics separately but in parallel with simpler trades.

The GPU design principles remain the same; only the scale and orchestration change.

Auditability and Reproducibility in a Parallel World

Regulators and internal risk committees demand not only fast VaR/ES but also transparent and reproducible numbers. GPU implementations must therefore address questions such as:

- Can we reproduce the same result if we rerun the engine with the same inputs?
- Can we trace back which scenarios and trades contributed most to a particular tail loss?
- Can we explain differences between today's and yesterday's VaR/ES?

Parallelism complicates these requirements, but they remain manageable with discipline:

- **Deterministic random numbers.** For Monte Carlo scenarios, use fixed seeds and stable scenario indexing so that each scenario is reproducible across runs and across hardware.
- **Stable algorithms.** For reductions and tail computations, use deterministic parallel algorithms that do not depend on thread scheduling or data races. This may require avoiding certain atomic-based shortcuts in favor of structured reduction trees.
- **Scenario identifiers.** Carry scenario IDs through the pipeline. When you identify a worst-case scenario in the tail, you can map it back to underlying factor shocks and historical dates.
- **Versioning inputs.** Store hashes or versions of all key inputs (positions, curves, vol surfaces, model parameters) so you can reconstruct the exact environment of a past run.

While strict bit-for-bit reproducibility may sometimes be relaxed (for example, when you upgrade hardware or libraries), maintaining an option for fully deterministic runs is valuable for validation and debugging.

Putting It All Together

By this point in the book, we have assembled the following GPU components:

- Monte Carlo path engines for derivatives and risk factors.
- Factor-model and covariance estimators.
- GPU-backed portfolio optimizers.
- PDE and FFT pricers for vanilla options.

The VaR/ES engine described in this section sits on top of these building blocks. Scenario generation draws on Monte Carlo and factor models; portfolio revaluation uses analytic, PDE, FFT, and Monte Carlo pricers; tail extraction uses generic GPU data-processing primitives.

The result is an end-to-end, GPU-native risk pipeline that can:

- scale to hundreds of thousands or millions of scenarios;
- handle portfolios with complex derivatives and path-dependent payoffs;
- support both intraday incremental updates and overnight full revaluations;
- produce VaR and ES metrics—and associated diagnostics—fast enough to be part of the daily trading and risk dialogue, not just a back-office report.

In this section we built a high-throughput GPU pipeline for VaR and Expected Shortfall by decomposing the problem into three stages:

- **Scenario generation** using historical resampling and Monte Carlo models on the GPU.
- **Portfolio revaluation** using parallel pricing kernels and GPU-friendly aggregation to scenario P&L.
- **Tail extraction** using sort, select, and reduction primitives to compute quantiles and tail means.

By reusing the pricing and modeling components introduced earlier, and by designing data layouts and kernels that respect GPU strengths, we can turn risk modeling into a real-time or near-real-time capability rather than a slow overnight batch job. In the final section of this chapter, we will extend this high-performance infrastructure to reinforcement and deep learning strategies, closing the loop between model discovery, portfolio construction, and risk-aware evaluation on GPUs.

5.6 Reinforcement & Deep Learning for Trading

Up to this point, the chapter has focused on *model-driven* analytics: Monte Carlo pricers, factor models, portfolio optimizers, and risk engines, all of which start from explicit stochastic or statistical assumptions. In practice, many modern trading strategies blend these with *data-driven* components, especially deep learning (DL) and reinforcement learning (RL).

Deep networks are already standard for problems like image and language recognition. In finance, they are increasingly used for:

- predicting returns or relative performance (supervised learning),
- detecting regimes, clusters, or latent factors (unsupervised learning),
- learning execution or portfolio policies that react adaptively to market dynamics (reinforcement learning).

GPUs are the default hardware for training such models. But in many shops, GPU use stops at the model itself: the surrounding backtest, execution simulator, and risk evaluation still run on the CPU, creating bottlenecks and inconsistencies.

In this section we close that gap. We show how to integrate GPU-native DL and RL components into backtests and risk loops, emphasizing three themes:

- keeping data and computation on the GPU as much as possible, not just the neural network;
- modeling execution and market impact realistically enough that learned strategies are not just fitted to a toy environment;
- building risk-aware evaluation loops, so that models are assessed on risk-adjusted performance and robustness, not just raw P&L.

Roles for Deep and Reinforcement Learning in a Quant Stack

It helps to differentiate three broad roles for learning-based models:

1. Predictive models. These estimate quantities like:

- expected short-horizon returns,

- volatility or correlation forecasts,
- the probability of certain events (for example, a spread widening, a default, or a regime switch).

They plug into factor models and optimizers as another source of expected returns or risk inputs.

2. Representation and regime models. These learn compressed or structured descriptions of the market:

- latent factors extracted by autoencoders or other dimensionality-reduction networks,
- clustering or regime indicators derived from deep embeddings,
- learned bases for yield curves, volatility surfaces, or order-book states.

These representations feed into both predictive models and risk systems.

3. Policy models (reinforcement learning). Here the output is not a prediction but an *action*, such as:

- trade sizes and directions for a portfolio strategy,
- slice sizes and timing in an execution algorithm,
- dynamic hedge adjustments in response to market moves.

These policies are trained to maximize long-run reward, typically a function of P&L, costs, and risk.

All three roles benefit from GPUs because they rely on large datasets and complex models. However, to avoid the classic pitfall of "beautiful models in unrealistic backtests," you want to integrate these learning components into a backtest and risk environment that is itself GPU-accelerated and financially faithful.

Making Backtests GPU-Native

Traditional backtests are often written in high-level languages and run largely on the CPU. They:

- iterate over time,
- update positions and P&L,
- call into pricing and risk modules,
- handle orders, fills, and transaction costs.

When you insert a deep network into this loop, you can end up with a pattern where:

- the CPU prepares features for a single time step,
- data are copied to the GPU to run a forward pass,
- outputs are copied back to the CPU to update the simulation.

This constant host-device ping-pong is expensive and wastes the GPU's parallel potential.

A GPU-native backtest turns this pattern around:

- You maintain the main state of the simulation—prices, positions, features, and, where possible, the environment—on the GPU.
- You process many paths or scenarios in parallel, not just a single historical path.
- You call neural network models and pricing kernels directly from within GPU-centric workflows, minimizing data transfer.

Conceptually, this makes the backtest look more like a Monte Carlo engine or a VaR pipeline than a sequential script:

- each GPU thread (or small group of threads) simulates one scenario or one environment instance;

- at each simulated time step, policy networks are evaluated in parallel for all scenarios;
- pricing and risk calculations are similarly vectorized.

This structure is especially powerful for RL, where you are constantly generating new trajectories under evolving policies.

Reinforcement Learning for Trading Policies

In reinforcement learning, an agent interacts with an environment in discrete time steps:

- At each step, the agent observes the current *state* (for example, positions, prices, order-book features, volatility estimates).
- It takes an *action* (for example, submitting orders, changing target weights, or adjusting hedge ratios).
- The environment transitions to a new state and returns a *reward* (for example, P&L minus transaction costs and risk penalties).

The agent's goal is to learn a policy that maximizes cumulative discounted reward over time.

Applying RL to trading raises specific challenges:

- Markets are non-stationary; relationships change over time.
- Data are limited: you cannot observe many independent paths of history.
- Actions affect the environment (especially in execution), so you must model impact and slippage.
- Risk is as important as return; a policy that occasionally "blows up" is unacceptable, even if its average P&L looks good.

These challenges make careful environment design critical.

Designing the environment. The environment should be rich enough to capture:

- Price dynamics: where do mid-prices and spreads come from in each step?
- Liquidity and impact: how do orders move prices and queues?
- Constraints: position limits, capital usage, regulatory and mandate requirements.
- Costs: explicit transaction costs, bid-ask spread, market impact, and slippage.

On the GPU, you can implement many parallel environments, each representing:

- a different historical period or market regime,
- a synthetic scenario generated by Monte Carlo or bootstrapping,
- a different initial portfolio or set of constraints.

Each environment instance is assigned to one thread block or a group of warps, which simulate its evolution in parallel with others. The RL agent's policy network is evaluated across all these environments at once: one batched forward pass per step.

Execution Modeling and Realism

A common failure mode in RL for trading is unrealistic execution. If your environment assumes that you can always trade at the mid-price with no impact, a naive agent will often learn very aggressive, unstable policies:

- buy heavily when the model predicts even a small up-move;
- flip positions frequently on marginal signals;
- ignore liquidity constraints and market depth.

To prevent this, you must embed execution effects directly into the environment's dynamics and reward structure. Key elements include:

1. Bid-ask spread and limit order book. Even a simple execution model should distinguish between:

- trading via market orders (immediate execution but crossing the spread),
- trading via limit orders (better prices but uncertain fills).

On the GPU, a lightweight representation of the order book or spread can be maintained per environment:

- a few levels of bid and ask depth,
- recent trade volume and volatility as proxies for liquidity,
- simple rules linking order size to execution price and fill probability.

2. Market impact. Larger trades should push prices, at least temporarily. Impact can be modeled as:

- a function of trade size relative to typical volume,
- a transient component that decays over subsequent steps,
- a permanent component that shifts the baseline price.

This impact model is applied in parallel across all environments and steps, using vectorized operations on the GPU.

3. Transaction costs and slippage. Every trade incurs:

- explicit fees,
- spread costs,
- adverse selection (for example, passive orders filled when the market moves against you).

These costs are subtracted from P&L at each step and therefore directly influence the RL reward. Encoding them into the environment discourages overtrading and encourages strategies that are robust to realistic friction.

Risk-Aware Reward Design

RL agents respond to the reward signals you give them. If reward is simply next-step P&L, they will focus on maximizing short-term gains without regard for risk or tail events. In finance, this is unacceptable.

To obtain risk-aware policies, you can shape rewards to include:

- penalties for high volatility or drawdowns,
- explicit costs for breaching risk limits,
- incentives for achieving smoother P&L with acceptable leverage.

Examples of risk-sensitive terms include:

- a negative term proportional to squared position size or risk contributions,
- episodic penalties when cumulative drawdowns exceed thresholds,
- state-dependent penalties that grow when volatility regimes spike.

On the GPU, computing these penalties across many parallel environments is straightforward: they are algebraic functions of existing state variables and can be updated efficiently at each step. The key is conceptual clarity: ensure the reward captures the true objectives and constraints of the strategy, not just raw return.

Stability: Data, Training, and Evaluation

Deep RL in finance is notoriously fragile. Overfitting, instability, and apparent "alpha" that disappears in realistic tests are real risks. GPU acceleration does not fix these issues by itself, but it enables better practices:

1. Larger, richer training sets. With GPU-accelerated backtests and scenario generation, you can:

- simulate many more episodes than would be practical on CPUs,
- vary regimes, parameters, and scenario seeds to encourage robustness,
- augment historical data with Monte Carlo trajectories consistent with your models.

This helps the agent generalize beyond specific market conditions.

2. Extensive validation and cross-validation. Training can be done on certain subsets of history or synthetic scenarios; evaluation should be done on:

- different time periods, including stress regimes,
- alternative models of impact and liquidity,
- slightly perturbed versions of features and transaction cost assumptions.

GPU-based pipelines make it feasible to run many such validation backtests in parallel.

3. Conservative deployment criteria. Before using an RL policy in production, you should demand:

- stable performance across validation scenarios, not just in-sample training episodes;
- acceptable risk metrics (VaR, ES, drawdowns) when plugged into the VaR/ES engine described earlier;
- transparent diagnostics, such as which features and states drive actions.

These evaluations can reuse GPU-accelerated VaR, ES, and scenario analysis, treating the learned policy as just another portfolio construction or execution rule.

Synchronizing Training with Backtesting

Training loops for DL and RL involve repeated cycles of:

- sampling data or episodes,
- computing losses or rewards,
- backpropagating gradients,
- updating model parameters.

To keep this efficient on a GPU-native stack, you want to:

- keep training data and replay buffers in GPU memory as much as possible;
- generate new experience (for RL) on the GPU by simulating environment steps without CPU intervention;
- integrate feature computation and normalization into the GPU workflow.

A typical pattern for RL might be:

- Run a batch of environments in parallel for several steps on the GPU, storing transitions (state, action, reward, next state) in a GPU-resident replay buffer.
- Sample mini-batches of transitions from this buffer and feed them directly to the policy and value networks, also on the GPU, to compute training updates.
- Periodically synchronize model parameters across devices if running on multiple GPUs.

For supervised and unsupervised learning, the pattern is similar: load large panels of features and labels into GPU memory; apply data augmentations and normalizations using GPU kernels; train networks using mini-batch updates without moving data back to the CPU.

Connecting Learned Models to Classical Components

DL and RL components should not live in isolation from the rest of your quant stack. Instead, they should both consume and feed information to classical models:

- Predictive DL models can output forecasts and confidence intervals that are fed into factor models and portfolio optimizers, which remain responsible for enforcing constraints and risk budgets.
- RL policies for execution can use as inputs the risk metrics and scenario analyses produced by the VaR/ES engine, adjusting aggression in line with current risk and liquidity conditions.
- Representation-learning models can produce lower-dimensional factor representations of curves and surfaces, which simplify and stabilize downstream covariance estimation and optimization.

On the GPU, these interactions are natural: all components—neural nets, Monte Carlo, covariance estimators, optimizers, and risk engines—operate on shared tensors and matrices in device memory. The host orchestrates which component to call when but does not need to shuttle large arrays back and forth.

Logging, Diagnostics, and Post-Mortems

A final but crucial aspect of integrating learning-based strategies is observability. When a classical model misbehaves, you can often trace the cause through its parameters and equations. For deep networks, this is harder, so careful logging and diagnostics are essential.

In a GPU-centric environment, you should:

- Log not only actions and P&L, but also key state variables, predicted values, and confidence measures at regular intervals for a subset of environments.

- Periodically snapshot model parameters and training statistics so that you can reconstruct the training trajectory and reproduce decisions.
- Use explainability tools (such as feature attribution or sensitivity analyses) adapted to time-series and trading contexts to understand how policies react to different inputs.

While logs are typically stored on disk by the CPU, you can pre-aggregate many metrics on the GPU—means, variances, histograms—so that only compact summaries need to be transferred. This keeps overhead manageable even when running large numbers of parallel environments.

In this section, we extended the GPU-accelerated toolkit of this chapter to deep and reinforcement learning for trading. The main messages are:

- GPUs should accelerate not only neural networks themselves, but also the surrounding backtest, environment, and risk evaluation logic.
- Reinforcement-learning environments must model execution, impact, and costs realistically, with risk-aware rewards, to produce strategies that can survive contact with real markets.
- GPU-native backtests enable parallel simulation of many scenarios and environments, yielding richer training data and more robust validation.
- Learned models should be tightly integrated with classical components—factor models, optimizers, and VaR/ES engines—forming a coherent, risk-aware decision-making pipeline.

With these pieces, you can build a research and trading platform where learning-based strategies are evaluated and deployed under the same GPU-accelerated, financially grounded framework as more traditional quant models, closing the loop between data, models, portfolios, and risk.

Chapter 6

Performance Engineering, Scaling & Production Deployment

You've already seen that GPUs can make backtests and pricing engines startlingly fast in isolation. This chapter asks a tougher question: can they stay fast when wired into messy real-world data, competing jobs, and risk systems-and still be transparent, testable and cheap to run? We'll move from intuition and ad-hoc timing to disciplined performance engineering, show how to design dataflows that keep the GPU fed instead of starved, and then push your research stack out onto multiple GPUs, clusters and the cloud. Along the way, you'll learn the operational tools-testing, CI/CD, governance-that separate a clever prototype from a desk-critical production system.

6.1 Performance Measurement, Roofline & Profiling

Up to this point, we have focused on how to formulate quant finance problems so they map well to GPUs and how to implement correct CUDA kernels. In this section we turn to a different question:

Given a working GPU implementation, how do you know whether it is actually fast, and why it runs as fast or as slowly as it does?

In a trading or risk environment this is not an academic issue. Overnight risk runs may compete for a limited window between market close and the next morning's opening meeting. Intraday analytics are only useful if they complete within a latency budget measured in milliseconds or seconds. "It feels fast" is not an acceptable measure of success.

We will build a structured way to think about performance, using three main tools:

- Clear, quantitative performance metrics that match common quant tasks.
- The roofline model, which tells you what is theoretically possible on a given GPU.
- Practical profiling with NVIDIA Nsight tools, which tells you what your code is actually doing.

The goal is to separate *algorithmic limits* (for example, you fundamentally do not have enough arithmetic per byte of data) from *implementation issues* (for example, your loads are uncoalesced, or you launch tiny kernels in rapid succession). Once you can tell these apart, optimization becomes much less of a guessing game and much more of a targeted, engineering exercise.

Performance Metrics for Quant Workloads

Before you can improve performance, you have to measure it in terms that matter to your users. For GPU-accelerated quant workloads, the following metrics are especially useful.

Latency vs. Throughput

Latency is the time from submitting a particular job to receiving its result. For example:

- Time from "run this intraday risk report" to "results ready".
- Time between "new market snapshot arrived" and "updated Greeks computed".

Throughput is the amount of work you can do per unit time once the system is fully loaded. Examples:

- Historical backtest: trading days simulated per second.
- Scenario risk: Monte Carlo paths processed per second.
- Cross-sectional factor model: instruments or portfolios evaluated per second.

Latency and throughput often trade off against each other. Large batch sizes can improve throughput but may hurt latency for small, urgent jobs. GPUs excel at throughput, but good engineering can also make latency highly competitive by reducing launch overheads and avoiding unnecessary data movement.

Tail Latency

In risk and compliance workflows, averages are not enough. You care about the rare slow jobs that arrive just before a board meeting or just after a market shock.

Tail latency refers to high-percentile latencies, for example:

- 95th percentile: 95% of jobs complete in this time or less.
- 99th percentile: 99% of jobs complete in this time or less.

A system where most jobs complete in 10 seconds but 1% of them take 5 minutes will cause operational headaches. GPU-accelerated backtesting and risk infrastructure should therefore be characterized not only by average performance but also by how often outliers occur and what causes them (for example, skewed data partitions, GPU contention, or pathological instruments).

Domain-Specific Rates

For day-to-day communication with desk heads and risk managers, it is helpful to express performance in domain-specific terms:

- **Simulations per second**: Monte Carlo paths or scenarios processed per second.
- **Years of history per second**: for historical backtests.
- **Portfolios per second**: for factor risk engines or cross-sectional signal calculations.

These metrics abstract away many technical details, and they make it easier to evaluate trade-offs. For example, if mixed-precision arithmetic doubles simulations per second while keeping pricing error within a pre-agreed tolerance, that is a clear win.

Cost-Normalized Performance

In a research cluster or cloud environment, compute is shared and metered. It is therefore useful to think in terms of *cost-normalized* performance:

- Simulations per dollar or per unit of internal chargeback.
- Backtest years per GPU-hour.

These metrics encourage engineering decisions that are not only fast but also economically sensible. For instance, it may be better to run a job on slightly slower, cheaper GPUs if the resulting cost per simulation is substantially lower and latency constraints are still met.

Why We Need a Model: Intuition vs. Measurement

Even experienced developers often misjudge where time is being spent. There are a few reasons for this:

- Humans focus on code that is complicated or "clever," not necessarily on code that runs the most often.
- GPU execution is highly parallel. Small inefficiencies that are repeated across many threads or warps can dominate, even if each instance looks trivial.
- Memory effects are non-intuitive. A kernel can look like "just a few loads and stores" yet be completely limited by memory bandwidth due to poor access patterns.

To overcome these biases, we use models and measurement tools. The roofline model gives us a simple picture of what is *possible* on a particular GPU. NVIDIA Nsight tools then show where our actual implementation sits within that picture.

The Roofline Model: A Mental Map of Performance

The roofline model is a way to reason about the maximum performance your kernel can achieve given:

- How fast the GPU can do arithmetic (its peak floating-point rate).
- How fast it can move data to and from memory (its memory bandwidth).
- How much arithmetic your algorithm does per unit of data it moves.

The key idea is to treat performance as the *minimum* of a compute ceiling and a memory ceiling:

- If your algorithm does a lot of arithmetic per byte of data, compute limits you.
- If your algorithm does only a little arithmetic per byte, memory bandwidth limits you.

Operational Intensity

The central quantity in the roofline model is *operational intensity*. Informally:

> How many useful arithmetic operations do you perform for each unit of data moved to or from main memory?

You can think of it using a simple analogy. Suppose you are running a kitchen:

- Fetching ingredients from the pantry is like loading from memory.
- Chopping, mixing, and cooking are like arithmetic operations.

If a dish requires repeatedly walking back and forth to the pantry for small items, the chef spends most of the time on movement, not cooking. This is a low-intensity workload - lots of data movement, not much compute. If a dish uses a few ingredients but requires long, complex preparation, the chef spends most time cooking: a high-intensity workload.

In GPU terms:

- A simple rolling-average over a long time series often has low intensity.
- A dense matrix factor model, where each load feeds many multiplications and additions, has higher intensity.

Performance vs. Intensity: The Roofline Plot

The roofline plot is a graph with:

- Horizontal axis: operational intensity (from low to high).
- Vertical axis: achieved performance (for example, billions of operations per second).

Two lines define the “roof”:

- A sloped line at low intensities: this is the memory ceiling. Performance here increases in direct proportion to intensity, because memory bandwidth is the bottleneck.

- A flat line at higher intensities: this is the compute ceiling, the maximum the GPU can perform even if data movement is no longer the issue.

Any realistic kernel will lie *under* or at best *on* this roof: you cannot exceed the hardware limits. Where your kernel lies relative to these lines tells you whether extra arithmetic optimizations can help, or whether you must focus on memory behavior.

Immediately after you introduce this model to colleagues, a natural question arises: what does this look like for our actual backtesting and risk kernels?

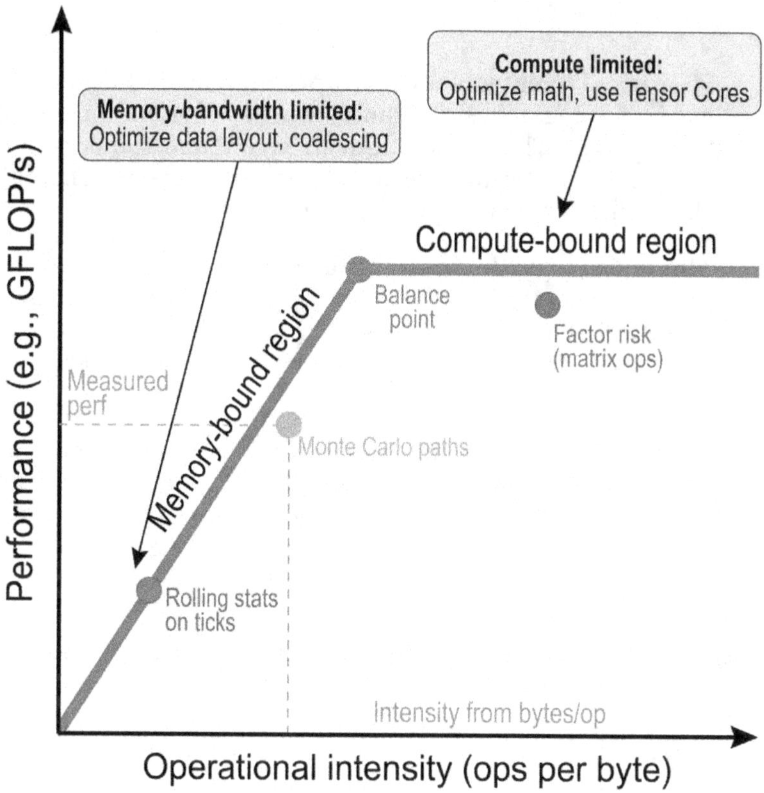

Placing Quant Kernels on the Roofline

To use the roofline model in practice, you proceed in three steps:

1. Estimate the operational intensity of your kernel. For example, count approximately how many arithmetic operations each thread performs per element it loads and stores.
2. Determine the peak compute rate and memory bandwidth of your GPU model. These are provided in vendor documentation.
3. Draw the roofline and mark your kernel's position based on its intensity and measured performance.

Some typical patterns:

- **Historical backtests with simple indicators** (for example, moving averages, basic technical signals) often have relatively low intensity. They stream through large volumes of price data, doing only a few arithmetic operations per data point. They usually fall in the memory-bound region.
- **Monte Carlo path simulations** that include path-dependent payoffs, stochastic volatility, or complex discounting logic often have medium intensities. Depending on implementation details, they may lie near the balance point or modestly into the compute-bound region.
- **Factor risk models and linear algebra heavy workloads** (for example, covariance estimation, principal component analysis, or large dense matrix multiplies) often achieve very high intensities and can approach the compute ceiling, particularly if they are implemented using highly optimized libraries.

Once the kernel is placed, the model guides your optimization priorities:

- If the kernel is well below the sloped memory line, you are not using memory bandwidth effectively. Work on coalesced accesses, caching, and data layout.
- If the kernel is well below the flat compute line at high intensity, you are not using compute resources efficiently. Work on branch divergence, instruction-level efficiency, and use of specialized units.

From Roofline to Measurement: NVIDIA Nsight Tools

The roofline model provides a high-level map. To navigate in detail, you need a profiler. NVIDIA's Nsight family of tools gives you two complementary views:

- **Nsight Systems**: a system-level timeline view.
- **Nsight Compute**: a detailed kernel-level analysis.

Together, they help you connect GPU behavior to the finance context: which part of a backtest, which portfolio, which data slice.

Nsight Systems: Seeing the Whole Timeline

Nsight Systems records a time-ordered view of what your application is doing across CPUs and GPUs. When you profile a backtest or risk run with it, you can answer questions such as:

- When the application appears to be "busy," is the GPU actually doing work, or is it idle waiting for data?
- Are kernels launched in a steady stream, or do they appear in bursts separated by long CPU-side processing gaps?
- Do multiple streams of work overlap effectively, or are they serialized?

In a typical quant backtest you might see patterns like:

- Long CPU preprocessing stages (for example, assembling cash-flow schedules or re-indexing tick data), followed by short GPU kernels. This suggests an opportunity to push more preprocessing onto the GPU or at least to overlap it with GPU computation.
- Many very small kernels launched in quick succession, each performing trivial work on small slices of data. This indicates kernel launch overhead could be a substantial fraction of the runtime; batching operations into larger kernels may help.
- Data transfer spikes over the PCIe or NVLink interconnect, where large copies host-to-device or device-to-host precede each compute segment. This suggests you should reorganize the data pipeline to keep more data resident on the GPU or reduce round-trips.

Nsight Systems also lets you align these events with application-level markers. For example, you can annotate the code to mark "rebalance step," "factor recomputation," or "VaR aggregation," and then see exactly how each stage consumes GPU time and data transfers.

Nsight Compute: Looking Inside Kernels

Once Nsight Systems has helped you identify which kernels matter, Nsight Compute lets you examine those kernels in depth. Some of the most useful categories of metrics are:

Achieved Occupancy

Occupancy tells you how many warps are active relative to what the GPU could theoretically support. While "higher is better" is only a rough rule, very low occupancy can signal issues such as:

- Blocks that are too small or too few.
- Excessive register usage per thread, which reduces how many threads fit.
- Overuse of shared memory per block, which limits concurrent blocks.

For a backtest kernel that updates many independent positions or scenarios, low occupancy may indicate you are not exploiting obvious parallelism.

Warp Stalls and Control-Flow Issues

Nsight Compute can show why warps are stalled:

- Waiting on memory (global, shared, or local).
- Waiting on synchronization within a block.
- Waiting due to control-flow divergence (different threads in a warp taking different branches).

For example, in a Monte Carlo early-exercise pricer, some paths may exercise early and exit a loop, while others continue. If you implement this with a literal `break` in the loop, threads within a warp stop progressing together. Nsight Compute will reveal increased divergence and lower effective utilization. That signals the need to restructure the logic, a topic we will return to in later sections on kernel optimization.

Memory Throughput and Efficiency

To connect to the roofline model, Nsight Compute provides:

- Actual bytes read and written from global memory.
- Derived measures of bandwidth utilization relative to theoretical maximum.
- Indicators of whether loads and stores are coalesced or scattered.

If your roofline analysis predicted that a kernel should be memory-bound and nearly saturate bandwidth, but Nsight Compute shows only a fraction of peak bandwidth being used, you likely have:

- Poor access patterns (for example, strided accesses over columns stored row-wise).
- Many small, unaligned loads instead of larger, aligned ones.
- Excessive local-memory traffic due to register spills.

These findings suggest concrete changes in data layout or in how loops are structured over instruments, time indices, or factors.

Instruction Mix and Arithmetic Utilization

Nsight Compute reports how much of the GPU's arithmetic capacity you are actually using:

- Fraction of cycles spent on floating-point operations.
- Use of specialized units (for example, Tensor Cores).
- Overhead from integer arithmetic, control instructions, and address calculations.

In a factor risk kernel dominated by matrix multiplications, if you see low utilization of floating-point units or no use of Tensor Cores where they would be appropriate, that points toward algorithmic or library-level changes rather than memory tuning.

Connecting Roofline and Profiling to Real Workloads

It is helpful to walk through how these tools guide you for typical quant workloads.

Example: Tick-Based Backtest with Simple Indicators

Suppose you have a backtest that processes raw tick data and maintains a set of simple indicators (moving averages, volatility estimates, order-book imbalances). The GPU kernel reads prices and volumes, updates per-instrument state, and writes results.

- **Roofline perspective**: Operational intensity is low: only a small number of arithmetic operations per tick. The kernel should be memory-bound. The maximum performance is limited by how fast you can stream tick data from memory.
- **Nsight Systems view**: Profiling shows that the GPU alternates between short bursts of compute and large host-to-device transfers as each chunk of ticks is copied. There are idle gaps between transfers.
- **Nsight Compute view**: Bandwidth utilization is well below peak. Loads are strided because the data is organized in an "array of structs" layout where each tick contains many fields, but the kernel only needs a subset.

From this, you conclude:

- The main bottleneck is not arithmetic; optimizing math will have almost no effect.
- You should change the data layout (for example, to a columnar format) and use larger, more coalesced transfers.
- You should set up asynchronous copy and compute so that while one chunk is processed, the next is already being transferred.

Example: Monte Carlo VaR with Complex Payoffs

Now consider a Monte Carlo Value-at-Risk engine with path-dependent payoffs and multiple risk factors.

- **Roofline perspective**: Each path involves many time steps and per-step operations (factor evolution, discounting, payoff logic). Operational intensity is moderate to high. The kernel might lie near or above the roofline's balance point.
- **Nsight Systems view**: The GPU is busy during simulation windows, with long, sustained kernels. Data transfers are largely confined to initial setup and final result aggregation.
- **Nsight Compute view**: You see:
  - Reasonable memory efficiency: bandwidth usage is near expectations.
  - Significant warp stalls due to branch divergence in payoff logic.
  - Modest arithmetic utilization; the GPU is not reaching its compute ceiling.

Here the combined picture tells you:

- Memory behavior is adequate; you are not clearly memory-bound.
- Divergence and control flow are limiting compute utilization.
- Refactoring the payoff logic (for example, splitting different payoff types into separate kernels, or using predication instead of complex branching) is likely to yield meaningful speedups.

Example: Factor Risk via Matrix Operations

Finally, consider a factor risk engine that constructs large exposure matrices and applies factor covariance matrices to compute portfolio risk.

- **Roofline perspective**: This is a high-intensity linear algebra workload. The maximum performance is bounded by the GPU's compute ceiling, assuming you use optimized matrix multiplication routines.

- **Nsight Systems view**: Most GPU time is spent in a few library calls (for example, GEMM operations). Data transfers are amortized over large batches; the GPU is kept busy.
- **Nsight Compute view**: When you profile the matrix kernels:
  - Arithmetic units are highly utilized.
  - Memory bandwidth is not the limiting factor.
  - Occupancy is decent, but there may still be some headroom to use better-tuned library parameters or mixed-precision variants.

Here, the model and measurements agree that you are close to compute-bound. Optimization efforts should therefore focus on:

- Using the best available vendor libraries and enabling Tensor Cores where appropriate.
- Considering mixed precision for intermediate results if numerical analysis shows it is safe.
- Possibly restructuring higher-level algorithms to reduce redundant matrix operations, rather than micro-optimizing memory accesses.

Letting Measurements Drive Decisions

The common thread in these examples is a disciplined workflow:

1. Define task-appropriate performance metrics: latency, throughput, tail latency, domain-specific rates, and cost-normalized measures.
2. Use the roofline model to set expectations: for a given algorithm and GPU, are you more likely to be memory-bound or compute-bound?
3. Profile with Nsight Systems to understand the end-to-end timeline: where kernels sit relative to data transfers and CPU work.

4. Profile key kernels with Nsight Compute to measure occupancy, stalls, memory efficiency, and arithmetic utilization.

5. Compare measurements to roofline expectations, and choose optimization strategies that address the *real* bottleneck.

This approach keeps you from wasting time on "optimizations" that do not move the metrics that matter. In the rest of this chapter, we will build on this foundation to show how to turn these insights into concrete kernel improvements, scaling strategies, and production deployment patterns that make GPU-accelerated research both fast and trustworthy.

6.2 Kernel Optimization & Mixed Precision

In the previous section we treated performance as something you can measure and reason about. You learned how to use the roofline model and NVIDIA Nsight to distinguish between memory-bound and compute-bound kernels, and to identify which specific kernels dominate runtime in a backtest or risk run.

We now assume you have that information. You know which kernels are the bottlenecks, and you have a sense of whether they are limited by memory or compute. The question becomes:

> How do you reshape those kernels to run faster, without turning them into an unmaintainable or numerically fragile mess?

This section focuses on four levers you can pull:

- **Improving occupancy** so the GPU always has useful work to do.

- **Reducing control-flow divergence** so warps move in lock-step.

- **Managing register and memory usage** to avoid hidden slowdowns.
- **Introducing mixed precision and Tensor Cores** in a controlled, auditable way.

We will ground each idea in typical quant workloads: Monte Carlo path updates, risk factor shocks, and rolling covariance or factor calculations. The emphasis is not on tricks, but on building an engineering mindset that turns profiling observations into systematic improvements.

Occupancy: Keeping the GPU Busy

You can think of a GPU as a factory with many identical production lines (the streaming multiprocessors, or SMs). Each production line processes groups of "items" in lockstep (warps of threads). Occupancy is a measure of how many of those lines are actually running work relative to the maximum the factory can support.

High occupancy helps the GPU hide latency. When one warp is waiting on a memory load, the SM can quickly switch to another warp that is ready to execute. If there are only a few warps available, the SM has nothing else to do while it waits, and the GPU sits idle.

What Controls Occupancy?

In CUDA, occupancy is shaped by three main choices:

- **Block size**: how many threads you put in each block.
- **Register usage**: how many registers each thread needs.
- **Shared memory usage**: how much on-chip shared memory each block consumes.

Each SM has fixed budgets for registers, shared memory, and active blocks. If each block is "heavy" (uses many registers or lots of shared memory), fewer blocks can reside on the SM at once, which limits how many warps it can keep active.

From the profiling section, you might see a Monte Carlo pricing kernel with low achieved occupancy. That is a sign that one of these resources is constraining how many warps can be scheduled.

Choosing Block Sizes for Quant Kernels

For many quant kernels, a good starting point is to choose block sizes that are multiples of the warp size (typically 32 threads) and that leave enough flexibility for the scheduler. Common choices are 128, 256, or 512 threads per block.

The right choice depends on the work each thread does:

- **Path-based Monte Carlo**: each thread may simulate one or several paths over many time steps. The work per thread is relatively large. You often want moderate block sizes like 128 or 256 to avoid oversized blocks that monopolize SM resources.
- **Cross-sectional factor calculations**: each thread may operate on a small number of instruments or factors. Work per thread is smaller; larger block sizes can help pack more warps on each SM.
- **Rolling covariance windows**: often involve tiling time-series into shared memory. Here, the block size is closely tied to the tile shape you choose. You should pick a tile size that both fits into shared memory and gives reasonable occupancy.

After picking a candidate block size, use Nsight Compute or the CUDA occupancy calculator to see whether occupancy is limited by block size, registers, or shared memory. If you see that only one block fits per SM and occupancy is low, consider reducing block size or resource usage.

Balancing Occupancy and Per-Thread Work

Occupancy is not an end in itself. Very high occupancy with extremely lightweight threads can be less efficient than moderate occupancy where each thread has enough work to amortize overhead.

A practical rule for quant workloads is:

> Ensure each thread does a meaningful chunk of financial work (for example, a full path, a full instrument, or a full

factor slice), then adjust block size and resource usage to get "good enough" occupancy.

"Good enough" usually means that when you profile, memory and arithmetic units are well utilized, and further tweaks to occupancy do not produce large speedups. It is common to see significant improvements when going from very low to moderate occupancy, but diminishing returns after that.

Taming Divergence: Keeping Warps Coherent

A warp is a group of threads that execute the same instruction at the same time, but on different data. Divergence occurs when threads within a warp take different branches in a conditional statement. The GPU then has to execute each branch path separately, masking off threads that are not taking that path. Some threads are idle while others work, reducing effective parallelism.

Quant finance kernels are full of branch-heavy logic:

- Early exercise rules in option pricing.
- Barrier conditions in structured products.
- Regime-switching or state-dependent dynamics.
- Instrument-type-specific payoff logic in a heterogeneous portfolio.

If you simply translate these rules directly into branch-heavy code, Nsight Compute will often show large fractions of cycles spent in divergent execution.

Common Patterns that Cause Divergence

Two patterns are especially common:

Mixed Instrument Types in a Single Kernel

Consider a risk engine that prices equities, vanilla options, and exotic derivatives in one kernel. Threads handle different instruments, and each instrument type has its own payoff and risk logic. Inside the kernel you might have a chain of conditionals based on instrument type.

Within a warp, some threads are equities, some are vanillas, some are exotics. Almost every branch diverges. Nsight Compute will show high divergence, and your compute roofline is unreachable.

Path-Dependent Early Exit

In Monte Carlo pricing of callable structures, some paths may knock out or exercise early. A naïve implementation lets each thread break out of the time loop as soon as its path is done.

Within each warp, a subset of threads exit early, while others keep going. The GPU effectively runs the loop for the maximum number of time steps among paths in that warp, but many threads are inactive for trailing iterations.

Strategies to Reduce Divergence

There are several practical strategies to tame divergence without changing the financial meaning of your code.

Data Partitioning by Behavior

Group together work items that follow similar control flow and run them in separate kernel launches. For example:

- Launch one kernel for equities, another for vanillas, another for exotics.
- Group barrier options with similar knock-out conditions together.

This does introduce more kernels and some extra bookkeeping, but it often leads to much more coherent warps in each kernel. Nsight Systems can help you verify that the additional kernels do not create intolerable launch overhead relative to the performance gains.

Predication Instead of Branching

Sometimes you can replace a branch with a conditional computation that always runs but is selectively applied. Rather than "if condition, do work, else skip," you compute the result and then multiply by a mask that is zero when the condition is false and one when it is true.

In finance terms, think of pricing an option that only pays off in certain states. You can always compute the payoff formula, but multiply it by an indicator that is one in the payoff region and zero elsewhere. All threads in the warp follow the same instruction path, reducing divergence. You do extra arithmetic, but you avoid control-flow overhead.

Predication is most attractive when the branch bodies are not too expensive and when divergence is severe. Profiling will tell you whether the trade-off is beneficial.

Uniform Decisions at Coarser Granularity

Sometimes you cannot avoid a complex branch, but you can move the decision to a point where it is uniform across threads in a warp or block. For instance, a regime-switching model might use different dynamics depending on the overall market regime (bull, bear, stressed). Instead of branching per path, you can compute the current regime once per kernel launch or block, and then launch different kernels or choose flags that are uniform within a warp.

This is particularly effective when the variability is driven by a small number of market-wide states rather than path-specific noise.

Managing Registers and Memory: Avoiding Hidden Slowdowns

Every thread has a set of registers for its variables. If you use more registers per thread than the hardware can allocate while maintaining high occupancy, or if the compiler runs out of registers, it spills variables to "local memory," which lives in global memory and is much slower.

From a quant developer's point of view, register pressure often comes from:

- Very long kernels that do many different tasks.
- Complex payoff logic with many intermediate variables.
- Large per-thread arrays or structures.

Signs of Register Pressure

Nsight Compute can show you:

- Registers used per thread.
- Local memory traffic, which usually indicates spills.
- The resulting effect on occupancy.

If you see high register usage, significant local-memory loads and stores, and reduced occupancy, you likely have a register pressure problem.

Simplifying Kernels

The simplest and often most effective way to reduce register pressure is to simplify the kernel:

- Split one enormous “do everything” kernel into a sequence of smaller kernels, each responsible for a coherent stage of work (for example, shock generation, path evolution, payoff evaluation, aggregation).
- Limit the number of live variables at any point by reusing temporaries when possible and keeping the scope of variables tight.
- Move infrequently used or invariant data out of per-thread scope and into constant memory or shared memory where appropriate.

There is a trade-off: more kernels mean more launches and possibly more global memory traffic between stages. But if the original kernel is heavily spilling and achieving low occupancy, the gains from simplification often dominate.

Using Shared Memory Thoughtfully

Shared memory is a small, fast, on-chip buffer that threads in the same block can use to collaborate. For rolling covariance or factor loading calculations, a common pattern is:

- Load a tile of the input data (for example, a block of instruments by time points) into shared memory.
- Have multiple threads reuse this tile to compute statistics or dot products.

This can significantly reduce global memory traffic and increase effective operational intensity. However, shared memory is also a limited resource. If each block uses a lot of shared memory, fewer blocks fit on an SM, which may hurt occupancy.

The engineering task is to:

- Choose tile sizes that give good reuse but still allow multiple blocks to reside on each SM.
- Lay out shared memory to avoid bank conflicts, which are another kind of memory stall Nsight Compute can report.

Again, profiling guides you: if using a larger shared-memory tile noticeably reduces global memory traffic and moves you closer to the memory roofline without destroying occupancy, it is likely a win.

Mixed Precision: Trading Bits for Speed Safely

Modern GPUs provide much higher throughput for lower-precision arithmetic (such as 16-bit or specialized 32-bit formats) than for full 64-bit double precision. Tensor Cores, in particular, can perform matrix operations in mixed precision extremely quickly.

This raises a natural question: in finance, where numerical accuracy and auditability matter, can we safely use these faster, lower-precision modes?

The answer is "yes, sometimes"—but only if you approach mixed precision as a controlled, measured experiment guided by an explicit error budget.

Precision Levels in Practice

For our purposes, three main precision levels matter:

- **Double precision** (64-bit): highest precision, but slowest and more resource-intensive on most GPUs.
- **Single precision** (32-bit): often much faster, with adequate precision for many intermediate calculations.

- **Lower precision formats** (such as 16-bit or specialized 32-bit formats): enable Tensor Cores and very high arithmetic throughput, but have fewer representable values and smaller dynamic range.

The key is to decide which parts of your computation need full precision and which parts can tolerate some rounding noise.

Designing an Error Budget

An error budget is a simple statement of how much numerical error is acceptable for a given use case. It often takes a form like:

- Option prices should not deviate from a double-precision reference by more than a small fraction of a cent.
- Portfolio expected return or volatility should be accurate to within a small relative percentage.
- Risk measures like Value-at-Risk should not show systematic bias beyond a specified tolerance when compared to a high-precision baseline.

Once you state an error budget, mixed precision becomes a constrained optimization problem: you try faster numerical schemes and check whether they stay within the budget.

Where Mixed Precision Tends to Work Well

In many GPU-accelerated quant workloads, the following patterns are promising for mixed precision:

Intermediate Linear Algebra

When computing factor exposures or applying covariance matrices, much of the heavy lifting is in matrix multiplications. You can often perform these products in mixed precision while accumulating results in a higher precision. Tensor Cores are particularly good at this pattern.

The intuition is that individual multiplicative errors tend to cancel out to some degree when aggregated, and the final accumulation in higher precision stabilizes the result.

Monte Carlo Path Evolution

Simulating paths step by step involves repeated arithmetic operations. The relative errors introduced by using single precision for increments and state updates are often small compared to the overall Monte Carlo sampling noise, especially if:

- You store key risk metrics or final payoffs in higher precision.
- You avoid subtracting nearly equal numbers (a numerically delicate operation) in low precision.

The right way to confirm this is empirical: run a representative set of simulations in double precision and in a candidate mixed-precision scheme, and compare the distributions of payoffs and risk metrics.

Where Caution is Needed

There are places where mixed precision can be dangerous:

- **Long accumulations**: Summing many small terms of varying magnitudes (such as cumulative PnL over long histories) is sensitive to rounding. Using low precision here can create noticeable drift.
- **Close-to-canceling quantities**: When computing differences of large, nearly equal numbers (for example, hedged portfolios), low precision can amplify relative errors.
- **Regulatory or accounting outputs**: Some outputs must exactly match established baselines within very tight tolerances; these are poor candidates for aggressive downshifts in precision.

For these components, it is usually safer to keep double precision or at least single precision with careful accumulation techniques.

Techniques to Control Numerical Drift

Several classic numerical techniques help you enjoy the speed of mixed precision while containing drift:

Compensated Summation

When summing many terms, you can use a summation algorithm that keeps track of small rounding errors and feeds them back into the sum. This reduces the accumulation of error, particularly when adding many small terms to a large total.

In a mixed-precision context, you might:

- Perform individual term calculations in lower precision.
- Perform the summation in higher precision with compensation.

This is particularly useful in portfolio-level aggregations of PnL or risk measures.

Periodic High-Precision Checkpoints

In long-running simulations, you can periodically re-evaluate key quantities in higher precision to "reset" drift. For example, every certain number of time steps, you re-compute a path's state or a portfolio's value in double precision and then continue with faster arithmetic.

This approach mirrors how risk systems sometimes reprice portfolios with a full revaluation at coarser frequency, even if they use cheaper approximations intraday.

Scaling and Normalization

For algorithms that suffer when variables grow over many orders of magnitude, rescaling inputs and intermediate values into a more moderate range can improve the effectiveness of lower precision. In finance, this often means:

- Working with log-prices or returns rather than raw prices when appropriate.
- Normalizing factor exposures or state variables before feeding them into mixed-precision linear algebra.

Putting It All Together: From Profile to Optimization Plan

Let us revisit the typical bottleneck kernels identified in the profiling section and outline what an optimization plan might look like.

Monte Carlo Path Update Kernel

Suppose Nsight shows:

- Moderate occupancy limited by high register usage.
- Significant divergence from early exercise logic.
- Compute-bound behavior with room to utilize more arithmetic throughput.

An optimization plan might be:

- Split the kernel into path evolution and payoff evaluation. This reduces register pressure and simplifies control flow in each part.
- Group instruments with similar payoff structures and run them in separate kernel batches to reduce divergence.
- Experiment with single-precision state updates while keeping final payoff computation and aggregations in double precision. Validate against a double-precision baseline using your error budget.
- If using matrix operations for factor shocks, switch those to Tensor Core-accelerated mixed-precision routines and re-measure throughput and error.

Rolling Covariance Calculation

Suppose profiling shows:

- Memory-bound behavior with underutilized bandwidth.
- Non-coalesced loads from an inconvenient time-series layout.

- Modest occupancy due to large shared-memory tiles.

Your plan could be:

- Reorganize input data into a columnar layout optimized for the access pattern in the kernel, and ensure coalesced reads for each time window.
- Adjust tile sizes in shared memory to balance reuse and occupancy, guided by Nsight's shared-memory usage and occupancy reports.
- If covariance is subsequently used in factor models, consider computing the covariance in single precision but storing the final matrix and performing eigen-decomposition or factor extractions in higher precision.

Factor Risk Matrix Operations

If the profiler reports:

- High arithmetic utilization but not close to peak.
- Predominant time spent in matrix multiplications.

You may:

- Replace custom matrix operations with vendor libraries tuned for your GPU generation.
- Enable mixed-precision modes and Tensor Cores for large matrix operations, while retaining double precision for final portfolio-level metrics.
- Validate that factor exposures, portfolio betas, and risk decompositions remain within your error budget relative to a full double-precision implementation.

An Optimization Mindset, Not a Bag of Tricks

The techniques in this section are effective only when used within the disciplined framework you developed earlier:

- Start from measurements: identify hot kernels and classify them as memory-bound or compute-bound.
- Choose the optimization levers that address the real bottlenecks: occupancy and memory layout for memory-bound kernels; divergence, register usage, and mixed precision for compute-bound kernels.
- Iterate experimentally: change one or two things at a time, remeasure, and compare against both performance baselines and numerical baselines.
- Document and validate: record configuration, precision choices, and observed errors so model validation and audit teams can understand and reproduce your results.

In the next section we will extend this thinking beyond a single GPU to multiple GPUs and distributed clusters, where communication, partitioning, and failure modes add new dimensions to the performance engineering problem.

6.3 Multi-GPU & Distributed Execution

So far we have focused on making a *single* GPU run as efficiently as possible. In many real trading and risk environments, however, a single device is not enough. You may face:

- Portfolios with hundreds of thousands of instruments across many asset classes.
- Monte Carlo risk reports with tens or hundreds of millions of paths.

- Tight overnight or intraday deadlines where wall-clock time, not just simulations per second, is the binding constraint.

In these situations, you need to scale horizontally: across multiple GPUs in one server, and across multiple servers in a cluster. Doing so effectively requires a different way of thinking about your workload. Performance is no longer just "how fast is this kernel," but also "how much communication is needed between GPUs," "how is the data partitioned," and "what happens when something fails halfway through an overnight run."

This section develops a mental model for multi-GPU and distributed execution tailored to quant finance. We will:

- Identify parallelization patterns that naturally fit backtests and risk analytics.
- Explain intra-node multi-GPU execution and communication using NCCL.
- Extend the picture to multi-node clusters coordinated by frameworks such as Dask or Ray.
- Highlight practical concerns: skewed partitions, idempotent tasks, checkpointing, determinism, and failure modes.

Throughout, assume that for each individual GPU we are already applying the profiling and kernel-optimization techniques from earlier sections. Scaling out adds more moving parts; our goal is to do so without losing the performance gains we worked so hard to achieve.

Parallelization Patterns in Quant Workloads

Before introducing tools and libraries, it is helpful to classify how your workloads can be partitioned. In distributed systems, the best strategies usually exploit *natural* independence in the problem.

Portfolio-Parallel and Scenario-Parallel Workloads

Many workloads are *embarrassingly parallel*, meaning that individual units of work do not depend on each other during computation:

- **Scenario-parallel Monte Carlo**: Each path, or each group of paths, can be evolved independently. Only at the end do you aggregate results into portfolio risk measures.
- **Portfolio-parallel analytics**: If you have many relatively independent portfolios or books, you can assign each to a different GPU and compute Greeks or factor risks independently, then merge results.

These workloads are usually the easiest to scale. Each GPU runs essentially the same code on a different chunk of data, with minimal communication until an aggregation stage.

Time-Partitioned Backtests

Historical backtests often operate on long time horizons. A natural strategy is to partition by time:

- GPU 0 simulates years 1-5.
- GPU 1 simulates years 6-10.
- And so on.

This works well when strategy state does not depend on future information and when you can properly handle initial conditions for later segments (for example, by passing final positions from one segment as initial conditions for the next).

Time-partitioning is particularly useful when your raw data is already sharded by date or when object stores or file systems arrange files in time-based directories.

Cross-Sectional Partitioning

Many factor and risk engines process large cross-sections of instruments or risk factors at a given time slice. You can partition by instrument universe or symbol:

- GPU 0 handles equities A-M.
- GPU 1 handles equities N-Z.
- Other GPUs handle fixed income, FX, or derivatives.

Cross-sectional partitioning is flexible, but beware of skew: some symbols or asset classes may be much more active or complex than others, leading to imbalanced loads across GPUs.

Single-Node Multi-GPU: NCCL and Collectives

On a single server with multiple GPUs, the hardware typically provides high-bandwidth connections between devices (for example, NVLink) and between devices and host memory (PCIe). NVIDIA's NCCL (NVIDIA Collective Communications Library) is designed to exploit these links efficiently.

The Role of Collectives

A *collective* operation involves a group of participants (GPUs) working together on a communication pattern. The most important collectives for quant workloads are:

- **All-reduce**: Each GPU has an array of values (for example, local PnL paths or partial Greeks). All-reduce combines them with an operation (such as sum or maximum) and leaves every GPU with the full, reduced result.
- **Reduce**: Similar to all-reduce, but only one GPU (or the host) receives the reduced result.

- **Broadcast**: One GPU has a buffer (for example, updated factor covariances) that needs to be sent to all other GPUs.

These operations appear whenever you have:

- Independent simulations or calculations on each GPU.
- A final aggregation or synchronization step (for example, computing total portfolio VaR from per-GPU contributions).

NCCL implements these collectives using communication topologies that match the physical links between GPUs. The main advantage for you as a quant developer is that you do not need to micromanage which GPU sends what to whom; you express the collective operation, and NCCL takes care of the details.

Multi-GPU Monte Carlo Within a Node

Consider a Monte Carlo VaR calculation where you need one hundred million paths. On a single GPU this might be marginal for your overnight window. With four GPUs in one server, a common pattern is:

1. Split the total number of paths into four equal or near-equal chunks, one per GPU.
2. Each GPU runs the same kernel on its assigned paths, using independent random number streams.
3. At the end, each GPU has partial statistics: sums of PnL, sums of squares, perhaps histograms or ordered lists for quantiles.
4. Use NCCL all-reduce to combine these partial statistics into a global result.

The bulk of work is embarrassingly parallel; the communication cost is concentrated in the final aggregation. If the amount of aggregated data is small compared to the simulation work (for example, a few arrays of statistics versus the entire path history), communication has minimal impact on overall runtime.

When Communication Becomes the Bottleneck

Even within a node, communication can limit scaling if you:

- Aggregate very large intermediate objects (for example, full path matrices or tick data) instead of reduced statistics.
- Perform frequent synchronization steps inside a time loop rather than once at the end.
- Use patterns that effectively serialize computation across GPUs (for example, GPU 1 must wait for data from GPU 0 at each time step).

Profiling tools can show you when GPUs are waiting on communication rather than computation. The remedy is usually to:

- Redesign the algorithm to keep data local as much as possible.
- Aggregate aggressively before communicating.
- Reduce the frequency of global synchronization.

From One Node to Many: Distributed Orchestration

Once you move beyond the confines of a single server, you face additional complexity:

- Communication between nodes is slower and less predictable than communication between GPUs in a node.
- Nodes may fail independently.
- You often want a flexible way to schedule and track many small tasks across a cluster.

Distributed execution frameworks such as Dask and Ray help manage this complexity. They provide:

- A central scheduler or set of schedulers that track available workers and assign tasks.
- A way to express computations as graphs of tasks with dependencies.
- Mechanisms for data distribution, serialization, and fault recovery.

In a GPU-centric quant environment, you typically run one worker process per GPU, and let the framework assign tasks (for example, "simulate these paths," "compute this factor slice") to workers.

The Two-Level View: Intra-Node vs. Inter-Node

It is helpful to think in terms of two layers:

1. **Intra-node**: GPUs within a single server cooperate using NCCL and high-bandwidth links.
2. **Inter-node**: Servers cooperate over the network, coordinated by Dask, Ray, or a similar framework.

Within a node, you want to exploit tight coupling and fast collectives. Across nodes, you assume higher latency and lower bandwidth, so you design algorithms to communicate less often and in coarser units.

Midway through this section is the right point to visualize the full architecture.

Task Graphs for Backtests and Risk Runs

Frameworks like Dask and Ray encourage you to think in terms of tasks and dependencies:

- **Input tasks**: load or receive a partition of data (for example, one symbol group or time window).
- **Compute tasks**: run a GPU-accelerated backtest or risk calculation on that partition.

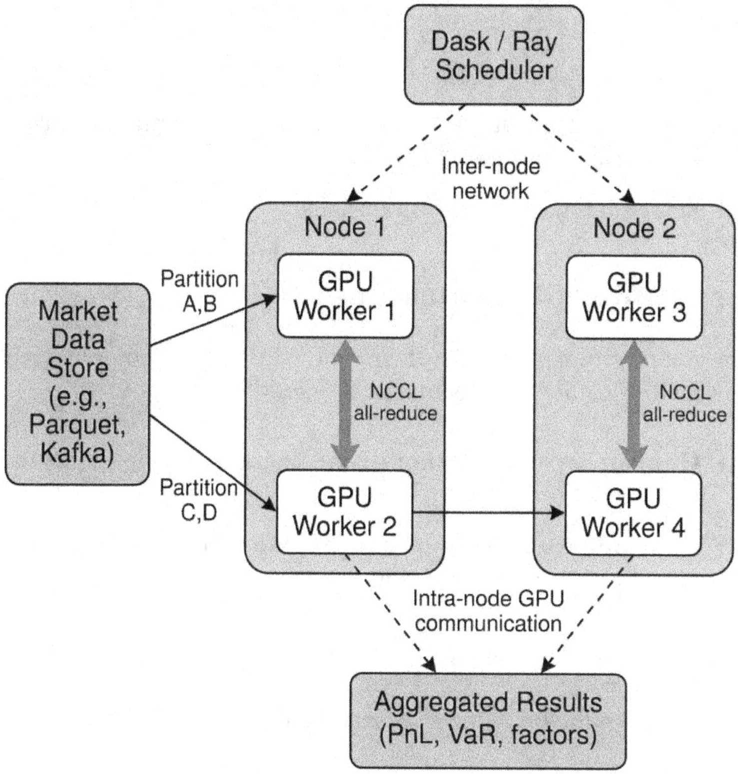

- **Aggregation tasks**: combine results across partitions into final metrics.

For example, a historical backtest over ten years of data might be represented as:

- Ten input tasks (one per year) that each feed a GPU backtest.
- Ten compute tasks, each running on a different worker.
- One or more aggregation tasks that merge performance statistics and risk metrics across years.

The scheduler is responsible for:

- Assigning compute tasks to workers with available GPUs.
- Moving data partitions to where tasks run, or arranging for workers to read from shared storage.
- Rescheduling tasks if a worker fails.

Partitioning Strategies and Skew

How you partition data across tasks and GPUs has a profound impact on overall efficiency. Two common sources of trouble are:

- **Uneven work per partition**: some partitions take much longer than others.
- **Data-dependent complexity**: some symbols or time periods are much more active or complex.

Symbol-Based Partitioning

When partitioning by symbol or instrument:

- Avoid putting very liquid or derivative-heavy names all into one partition. That partition will dominate runtime.
- Consider grouping symbols by approximate "weight" (for example, past trading volume, number of trades, or complexity of instruments) and then balancing total weight per partition.

In practice, you might compute a simple score per symbol and then greedily assign symbols to partitions to equalize total scores.

Time-Based Partitioning

When partitioning by time, some periods—such as crisis days or eventful weeks—may be far more computationally heavy, due to higher volatility, more trades, or complex path behavior. If you simply assign equal time intervals to each node, you may end up with one node processing the most turbulent periods while others finish early and sit idle.

Possible remedies include:

- Using smaller time chunks as tasks (for example, days instead of years) so that the scheduler can spread heavy days across different workers.
- Dynamically adjusting partition sizes based on historical volume or volatility measures.

Handling Failure and Designing Idempotent Tasks

In a single-node, single-GPU context, you typically assume that if your program runs to completion, the result is available; failures are relatively rare and often handled by rerunning the whole job.

In a distributed cluster, failures are more common: a node might be preempted in the cloud, a network hiccup might disconnect a worker, or a GPU might reset due to an error. You want your system to treat these as routine events, not crises.

Idempotent Tasks

A task is *idempotent* if running it multiple times with the same inputs produces the same result and has no harmful side effects. Idempotent tasks make failure handling straightforward:

- If a worker fails mid-task, the scheduler can resubmit the task to a different worker.
- You do not need to coordinate partial states or worry about duplicate contributions.

For quant workloads, this means:

- Each backtest or simulation task should produce results that can be recomputed from scratch from its input data and random seeds.

- Tasks should not directly commit trades, modify shared state, or write to global tables in a way that depends on how many times they ran.

Checkpointing Long-Running Tasks

Some tasks are too large or too long to rerun cheaply. For example, simulating one hundred million paths for a complex exotic book might take hours even on a GPU cluster.

In these cases, you can implement checkpointing:

- Periodically save intermediate results to durable storage (for example, partial path statistics, state of random number generators, or partial PnL distributions).

- On failure, resume from the last checkpoint instead of restarting from scratch.

Checkpointing is a trade-off: writing checkpoints incurs overhead. The right frequency depends on your tolerance for lost work and the expected failure rate in your environment.

Determinism and Reproducibility at Scale

Earlier we discussed reproducibility on a single GPU: controlling random seeds, reconciling against CPU baselines, and logging configuration. In a distributed setting, these concerns become more subtle.

Randomness Across GPUs and Workers

To reproduce a Monte Carlo run spread across many GPUs:

- Use a parallel-friendly random number generator that allows you to assign independent, non-overlapping streams to different workers or GPUs.
- Derive seeds in a systematic way from a master seed plus identifiers such as worker index, GPU index, and partition index.
- Log these seeds and mappings so you can reconstruct which paths were simulated where.

This ensures that if you rerun the same job with the same configuration and cluster layout, you get bit-identical results. Even if the physical node assignment changes, you can maintain logical mapping between partitions and random streams.

Aggregation Order and Floating-Point Differences

In a distributed system, the order in which partial results are combined may vary between runs, especially if tasks complete in different orders due to scheduling or load. Since floating-point addition is not strictly associative, this can lead to tiny differences in aggregated results.

Whether these differences matter depends on your tolerance and regulatory environment. If you need strict bit-for-bit reproducibility, you may:

- Impose a deterministic aggregation order (for example, always sort partial results by partition key before reducing).
- Use higher precision for final aggregations.
- Record not only seeds but also the reduction plan used.

In many practical cases, the differences are smaller than your numerical error budget and can be accepted as noise, provided you have documented and validated this.

End-to-End Examples

To make these ideas concrete, consider two representative workflows.

Overnight Multi-Asset Monte Carlo VaR

You need to compute a full revaluation Monte Carlo VaR for a large, multi-asset portfolio every night, targeting completion by a fixed time.

A plausible architecture:

- **Data preparation**: A CPU-based pipeline prepares market data slices and instrument definitions and stores them in a shared object store or database, partitioned by instrument group.
- **Task graph construction**: A central scheduler (Dask or Ray) creates tasks, each representing "simulate this subset of instruments and scenarios on one GPU."
- **Node-level execution**: Each node runs one worker per GPU. Within a node, NCCL all-reduce may be used to aggregate partial statistics across GPUs before sending them back to the scheduler.
- **Cluster-level aggregation**: Aggregation tasks on the scheduler or on designated nodes combine per-partition results into global PnL distributions and risk measures.
- **Checkpointing and fault tolerance**: Long tasks checkpoint periodically; failures cause tasks to be rescheduled from the last checkpoint.

Here, most computation is scenario-parallel and instrument-parallel. Communication is concentrated in the final aggregation stages and in the relatively small metadata and market data exchanges.

Cross-Sectional Factor Risk Across a Universe

You compute factor exposures and factor risk for a very large equity universe intraday.

A sensible design:

- **Partitioning**: Divide the universe into balanced symbol partitions based on trading volume or complexity.

- **Broadcast**: Use a broadcast (across nodes) to distribute updated factor covariances and model parameters to all GPU workers.
- **Local compute**: Each worker reads its symbol partition, runs a GPU-accelerated factor engine to compute per-instrument exposures and specific risk.
- **Portfolio assembly**: For each portfolio or desk, aggregation tasks fetch exposures from the relevant partitions and assemble portfolio-level risk metrics.

The heavy linear-algebra work occurs locally on each GPU with minimal inter-worker communication. The main cluster-level communication is broadcasting the factor model parameters and collecting the relatively small exposure matrices and risk measures.

A Practical Checklist for Scaling Out

When you decide to move from a single GPU to multi-GPU and distributed execution, keep the following checklist in mind:

- **Parallelization pattern**: Is the workload scenario-parallel, portfolio-parallel, time-partitioned, cross-sectional, or a mix?
- **Intra-node design**: How will GPUs within a node cooperate? Where do you use NCCL collectives, and how often?
- **Inter-node design**: What data is exchanged across nodes, and how often? Is this minimized and aggregated?
- **Partitioning strategy**: How are data and tasks partitioned to avoid skew and imbalance?
- **Task properties**: Are tasks idempotent and large enough to amortize overhead but small enough for good load balancing?
- **Failure handling**: How do you detect and recover from worker or node failures? Do you need checkpointing?

- **Determinism**: How are random seeds assigned? How are aggregations performed? What level of reproducibility do you require?

Bringing these pieces together allows you to extend the disciplined, measurement-driven approach you developed for single GPUs to the cluster level. In the following sections we will look at the data engineering and infrastructure needed to keep such distributed GPU systems reliably fed and governed in a production setting.

6.4 Data Engineering for GPU Workflows

In the previous sections we treated the GPU and the cluster as powerful engines for computation. We profiled kernels, optimized them, and scaled them across multiple devices and nodes. In practice, those engines are only as useful as the data they receive. An exquisitely tuned Monte Carlo kernel that sits idle waiting for market data is not a success.

This section focuses on the "plumbing" that keeps GPUs continuously and correctly fed with data. In a quant shop, that plumbing must satisfy three demands at once:

- **Throughput**: Move large volumes of historical and live market data fast enough to keep GPUs busy.
- **Efficiency**: Minimize unnecessary data movement, especially across the relatively slow host-device boundary.
- **Correctness over time**: Preserve event-time semantics so that timestamps, ordering, and late or out-of-order events are handled in a way that keeps backtests and analytics meaningful.

We will walk step by step from raw data storage, through ingestion and preprocessing, to GPU-based resampling and feature engineering, and finally to downstream backtests and live analytics. Along the way we will highlight where data crosses critical boundaries (notably PCIe or

NVLink), and how to structure pipelines so most heavy lifting happens on the device.

Why Data Engineering Matters for Performance

When you profile a real backtest or risk run in a multi-GPU environment, it is common to discover that:

- A large fraction of wall-clock time is spent in I/O and data preparation rather than in GPU kernels.
- The same data is copied back and forth between CPU and GPU multiple times.
- Tick data is repeatedly parsed, filtered, and reassembled in slightly different ways for different strategies.

The result is a system where the GPU appears underutilized despite apparently heavy workloads. To fix this, you must design data flows with the same discipline you brought to kernel optimization:

- Use storage formats aligned with GPU-friendly access patterns.
- Push transformations as close as possible to where the data will be consumed.
- Batch and stream data to overlap I/O and compute.
- Make event-time a first-class concept so you do not compromise the integrity of time series when you parallelize.

We begin with an overall picture of such a pipeline.

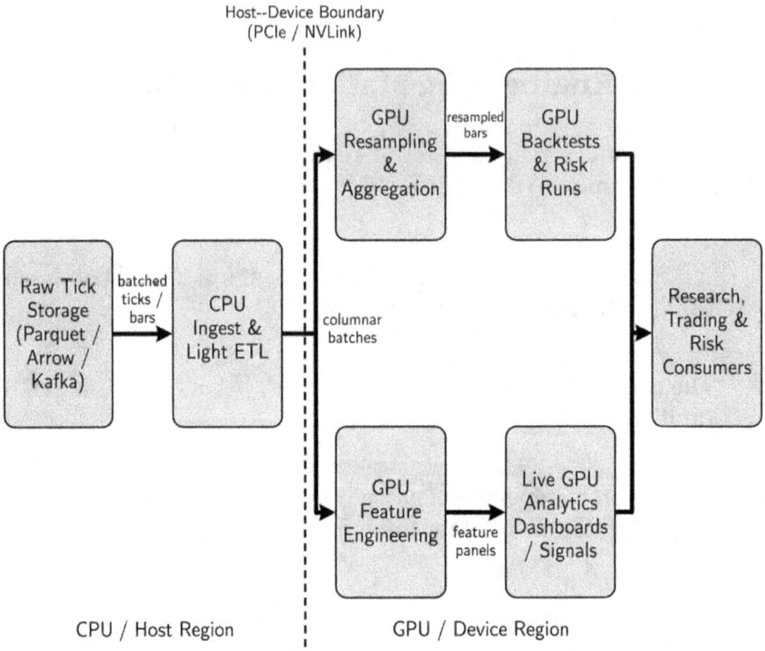

This diagram will guide the narrative that follows.

Storage Formats and Ingestion

The starting point for any pipeline is how data is stored. For GPU analytics, columnar formats are natural allies.

Columnar Storage: Parquet and Arrow

In a columnar format, data is stored column by column rather than row by row. For time-series and cross-sectional financial data, this has several advantages:

- You can read only the columns you need (for example, price, volume, and timestamp) instead of loading entire records.
- Values in a column are contiguous in memory, which maps well to GPUs' preference for coalesced memory accesses.
- Compression and encoding schemes can exploit repeated patterns in columns (for example, repeated symbols or similar prices), further reducing I/O.

Formats such as Parquet and Arrow are widely used in data lakes and are supported by GPU-aware libraries. When a GPU kernel computes a simple transform like log returns or volume-weighted average price, it often processes one or a few columns at a time—exactly what columnar layouts provide efficiently.

Encoding Market Data for GPU Consumption

How you encode prices, volumes, and related fields in storage affects how easily and efficiently you can transform them on the GPU. Practical considerations include:

- **Numeric types**: Choose consistent numeric types that balance precision and storage cost. For many intermediate analytics, 32-bit floating point is enough, with separate high-precision storage for final valuations if needed.
- **Time encoding**: Use a clear scheme for timestamps (for example, nanoseconds since epoch, along with separate columns for trading day or session) so that time-zone conversions and calendar joins can be applied systematically.
- **Corporate actions**: Encode splits, dividends, and other events in ways that make common adjustments simple. For example, include both raw and adjusted prices or store corporate-action factors that can be applied as multiplicative adjustments in GPU kernels.

If you standardize these conventions across datasets and desks, you avoid repeated one-off transformations that add complexity and I/O.

CPU Ingest and Light ETL

Even in a GPU-centric architecture, some work is best done on the CPU during ingestion:

- **Parsing**: Converting raw exchange feeds, FIX messages, or CSV files into structured columns.
- **Basic validation**: Checking for malformed records, impossible timestamps, or obviously bad values.
- **Row-level filtering**: Discarding instruments or markets not relevant to a particular backtest or risk run.

The goal of this stage is not to perform heavy analytics, but to produce clean, columnar batches ready for GPU processing. Ideally, these batches are already partitioned in ways that match downstream parallelism: by symbol group, by time window, or both.

Crossing the Host-Device Boundary Efficiently

Transferring data between host memory and GPU memory is often much slower than operating on data already on the GPU. Your pipeline should therefore:

- Minimize the number of transfers.
- Maximize the amount of useful work done per transferred byte.
- Overlap transfers with computation wherever possible.

Batching and Pinned Memory

Rather than moving ticks one by one, you should batch them into sizable chunks:

- For historical backtests, one batch might represent a day or a week of data for a set of symbols.
- For live analytics, batches might contain all ticks arriving in a short time window.

Using pinned (page-locked) host memory for these batches allows the GPU to perform direct memory access (DMA) more efficiently. Combined with asynchronous copy operations, you can start transferring the next batch to the GPU while the previous batch is still being processed.

Keeping Data on the GPU

Once data reaches the GPU, try to keep it there for as many stages of the pipeline as possible:

- Perform resampling (ticks to bars), feature engineering (rolling statistics, cross-sectional z-scores), and even intermediate aggregations on the GPU.
- Only copy back results that must be consumed by CPU-based systems, and even then aim to send compact summaries rather than full intermediate states.

This approach turns the GPU into a "data gravity" center: raw data flows in, high-value analytics flow out.

Resampling Tick Data on the GPU

Tick data are irregular: trades and quotes arrive at uneven intervals, and different symbols have very different levels of activity. Most backtests and risk engines, however, operate on regular time grids (for example, one-second or one-minute bars) or at least on well-defined event sequences (such as trades only).

From Irregular Events to Bars

Resampling tick data into bars involves:

- Grouping ticks into time buckets (for example, all trades between 10:00:00 and 10:00:59).
- Computing aggregate fields per bucket (open, high, low, close, volume, VWAP).
- Handling buckets with no ticks (carrying forward previous prices or marking gaps).

On a GPU, you typically:

- Map each symbol or symbol-time bucket to a set of threads.
- Use parallel reductions within blocks to compute aggregates efficiently.

Because this stage is often memory-bound—streaming through a large number of ticks with simple arithmetic—it benefits greatly from columnar layouts and coalesced accesses. It also benefits from doing as much as possible in one pass: compute all required bar statistics in the same kernel rather than launching separate kernels for each statistic.

Maintaining Event-Time Semantics

Event-time semantics mean that you process data in the order events actually occurred, not merely in the order they were received or processed. This is crucial for:

- Accurately simulating latency-sensitive strategies.
- Handling late or out-of-order ticks.
- Ensuring that bars and features reflect the true market evolution.

When you resample on the GPU:

- Ensure that input data batches are sorted by event time, at least within each symbol or partition.
- For streaming systems, maintain per-symbol buffers that can reorder a limited amount of out-of-order data based on timestamps before handing them to GPU kernels.
- When you parallelize across time or symbols, design partitions so that ticks for a given symbol and time range are not split across tasks in ways that break ordering assumptions.

If late ticks arrive after a bar has been computed, you must decide whether to adjust historical bars (and how that affects auditability) or to treat them separately, for example as corrections or as part of a delayed feed.

GPU-Based Feature Engineering

Once you have resampled bars or other structured data on the GPU, you can derive features that feed into strategies, risk models, or machine learning pipelines.

Common Rolling and Cross-Sectional Features

Typical GPU-friendly features include:

- **Rolling statistics**: moving averages, standard deviations, maximum drawdowns over fixed windows.
- **Volatility and liquidity measures**: realized volatility, bid-ask spread statistics, turnover.
- **Cross-sectional scores**: z-scores of returns or fundamental ratios across a universe at a given time point.
- **Microstructure features**: order-book imbalance, trade intensity, short-term order-flow measures.

These features often involve:

- Repeated patterns over contiguous time windows (good for shared-memory tiling).
- Simple arithmetic operations (well-suited to GPUs' parallel lanes).
- Natural independence across symbols or risk factors (good for partitioning across threads and blocks).

By chaining such operations on device, you avoid copying intermediate feature matrices back to the CPU.

Chaining Operations with GPU DataFrames and Custom Kernels

High-level libraries inspired by pandas but implemented on top of GPU primitives (for example, DataFrame-like APIs built on CUDA) let you:

- Express sequences of operations such as grouping, rolling windows, and joins.
- Rely on underlying kernels that are already tuned for GPUs.

Where these abstractions fall short, you can insert custom kernels that operate on the same columnar buffers. The design goal is to maintain a pipeline where data remains in GPU-native structures from the moment it crosses the host-device boundary until it is either stored or consumed.

Batch vs. Streaming Pipelines

So far, the description applies naturally to batch processing of historical data: you have a fixed dataset and want to run a backtest or risk report over it. Many quant shops also need near-real-time analytics: signal calculation, live risk dashboards, or intraday stress tests.

The main difference between batch and streaming pipelines lies not in the structure of GPU computation but in how data pieces are triggered and combined over time.

Batch Pipelines for Historical Backtests

In a batch pipeline:

- You read large chunks of historical data from storage, often partitioned by day, month, or year.
- Each chunk becomes a unit of work in a distributed task graph, as discussed in the multi-GPU section.
- GPU kernels run to completion on each chunk, and results are written back to storage or aggregated into final backtest metrics.

Batch pipelines are easier to reason about because there is no concept of "late data"; the dataset is fixed. Your main concerns are throughput, memory footprint, and partitioning.

Streaming Pipelines for Live Analytics

In a streaming pipeline:

- Data arrives continuously from sources such as exchange feeds or internal tick buses.
- You process data in small batches or micro-batches, perhaps every few hundred milliseconds or seconds.
- You maintain state across batches (for example, last price, rolling windows, accumulated PnL).

Two time concepts become critical:

- **Event time**: when an event (trade, quote) actually occurred in the market.
- **Processing time**: when your system saw and processed the event.

Because network latencies and system hiccups can cause events to arrive late, a strict "process-as-you-see" approach can produce inconsistent results. Many streaming frameworks introduce *watermarks*: markers that say "we believe we have seen all events up to time T, except for rare late ones." You can adopt similar concepts:

- Maintain per-symbol or per-venue buffers for recent events.
- Periodically flush buffered events to the GPU for resampling and feature computation when you are confident most events for the interval have arrived.
- Decide policies for handling genuinely late events: adjust later, ignore, or record as corrections.

Managing Memory and Data Movement at Scale

In multi-GPU and distributed environments, data engineering includes careful memory management and awareness of where data resides physically.

Host and Device Memory Budgets

Each GPU has limited device memory; each node has finite host memory. You must design batches and partitions that fit comfortably within these budgets:

- For historical data, this may mean loading only a subset of symbols or time at once, processing, then moving to the next subset.
- For streaming data, this may mean bounding the size of per-symbol buffers and the duration of rolling windows for which you maintain full histories on the GPU.

Profiling tools can show you when kernels are limited by memory capacity or cause spills to slower levels of the memory hierarchy. Data engineering choices–such as how many symbols to batch together–directly impact these profiles.

Minimizing Cross-Node Data Movement

In a cluster, moving large volumes of raw data across nodes is expensive. Good data engineering therefore aims to:

- Store data in a shared location (for example, a distributed file system or object store) that all nodes can access directly.
- Partition data so each node can read the partitions it is responsible for without copying them from other nodes.
- Exchange only compact, aggregated results between nodes, not raw tick streams.

This aligns with the principle "ship computation to data, not data to computation." Each worker node and its GPUs become responsible for local slices of the data lake.

Putting It All Together: A GPU-Oriented Dataflow

Let us summarize a typical end-to-end pipeline for a GPU-heavy quant research platform, combining batch and streaming aspects:

1. **Raw ingestion and storage**:
    - Exchange feeds and other sources are parsed by CPU-based ingest services.
    - Cleaned ticks, corporate actions, and reference data are stored in partitioned Parquet or Arrow files, organized by time and symbol, and optionally also streamed on a message bus for live processing.
2. **CPU-side preparation**:
    - For a requested backtest or risk run, a coordinator determines which time and symbol partitions are needed.
    - It reads metadata and constructs batches of columnar data tailored to GPU memory limits and parallelization strategy.
3. **Host-device transfer and GPU resampling**:

- Batches are copied to GPUs using pinned memory and asynchronous transfers.
- GPU kernels resample ticks into bars, maintaining event-time order within symbols and handling empty intervals as specified.

4. **GPU feature engineering**:
    - Subsequent kernels compute rolling statistics, cross-sectional scores, and microstructure features entirely on device.
    - Where necessary, intermediate results are stored in GPU-native columnar formats to be reused by multiple strategies.

5. **Downstream consumption**:
    - GPU backtests and risk models read feature panels directly from device memory or from GPU-resident caches.
    - Only high-level results (PnL paths, risk summaries, factor exposures) are copied back to the host for storage, reporting, or further aggregation across nodes.

6. **Streaming loop for live analytics**:
    - A parallel streaming pipeline ingests live ticks, maintains per-symbol buffers, and periodically dispatches micro-batches to GPUs for incremental updates to features and risk metrics.
    - Watermarks and event-time logic ensure that analytics reflect the temporal reality of the market as closely as possible.

A Data-Engineering Mindset for GPU Quant Systems

Designing data pipelines for GPUs is not glamorous, but it is foundational. The most successful GPU-accelerated quant platforms share several traits:

- They treat storage formats, partitioning schemes, and host-device transfers as first-class design decisions, not afterthoughts.
- They maximize the work done per byte moved: once data is on the GPU, it goes through as many useful transformations as possible before leaving.
- They respect time: event-time ordering, late data, and calendar idiosyncrasies are handled systematically, so that speed does not come at the expense of correctness.
- They are observant: logs and metrics capture not only compute performance but also data flow characteristics—throughput, queue lengths, buffer utilization—so bottlenecks in the pipeline can be found and fixed.

In the remaining sections of this chapter we will focus on validation, reproducibility, and infrastructure. Those topics build directly on the pipeline concepts introduced here: to test and govern a GPU-accelerated quant platform, you must know exactly how data flows through it and where the critical boundaries and assumptions lie.

6.5 Validation, Testing & Reproducibility

By now we have treated performance engineering, scaling, and data pipelines as first-class topics. We have fast kernels, multi-GPU clusters, and carefully designed data flows. The remaining question is whether you can *trust* the numbers coming out of this machinery.

In a research notebook, a rough sanity check might be enough. In a trading or risk platform, it is not. Regulators, auditors, risk committees, and even your own future self will at some point ask:

> Can we reproduce this result? How do we know it is numerically sound and not an artifact of GPU quirks?

This section builds a reliability toolbox for GPU-accelerated quant systems. We will cover:

- Testing strategies at multiple levels: unit tests, property-based tests, and full-pipeline "golden" comparisons.
- Numerical reconciliation between GPU implementations and established CPU baselines.
- Randomness control and logging for simulations running across many GPUs and nodes.
- How these practices feed into model validation and audit workflows.

The guiding principle is simple: high performance is only valuable if it comes with confidence in correctness and reproducibility.

Why GPUs Need a Deliberate Validation Strategy

GPU implementations introduce several sources of subtle risk that may not exist, or may be less pronounced, in traditional CPU code:

- **Parallel execution order**: Reductions and aggregations proceed in different orders than in scalar code, affecting floating-point rounding.
- **Aggressive optimizations**: Use of mixed precision, Tensor Cores, or fused kernels can make numerical behavior more complex to reason about.
- **Concurrency**: Race conditions or synchronization bugs may only appear under certain workload sizes or hardware configurations.
- **Distributed variation**: Multi-GPU and multi-node setups can aggregate results in different orders or split work differently from run to run.

You cannot rely on "if it compiles and seems fast, it must be correct." Instead, you need systematic tests and reconciliation that explicitly acknowledge these issues and bound their impact.

Layered Testing: From Kernels to Full Pipelines

A robust approach layers several kinds of tests, each with different scope and purpose. Collectively they form a "defense in depth" against errors.

Unit Tests for Kernels and Utilities

At the innermost layer, you test individual CUDA kernels and device-level utilities in isolation. The goals here are:

- Confirm that kernels produce expected results on small, carefully constructed inputs.
- Catch off-by-one indexing errors, boundary-condition bugs, and synchronization mistakes early.
- Make it easier to refactor performance-critical kernels without fear of silent behavior changes.

For example, you might unit-test:

- A kernel that computes rolling means and variances over short synthetic time series, where you know the exact answers.
- A kernel that applies factor shocks to instrument-level sensitivities, verified on a small matrix where you have hand-checked the results.
- A device-side random-number generator wrapper, checked for repeatability given fixed seeds and stream IDs.

These tests usually operate on tiny data sizes and run in milliseconds. They are ideal for integration into continuous integration (CI) pipelines; every change to the GPU codebase runs these tests automatically.

Property-Based Tests: Checking Invariants

Unit tests check specific examples. Property-based tests go one level deeper: they verify that core invariants hold across many randomly generated inputs. Rather than hard-coding dozens of cases, you define properties such as:

- *No-arbitrage*: For a given pricing kernel, prices should satisfy basic inequalities. For example, a call option on a non-dividend-paying stock should never be worth less than zero and never more than the underlying price.
- *Conservation of cash flows*: In a simulation kernel that models trades and funding, the total quantity of an asset plus cumulative trades should equal initial holdings plus net purchases.
- *Monotonicity*: Portfolio value under a strictly higher underlying price path (all else equal) should be at least as high as under a lower path for long-only positions.

A property-based testing framework can then generate many random inputs (different price paths, volatility levels, trade sequences) and check that your GPU implementation respects the properties. When a counterexample appears, the framework typically shrinks it to a minimal failing case, making debugging much easier.

These tests are particularly powerful for uncovering edge cases that you did not anticipate: extreme volatilities, thinly traded names, or rare timing patterns.

Golden-File Tests: End-to-End Regression Guardrails

At the outermost layer, you want tests that cover the entire pipeline: from data ingestion and preprocessing, through GPU simulation or analytics, all the way to portfolio-level metrics.

A common approach is to maintain *golden files*:

- Choose a few canonical datasets: for example, one normal trading period, one crisis week, one multi-asset stress period.
- Run your full production or near-production pipeline (perhaps originally on CPU) and store the outputs: PnL paths, risk measures, factor exposures, key Greeks.
- Treat these outputs as reference "golden" results. They represent a numerically and conceptually validated baseline.

Whenever you change GPU code, data engineering logic, or orchestration, you:

- Re-run the pipeline on the same inputs.
- Compare outputs to golden files within predefined tolerances.

If differences exceed tolerances, the change is flagged for review. This practice catches regressions that might slip past unit and property-based tests—such as a subtle alteration in how corporate actions are handled or in how paths are aggregated across GPUs.

Numerical Reconciliation with CPU Baselines

For many quant shops, existing CPU-based implementations are considered the "source of truth," at least initially. GPU acceleration is adopted to improve performance, not to change model behavior. This makes reconciliation between CPU and GPU implementations central.

What to Compare

You should design reconciliation harnesses that compare not just final aggregate metrics, but intermediate statistics:

- **Instrument-level results**: prices, Greeks, and risk decompositions for a sample of instruments across the portfolio.
- **Path-level statistics**: for Monte Carlo, distributions of payoffs or PnL for selected instruments or netting sets.
- **Aggregation consistency**: portfolio PnL or risk metrics computed bottom-up from instrument-level numbers should match those computed directly at the portfolio level.

By looking at multiple levels, you can quickly localize discrepancies. If individual instrument prices match but portfolio VaR does not, the bug likely lies in aggregation or portfolio-specific logic. If path-level distributions diverge, the issue may be in simulation or random number handling.

Defining Tolerances

Floating-point arithmetic on parallel hardware will rarely yield bit-identical results to a serial CPU implementation, even when using the same precision. You must therefore define explicit tolerances:

- **Absolute tolerances**: acceptable differences in units (for example, option price differences less than a fraction of a cent).
- **Relative tolerances**: acceptable percentage differences (for example, risk measures matching within a small fraction of a percent).

Tolerances should be motivated by the financial context:

- For a liquid at-the-money option, a half-cent difference may be immaterial.
- For a deeply out-of-the-money option with tiny absolute value, relative error may be a better measure.
- For regulatory capital, you may require much tighter bounds than for exploratory research backtests.

It is important to document these tolerances and apply them consistently across reconciliation tests. Overly strict tolerances will produce constant noise and reduce trust in the tests; overly loose ones may hide genuine problems.

Drift Detection Over Time

Even if a GPU implementation initially reconciles well with the CPU baseline, later changes may slowly degrade accuracy. To prevent "drift" from accumulating unnoticed:

- Run reconciliation tests regularly (for example, nightly or as part of CI) using stable input datasets.
- Track differences over time and set alerts if they trend upward, even if they remain within tolerances.
- Periodically revisit tolerances in light of observed drift and business needs.

This practice is analogous to monitoring performance regressions: you not only care when something suddenly breaks, but also when a series of small changes collectively push the system close to its risk limits.

Randomness Control in Parallel Simulations

Randomness is central to Monte Carlo pricing, stress testing, and many other simulations. In a multi-GPU, distributed environment, random number generation becomes a system-level concern rather than a local detail.

Parallel-Friendly Random Number Generators

On a single CPU, you might use a simple pseudo-random number generator and iterate through its sequence in order. On a GPU cluster you need generators with better properties:

- **Stream partitioning**: You can assign non-overlapping subsequences ("streams") to different threads, warps, kernels, GPUs, or nodes without risk of correlation artifacts.
- **Skip-ahead capability**: You can jump ahead in the sequence to start at different points for different tasks.
- **Statistical quality**: The distribution and independence of samples meet the demands of risk modeling.

Libraries designed for parallel random number generation provide these capabilities. Your task is to use them in a structured way.

Seeding Strategies

To make simulations reproducible and auditable, you must define and log seeding strategies. A common pattern is:

- Start from a *master seed* for the entire simulation run.
- Derive sub-seeds deterministically as a function of:

- GPU or worker index.
- Kernel or task identifier.
- Partition identifier (for example, path range or instrument group).

- Use these sub-seeds to initialize independent random streams for each parallel worker.

This structure ensures that given the same master seed and configuration, you can reproduce the entire simulation run, even if the physical mapping of tasks to GPUs changes. It also allows you to trace back from a suspicious path or scenario to the exact seeds that produced it.

Logging and Metadata

Randomness control is meaningless if you do not log the relevant metadata. For every major simulation or risk run, you should record at least:

- Master seed and scheme for deriving sub-seeds.
- Version identifiers for the random number generator implementation and library.
- Mapping from partitions or tasks to GPUs and workers, where applicable.

This metadata belongs alongside more traditional run information (code version, configuration files, hardware identifiers) in a reproducibility report, which we discuss shortly.

Reproducibility Reports and Audit Trails

For major production runs—end-of-day risk, capital calculations, significant backtests used in model approval—you should be able to rerun the job months or years later and obtain numerically consistent results (within agreed tolerances). Achieving this requires more than saving code; you must capture the entire environment and configuration.

What to Capture

A well-designed reproducibility report for a GPU-accelerated run includes:

- **Code and model versions**:

- Git commit hashes or similar identifiers for all relevant repositories.
- Model configuration versions (for example, factor model version, calibration sets).

- **Hardware and system details**:

- GPU model(s), driver version, and CUDA toolkit version.
- Container or environment image identifiers, if using containerization.
- Cluster configuration (number of nodes, GPUs per node).

- **Data inputs**:

- Paths or identifiers for input datasets (market data snapshots, reference data, trade books).
- Timestamps or versions for data extracts.

- **Run configuration**:

- Simulation parameters (number of paths, time steps, seeds).
- Partitioning schemes (symbol groups, time ranges).
- Precision settings (which parts of the pipeline used mixed precision).

- **Randomness and aggregation**:

- Master seed and seeding scheme.
- Aggregation order constraints or guarantees, if any.

These reports should be stored durably along with high-level outputs (risk numbers, PnL distributions), not discarded once the job completes.

Replaying Historical Runs

When a regulator or internal committee asks you to reproduce a historical risk run, the process should be:

1. Retrieve the reproducibility report and corresponding inputs from archival storage.
2. Provision an environment that matches the recorded hardware and software as closely as possible (containers help).
3. Execute the job with the same configuration and seeds.
4. Compare outputs to the original, using the same reconciliation tolerances.

If you are using cloud or dynamically scheduled resources, exact hardware matching may not be possible. In that case, you should at least demonstrate that results remain within documented tolerances across equivalent GPU generations, and note any small differences due to hardware changes.

Integrating Validation into the Development Flow

Validation and testing only work if they are part of everyday development, not a separate "compliance exercise" performed once before go-live. Practically, this means:

CI Pipelines with GPU-Aware Tests

Your continuous integration system should:

- Build GPU code and run unit tests on every change.
- Run selected property-based tests with modest sample sizes to catch blatant violations quickly.
- Periodically (for example, nightly) run golden-file tests and CPU-GPU reconciliation on dedicated GPU resources.

Since some tests may be too heavy for every commit, you can tier them:

- Fast tests for every change.
- Medium tests for changes to sensitive modules.
- Full regression suites for integration branches or before major releases.

Change Management and Model Validation

From a governance perspective, you should categorize changes by their potential impact:

- **Performance-only changes**: Kernel refactorings, launch parameter tuning, or memory-layout adjustments that are intended not to change numerical results except for rounding differences.
- **Model behavior changes**: Algorithmic changes, calibration updates, or alterations to financial logic.

For performance-only changes, passing reconciliation and golden-file tests may be sufficient for sign-off. For model behavior changes, you typically need additional model validation work—benchmarks, theoretical justification, and perhaps parallel run periods where old and new models run side-by-side.

In both cases, GPU-specific considerations (mixed precision, distributed aggregation order, random stream management) should be part of the validation checklist, not treated as low-level implementation details.

A Reliability Mindset for GPU-Accelerated Quant Systems

The reliability toolbox described in this section is not about mistrusting GPUs; it is about recognizing that powerful parallel hardware amplifies both strengths and weaknesses. Bugs can manifest at scale in surprising ways, and performance optimizations can have unintended side effects if not carefully checked.

A mature GPU-accelerated quant platform therefore:

- Uses layered testing to catch errors as close as possible to their source.
- Maintains well-defined numerical tolerances and monitors drift over time.
- Treats randomness as a managed resource, with structured seeding and logging.
- Produces reproducibility reports that make historical runs explainable and rerunnable.
- Integrates these practices into everyday development, CI/CD, and model validation processes.

With these foundations in place, the performance engineering, scaling, and data-pipeline work from earlier sections becomes genuinely valuable: not just fast, but also reliable enough to support real capital and real decisions. The final section of this chapter will connect these technical practices to organizational infrastructure and governance, completing the picture of what it takes to operate GPU-accelerated quant research and production systems at scale.

6.6 Infrastructure, CI/CD & Governance

The previous sections have focused on the technical core of GPU-accelerated quant research: kernels, scaling, data pipelines, and validation. To use these capabilities in production day after day, under changing markets and evolving models-you also need solid infrastructure and organizational scaffolding.

Without this scaffolding, you eventually see patterns like:

- A backtest that ran yesterday cannot be reproduced today because the CUDA driver auto-updated.
- A performance "optimization" silently degrades numerical accuracy in production because it bypassed proper testing.

- Two desks contend for the same GPU servers, starving overnight risk jobs as an unplanned research sweep runs.

This section explains how to avoid those situations. We will cover:

- Containers and environment management for GPUs.
- CI/CD pipelines tailored to GPU code and quant workflows.
- Observability: metrics, logging, and tracing for GPU workloads.
- Cost controls in shared GPU environments.
- Governance: processes and responsibilities around models, code, and infrastructure.

The central idea is to treat your GPU research platform as a product: something with users, SLAs, change controls, and clear ownership, not just a pile of fast machines.

Containers and Environment Management

GPU software stacks are sensitive. CUDA versions, driver versions, math libraries, and Python packages interact in ways that can be brittle. To achieve reproducibility and reduce operational surprises, you should standardize environments using containers.

Why Containers Matter More with GPUs

On a CPU-only cluster, you might tolerate a degree of diversity: different machines running slightly different OS versions or library stacks. With GPUs this is more dangerous:

- Kernel performance and even correctness can depend on compiler and library versions.
- Some models or kernels may rely on features present only in certain CUDA or driver versions.

- Upgrading drivers on a live cluster can affect all workloads at once.

Containers allow you to:

- Bundle your application code, libraries, and CUDA toolkit into an image that behaves consistently wherever it runs.
- Test new stacks in isolation before rolling them out.
- Run multiple stacks side by side (for example, an older stable image for production, a newer one for experimental research).

Designing Base Images

A practical approach is to maintain a small set of curated base images, for example:

- **Research image**: Includes Jupyter, GPU-aware DataFrame libraries, visualization tools, and common quant libraries. Intended for exploratory work and development.
- **Batch backtest / risk image**: Leaner image optimized for running large backtests, risk simulations, and production-like workloads.
- **Service image**: For long-running microservices (for example, intraday risk APIs or signal servers) with narrower dependency sets and stricter security hardening.

All these images should:

- Use a consistent base OS and CUDA toolkit compatible with your fleet of GPUs.
- Include clear versioning in tags (for example, `gpu-research:2025-03`) so you can tie runs to specific images.
- Be built via repeatable scripts or configuration files, not manually assembled.

Handling Heterogeneous Hardware

Large organizations often have a mix of older and newer GPUs, sometimes spread across on-prem and cloud. To manage this:

- Define a minimum supported GPU capability (for example, compute capability level). Kernels and libraries should be compiled against that baseline.
- Use container runtimes that expose device capabilities cleanly to the container, with driver versions on the host coordinated with CUDA versions in the image.
- Tag nodes or clusters with their GPU types and schedule workloads accordingly: heavy linear-algebra workloads to Tensor Core-rich devices, lighter backtests to older GPUs.

This avoids surprises where a container image runs fine on one set of machines but fails or underperforms on others.

CI/CD for GPU Code and Quant Pipelines

Continuous integration and continuous delivery (CI/CD) are standard in software engineering, but GPU-accelerated quant systems need some special attention.

What CI Looks Like for GPU Workloads

A GPU-aware CI pipeline typically includes:

- **Build stage**:
  - Compile CUDA code and build container images.
  - Run static checks and basic linting on quant code (Python, C++, etc.).
- **Unit and property-based tests**:
  - Execute GPU unit tests for kernels and utilities.

    - Run targeted property-based tests that check invariants (as described in the validation section).

- **Numerical regression tests**:
    - For changes in critical components, trigger CPU-GPU reconciliation tests on small canonical datasets.
    - Compare against golden-file outputs, enforcing tolerances.
- **Performance smoke tests**:
    - Run short, standardized benchmarks (for example, a miniature Monte Carlo and a small factor risk run) and compare performance against stored baselines.
    - Flag large regressions in runtime or GPU utilization.

Because GPU resources are limited and expensive, you may not want every developer branch to run the full suite. Prioritize:

- Fast tests (unit, basic properties) for every change.
- Deeper numerical and performance tests for main branches and release candidates.

Continuous Delivery and Promotion Pipelines

On the delivery side, you should think in terms of promotion stages rather than direct deployment:

- **Research / staging**: New changes are deployed to an environment with production-like data and hardware but isolated from real trading or risk decisions. Researchers can run realistic workloads and compare against production behavior.
- **Shadow or parallel runs**: For major model or infrastructure changes, you run the new version side-by-side with the old one on production data. Outputs are compared, but only the old system's numbers are used in official reports.

- **Production**: After validation, changes are deployed to production clusters with clear rollback plans.

Each stage should be gated by checks:

- Test suites must pass.
- Numerical differences must be within agreed tolerances.
- Performance must not degrade beyond acceptable thresholds.

Automation helps, but final sign-off on production promotion, especially for risk-critical models, is often a human decision involving model validation and risk management.

Observability: Making GPU Systems Transparent

You cannot manage what you cannot see. Observability for GPU workloads means having enough visibility to diagnose issues like:

- Why did last night's risk run finish late?
- Which strategies are consuming the most GPU time?
- Are we seeing hardware errors or memory pressure on particular nodes?

Metrics: What to Measure

At a minimum, you should collect:

- **GPU-level metrics**:
  - Utilization (compute and memory).
  - Memory usage and allocation failures.
  - Temperature and power draw.
  - Hardware error counts (for example, ECC errors).

- **Application-level metrics**:
  - Job durations (per backtest, per risk run).
  - Throughput (paths per second, instruments per second, bars per second).
  - Queue lengths and scheduling delays for GPU jobs.
- **Data pipeline metrics**:
  - Input rates (ticks per second, bytes per second).
  - Host-device transfer volumes.
  - Cache hit/miss rates if you cache GPU-resident data.

These metrics should feed into an existing monitoring stack, allowing you to set alerts (for example, "GPU utilization below X% on cluster Y during expected busy windows" or "overnight risk job exceeded SLA by N minutes").

Logging and Tracing

Beyond metrics, you need logs that tie GPU activity to business concepts:

- Which portfolios and strategies ran on which GPUs, at what times?
- For each job, which image, code version, seeds, and configuration were used?
- If an error occurred, which kernel or data partition was involved?

Structured logs (for example, JSON-formatted) with consistent fields-job ID, portfolio ID, cluster, node, GPU index, and so on-make it easier to query and correlate events across systems.

Tracing tools can go further by:

- Representing a backtest or risk run as a trace with spans for each major stage (data load, feature engineering, path simulation, aggregation).

- Overlaying GPU metrics on these spans to visualize where time and resources were spent.

This is especially useful when diagnosing intermittent latency spikes or understanding the impact of code changes on end-to-end performance.

Cost Management in Shared GPU Environments

GPUs are expensive resources. In a quant firm, they are typically shared across desks, strategies, and functions (research, production, risk). Uncontrolled, this leads to:

- “Noisy neighbor” problems: one team’s large experiment starves others of capacity.
- Surprising cloud bills when burst capacity is overused.
- Tensions between short-term PnL activities and long-term research.

A thoughtful cost-management strategy reduces these frictions.

Quotas, Reservations, and Scheduling Policies

You can manage access using:

- **Quotas**: Each team or business line has a maximum number of GPUs or GPU-hours they can consume over a period, with monitoring and alerts as usage approaches limits.
- **Reservations**: Critical workloads (for example, overnight risk) have reserved capacity that is not preempted by lower-priority jobs.
- **Priority scheduling**: Jobs are assigned priorities; the scheduler prefers higher-priority jobs when contention exists and can preempt or delay lower-priority work.

These mechanisms can be implemented using cluster schedulers, container orchestration systems, or custom job queues. The key is that policies are clear, documented, and transparent to users.

Tagging and Chargeback

To make GPU costs visible and encourage responsible use:

- Require jobs and containers to carry tags indicating desk, strategy, or project.
- Aggregate usage statistics by tag and publish regular reports showing GPU consumption and, if applicable, estimated monetary cost.
- Use these reports to support internal chargeback or at least to inform budget discussions.

This does not mean charging researchers for every experiment, but it does create an environment where teams see the resource implications of their choices and can prioritize accordingly.

Governance: Processes, Roles, and Controls

Technical infrastructure is only half the story. The other half is organizational: who owns the platform, who approves changes, and how you balance innovation with control.

Platform Ownership and Responsibilities

It is helpful to define a "GPU platform team" (or similar construct) with clear responsibilities:

- Maintain GPU hardware, drivers, and base images.
- Operate shared clusters and manage capacity.

- Provide libraries, APIs, and documentation for using GPUs in backtests and risk systems.
- Collaborate with quant teams on performance tuning and troubleshooting.

This team is not the only user of GPUs, but it is accountable for the health and evolution of the platform itself.

On the other side, quant and risk teams remain responsible for:

- Model design, calibration, and conceptual soundness.
- Correct use of GPU libraries and adherence to validation practices.
- Specifying accuracy requirements and performance targets.

Clear boundaries reduce confusion about who should address which kinds of issues.

Change Management and Review Processes

Given the potential impact of GPU code and models, changes should follow structured review processes:

- **Code review**: Peer review of changes to kernels, data pipelines, and orchestration logic, with attention to both performance and correctness.
- **Model review**: Independent validation of new or significantly modified models, including tests on historical periods, stress scenarios, and comparisons with existing models.
- **Risk and compliance review**: For changes that affect regulatory or capital metrics, involvement of risk management and Compliance to ensure requirements are met.

Change tickets or pull requests should link to test results: unit tests, reconciliation outputs, performance benchmarks, and, where relevant, shadow-run comparisons.

Emergency Procedures and Rollbacks

No matter how careful you are, some changes will behave badly in production. You need plans for:

- **Rapid rollback**: Ability to revert to a previous container image or configuration quickly, ideally via a single orchestrated action.
- **Safe fallbacks**: For critical reports (for example, end-of-day VaR), having a slower but well-tested CPU path as a last-resort fallback can be invaluable.
- **Post-incident analysis**: After resolving an incident, conducting a blameless review to understand root causes and improve processes or tests.

These procedures should be rehearsed occasionally, not just written down. A rollback plan that no one has tried is a risk in itself.

Bringing It All Together

This chapter has described how to engineer performance, scale across GPUs and clusters, design data pipelines, validate numerical behavior, and now, how to provide infrastructure and governance. When these elements are aligned, you obtain a platform with the following characteristics:

- **Fast**: Kernels and clusters are tuned for the workloads that matter, and data pipelines keep them fed.
- **Scalable**: You can add GPUs or nodes and know how backtests and risk runs will take advantage of them.
- **Reliable**: Layered tests, reconciliation, and randomness control keep numerical results trustworthy.
- **Reproducible**: Containers, environment capture, and reproducibility reports mean you can replay important runs under scrutiny.

- **Manageable**: Observability, cost controls, and quotas turn GPUs into a shared resource that supports both research and production without chaos.
- **Governed**: Clear roles, review processes, and emergency procedures align technology with the firm's risk appetite and regulatory obligations.

Ultimately, GPUs are just another tool. What makes them valuable in quant finance is not only their raw speed, but the ability to harness that speed systematically, safely, and repeatably in the service of robust research and disciplined risk-taking.

Chapter 7

Case Studies & Reusable Templates

This chapter is about reuse, not heroics. Instead of one-off CUDA experiments that die on a laptop, we'll walk through complete GPU-accelerated VaR and backtesting pipelines, show exactly how much speed you can claim (and how to prove it), and then distill the hard-won patterns into small, composable templates your team can drop into new projects-without blowing up model risk or your audit trail.

7.1 Benchmarking & Fair Baselines

In earlier chapters we focused on what GPUs can do for quantitative finance: more paths, more scenarios, richer cross-sectional models. In this section we turn to a simpler but more delicate question: *how do you know the GPU is actually helping?*

Answering that question rigorously is not glamorous, but it is what separates a convincing research result from a pretty slide. A claim like "our VaR engine is 50 times faster on GPU" needs to survive basic scrutiny: what exactly was measured, against which CPU baseline, with what compiler settings, on what data, and with which accuracy tolerances?

This section gives you a practical protocol for building and interpreting benchmarks that quants, engineers, and risk managers can all trust. We will:

- Define what we mean by speedup and which metrics matter in a quant context.
- Explain how to construct truly comparable CPU and GPU baselines.
- Highlight common benchmarking traps and how to avoid them.
- Show how to build a small, reproducible benchmark harness that you can reuse throughout the book's case studies and in your own work.

The goal is not to turn you into a performance engineer, but to give you a checklist and some intuition so you can tell when a reported speedup is meaningful and when it is just a measurement artifact.

What Are We Actually Measuring?

When people say "the GPU is faster," they usually have one of three things in mind:

- **Latency:** How long it takes to complete one job (for example, compute VaR for one trading day, or run one backtest).
- **Throughput:** How many jobs per unit time you can complete when the system is saturated (for example, VaR runs per hour or backtests per day).
- **Cost efficiency:** How much it costs to process a fixed number of jobs (hardware, cloud time, energy).

In finance we often care about both latency and throughput. Risk teams may have a daily VaR deadline, which is a latency requirement. Research teams may want to run hundreds of backtests overnight, which is mostly about throughput.

Latency and its distribution

A single runtime number like "this VaR run takes 2 seconds" hides a lot of information. In real systems you see variability: cache effects, noisy neighbours on shared hardware, background processes, occasional operating system interruptions.

Instead of quoting a single runtime, you should think in terms of a *distribution*:

- Minimum (often unrealistic, but a lower bound).
- Median (a robust central tendency).
- Tail values, such as the 95th or 99th percentile (how bad can it get when the system is under stress).

For trading or intraday risk analytics, those tail latencies are often more important than the median. A GPU that is usually very fast but occasionally produces large delays may be less attractive than a CPU system that is merely fast but very predictable.

Throughput, utilization, and batching

Throughput becomes important when you run many independent jobs: for example, scenario-based stress testing or a calibration loop that evaluates a model against many parameter guesses.

Here, the relevant questions are:

- How many independent jobs can you keep in flight at once?
- How well can you keep the GPU's compute units busy?
- What batching strategy do you need to reach high utilization?

GPUs typically shine when you can process large batches of similar work. A single tiny job may be slower on the GPU once you include data transfers and kernel launch overhead. But if you can send thousands of similar paths, options, or scenarios at once, the GPU's massive parallelism can dominate.

End-to-end vs. kernel-only timing

Another frequent source of confusion is *what exactly you time*. Common possibilities include:

- Pure compute time on device (kernel-only).
- Compute time plus host–device data transfers.
- Full end-to-end runtime from "submit a job" to "receive the result," including any pre- and post-processing.

For model risk and production discussions, end-to-end timing is usually the only number that really matters. Within a performance study, it can still be useful to break down the components to see where time is spent, but you should never present kernel-only times as if they represent full production performance.

Throughout this book we will be explicit: when we present GPU speedups, we mean end-to-end latency for a clearly defined task, compared against a clearly specified CPU implementation.

Designing Fair CPU and GPU Baselines

A benchmark is only as good as its baselines. A GPU implementation that is compared against an unoptimized, debug-compiled CPU reference will look amazing on paper but tells you very little about the true trade-offs. Likewise, a CPU implementation compiled with aggressive math relaxations that would never be accepted in production is not a realistic baseline either.

Same math, same tolerances

The first rule of a fair baseline is *same algorithm, same numerical goal*. When you compare a GPU VaR engine to a CPU VaR engine, they should:

- Use the same model (for example, same factor distribution and correlation structure).

- Aggregate P&L in the same way.
- Use consistent numerical tolerances (for example, same confidence level for VaR, same convergence criteria for any iterative solver).

If you change the algorithm (for example, by using a different approximation or a different optimization trick on one side only), then you are measuring algorithmic improvements and hardware differences at the same time. That is not "wrong," but it makes it much harder to attribute where the gains are coming from and whether a slower but more accurate algorithm might be preferable.

Random seeds and Monte Carlo reproducibility

Many of the workloads in this book are Monte Carlo based. This introduces a subtlety: *Monte Carlo noise* can easily mask or mimic performance or accuracy differences if you are not careful.

At a minimum:

- Use fixed random seeds so that repeated runs are directly comparable.
- Where reasonable, use the same random sequence on CPU and GPU (or at least the same family of generators with similar statistical quality).
- When comparing numerical outputs (for example, VaR levels), distinguish between differences due to random sampling and differences due to floating-point rounding or implementation details.

For many problems, it is sufficient to show that the CPU and GPU results are statistically indistinguishable at the path counts of interest. You do not need bit-identical results, but you do need to quantify the difference rather than just eyeballing numbers.

Compiler and build settings

Another common pitfall is to benchmark a GPU kernel compiled with full optimization against a CPU baseline compiled in debug mode or with conservative settings. For both sides you should:

- Use a release build with optimizations enabled.
- Explicitly document any flags that affect numerical behaviour, such as "fast math" options, fused multiply-add usage, or denormal handling.
- Ensure that any special-case optimizations (for example, using vector instructions on CPU) are either enabled on both sides or clearly explained if they cannot be matched.

The goal is not to handicap the CPU; a strong GPU result that survives comparison against a well-tuned CPU implementation is far more convincing than one obtained against a naive baseline.

Data layout and cache friendliness

Fair baselines also extend to how you layout your data. On GPUs we spend a lot of effort ensuring coalesced memory access patterns and avoiding unnecessary transfers. You should grant the CPU the same courtesy:

- Use contiguous, cache-friendly layouts on CPU, not overly abstract data structures that you would never choose for production.
- Avoid designs that artificially hurt the CPU, such as repeatedly allocating and freeing memory in a tight loop if the GPU version uses preallocated buffers.

Think in terms of what a reasonably competent C++ engineer would implement if asked to productionize the CPU version. That is your reference point.

Scaling Problem Sizes and Understanding Regimes

GPUs and CPUs have different strengths. GPUs have large parallel capacity but also fixed overheads: moving data to the device, launching kernels, and managing context. CPUs have fewer cores but lower overhead and stronger single-thread performance.

As a result, the relative performance depends strongly on the *problem size*. For very small tasks, the overhead of using the GPU can dominate, making it slower than a well-implemented CPU. For larger tasks, the GPU often wins by a large margin.

When you design benchmarks, you should always sweep across a range of problem sizes:

- Small sizes where GPU overhead dominates.
- Medium sizes where the two are comparable.
- Large sizes where the GPU is fully utilized.

This gives you a more honest picture than quoting a single speedup at a hand-picked size that flatters one side. It also helps with planning: if you know that your production workload is likely to be on the "small" side, investing heavily in GPU acceleration may not be worthwhile.

Right after this conceptual point, it is useful to visualize how latency and throughput evolve with problem size for both CPU and GPU.

CPU vs GPU Latency and Throughput for a Sample Quant Workload

The left panel illustrates a pattern you will see repeatedly: for very small problems the GPU's latency is worse than the CPU's because fixed overheads dominate. As the problem grows, the GPU's curve flattens relative to the CPU's, and the speedup becomes substantial. The right panel shows that, once you are in the "large problem" regime, the GPU can deliver much higher throughput.

Avoiding Common Benchmarking Traps

Even with clear metrics and fair baselines in mind, there are several easy ways to mislead yourself or others.

Ignoring warm-up and caching effects

GPUs and modern CPUs both have warm-up behaviour:

- Just-in-time compilation or driver-level caching may make the first run slower.
- Data and code paths become hot in caches after a few repetitions.

If you only measure the first run, you may dramatically understate steady-state performance. A simple rule is:

- Run one or more unmeasured warm-up iterations.
- Then run a reasonable number of measured iterations (for example, 10–50), and compute median and tail latencies from these.

This is particularly important when presenting results to non-technical stakeholders; you do not want a manager to rerun your benchmark once and see a different number.

Measuring in a noisy environment

On shared research machines or cloud instances, background activity can distort measurements: other users' jobs, operating system maintenance, and so on. While you cannot always get perfect isolation, you should:

- Avoid benchmarking on heavily loaded shared boxes at peak times.
- Repeat benchmarks and check for consistency; large variability is a warning sign.

- Log system load and any notable events for later interpretation.

Again, the goal is not absolute perfection but enough care that your numbers are stable and replicable.

Cherry-picking favourable cases

It is easy to pick a problem size or configuration that makes your preferred implementation look good. To guard against this, adopt a simple discipline:

- Predefine a grid of problem sizes and parameters that are relevant for your use case.
- Run the benchmark across the entire grid.
- Report the full picture, not just the most flattering point.

This pays off when you need to answer a skeptical question like "what happens if we run only half as many scenarios?" or "what if we double the number of assets?" You can then point to specific data rather than speculate.

Forgetting accuracy and risk relevance

Speed without correctness is useless in finance. A faster GPU implementation that subtly degrades tail risk estimates is not an improvement; it is a hidden model change. For each benchmark you should therefore:

- Always pair performance numbers with accuracy checks against a trusted CPU reference.
- Express differences in business-relevant terms, such as basis points of VaR or changes in exception counts.
- Make it clear where numerical differences are negligible relative to model uncertainty and where they could matter.

In later sections, when we run backtests of GPU-based VaR or scenario engines, we will explicitly show both the performance and the risk metrics side by side.

Building a Reproducible Benchmark Harness

To make these ideas concrete and reusable, it helps to standardize how you run and record benchmarks. Think of this as a small experiment-tracking framework tailored to performance measurements.

Fixed configuration files

Instead of hardcoding parameters in your code or typing them manually each time, define benchmark configurations in small, human-readable files. Each configuration should at least specify:

- Problem size (for example, number of paths, assets, or events).
- Model parameters (for example, volatility levels, correlation assumptions).
- Hardware and software identifiers (for example, GPU model, CPU model, compiler version).
- Random seeds and any numerical tolerances used.

When you run a benchmark, the program reads one of these configuration files and records which one was used alongside the results. This makes it much easier to rerun a specific experiment later.

Scripted runs

Run benchmarks via scripts rather than by hand from an interactive environment. A script can:

- Loop over a set of configurations.
- Perform warm-up runs and timed runs consistently.

- Capture runtimes, accuracy metrics, and hardware usage statistics.

This reduces the chance of accidental changes between runs ("I forgot to turn off debugging this time") and makes it easier to share the benchmark with colleagues or auditors.

Automated tables and plots

Finally, automate the generation of tables and plots from your benchmark logs. Rather than copying and pasting numbers into a spreadsheet, have a small reporting tool that:

- Reads the raw benchmark output.
- Computes summary statistics (median, percentiles, speedups).
- Produces standardized charts, such as the latency and throughput comparison shown earlier in this section.

This does not need to be elaborate. The important point is consistency: every time you change the implementation or hardware, you can rerun the same scripts and regenerate the same style of reports.

Communicating Results to Different Audiences

The same benchmark can be interpreted very differently depending on who is reading it. A trading desk quant, a platform engineer, and a model risk officer will focus on different aspects.

For quants and researchers

Quants are usually interested in:

- How much faster can I iterate on models and backtests?
- Does the GPU version change the numbers I rely on for strategy design?

When presenting to this audience:

- Emphasize latency and throughput improvements in the specific workflows they care about.
- Show simple accuracy comparisons: side-by-side distributions, scatter plots of CPU vs GPU outputs, and basic statistical tests when appropriate.

For engineers and infrastructure teams

Engineers care more about:

- Resource utilization, scalability, and operational complexity.
- How the GPU workload coexists with other processes.

For them, you should include:

- More detailed performance breakdowns: compute vs transfer time, utilization levels, memory consumption.
- Sensitivity to configuration changes, such as batch sizes or concurrency.

For risk managers and model governance

Risk and governance stakeholders want to know:

- Whether the GPU implementation is functionally equivalent to the existing model from a risk perspective.
- Whether the performance envelope and failure modes are well understood and documented.

For this audience, focus on:

- Clearly written summaries of how the GPU changes, or does not change, the model logic.

- Backtests that show that risk metrics (such as VaR exceptions) remain consistent.
- Conservative statements about performance: for example, "for production risk runs of size X, we observe a speedup between A and B times across recent test windows," rather than promising a single headline number.

Summary and Checklist

Benchmarking GPU-accelerated quant code is as much about discipline as it is about measuring raw speed. A fair baseline requires:

- Clear, end-to-end definitions of latency and throughput.
- Comparable CPU and GPU implementations with the same math and tolerances.
- Consistent random seeds and controlled Monte Carlo noise.
- Proper build settings and reasonable optimization on both sides.
- Benchmarks across a meaningful range of problem sizes to reveal where the GPU helps and where it does not.

On top of that, you should:

- Warm up systems before measuring.
- Avoid noisy environments when possible and rerun tests for stability.
- Automate configuration, execution, and reporting.
- Tailor the presentation of results to quants, engineers, and risk managers without changing the underlying facts.

The rest of this chapter will reuse this benchmarking framework in concrete case studies: Monte Carlo VaR, event-driven backtesting, and a reusable CUDA finance toolkit. By applying the same standards repeatedly, you will develop an intuition for when a GPU speedup is meaningful, how to argue for it internally, and when a CPU might still be the right tool for the job.

7.2 Case Study: Monte Carlo VaR on GPUs

In the previous section we built a discipline for benchmarking: define clear metrics, construct fair CPU and GPU baselines, and report speedups in a way that would withstand scrutiny. We now put that discipline to work in a concrete and important application: Monte Carlo Value-at-Risk (VaR).

VaR is one of the most natural places to apply GPU acceleration. It is path-based, heavily numerical, and often runs under tight time constraints. At the same time, it is subject to model risk governance: changing how you compute VaR is not just an engineering decision; it has regulatory and risk implications. This makes it an ideal test bed for everything you have learned so far.

Our objective in this section is to design and evaluate an end-to-end Monte Carlo VaR engine on the GPU. "End-to-end" means:

- Starting from a specified portfolio and risk factor model.
- Simulating many scenarios of market moves.
- Revaluing the portfolio under each scenario.
- Aggregating the simulated profit and loss (P&L) into VaR and Expected Shortfall.
- Backtesting those risk measures against historical P&L.
- Comparing performance and numerical behaviour against a carefully tuned CPU implementation using the benchmarking framework from the previous section.

We will deliberately keep the financial model simple enough to be transparent, while making the computational structure realistic enough that the patterns carry over to more complex production systems.

The Monte Carlo VaR Workflow

Before mapping anything to the GPU, it is helpful to outline the logical steps of a Monte Carlo VaR calculation. At a high level:

1. **Specify the portfolio.** We define positions in instruments whose values depend on a set of underlying risk factors. For example, a portfolio of equities and options depending on underlying stock prices and possibly a volatility surface.
2. **Specify the risk factor model.** We choose a joint distribution for daily (or multi-day) changes in these risk factors, often represented by a vector of means, volatilities, and a correlation matrix.
3. **Generate simulated shocks.** We draw many independent samples from this joint distribution, each representing a possible market move over the risk horizon.
4. **Revalue the portfolio per scenario.** For each simulated shock we transform today's market state into a shocked state and compute the portfolio value under that scenario.
5. **Aggregate to a P&L distribution.** We subtract the current portfolio value from the shocked value to get scenario P&L, and we collect these across all paths.
6. **Extract risk measures.** We compute VaR as a lower quantile of the P&L distribution and Expected Shortfall as the average of losses in the tail beyond that quantile.

This loop—simulate, revalue, aggregate—fits very well with GPU-style parallelism: each simulated path is mostly independent of the others. The main challenge is to arrange the work and data so that the GPU can process many paths efficiently, while keeping the implementation faithful to a CPU reference.

Mapping Monte Carlo VaR to the GPU

Using the concepts from the benchmarking section, we want a GPU design that is:

- Close in mathematics to a reference CPU implementation.
- Well suited to large batches of similar, parallel work.
- Conscious of end-to-end performance, including random number generation and data movement.

We will focus on three core components of the GPU engine:

1. Random scenario generation using cuRAND.
2. Batched portfolio revaluation.
3. Parallel quantile and tail estimation.

Random scenario generation with cuRAND

On the CPU, you might use a standard pseudo-random generator to produce a stream of independent normal draws and then apply a correlation structure via a Cholesky factor. On the GPU, the idea is the same, but we use cuRAND, NVIDIA's library for random number generation on the device.

Conceptually, we proceed as follows:

- **Allocate a random state per path or per thread.** Each thread that will produce random numbers has its own state, initialized with a seed and an index so that streams do not overlap.
- **Generate independent standard normals.** We fill a large device array with independent draws for all risk factors and all paths.
- **Impose correlations.** For each path, we transform the vector of independent normals into correlated shocks using a precomputed matrix factor, just as on CPU. This is a matrix–vector multiplication per path, which can itself be parallelized.

From a risk governance perspective, two points are critical:

- The random generator type and parameters should be documented and, ideally, comparable to those used on CPU in terms of statistical quality.

- Seeds and stream indices must be logged so that if you rerun the same VaR job in the future, you can reproduce the exact same scenarios on both CPU and GPU for validation purposes.

Batched portfolio revaluation

Given a large array of risk factor shocks, the next step is to revalue the portfolio under each shocked scenario. This is where batching on the GPU shines.

Think of the portfolio as a collection of instruments, each of which has a pricing function that maps risk factors to a value. Many of these pricing functions share a similar structure—for example, Black-Scholes formulas for vanilla options or simple discounting for bonds. The batched approach on the GPU is:

- **Organize instruments by type.** Group instruments that share a pricing formula and similar input requirements.
- **For each type, process many instruments and scenarios together.** For example, you may evaluate all equity options across all simulated paths in one or a few large GPU kernels.
- **Ensure data is laid out for coalesced access.** Store risk factor states and instrument parameters in contiguous arrays so that adjacent GPU threads read adjacent memory locations, maximizing memory bandwidth.

From a latency perspective, we care about limiting the number of kernel launches and avoiding small, fragmented batches. From a numerical perspective, we ensure that the formulas used for pricing are the same as on the CPU implementation, so that any differences in results are attributable only to floating-point rounding or the random sequence, not to a change in the underlying model.

Parallel quantile and tail computation

Once we have the scenario P&L array on the GPU, we need to extract VaR and Expected Shortfall. There are several ways to compute quantiles, each with different performance and accuracy trade-offs. Conceptually, two patterns are common:

- **Sorting-based:** Sort the P&L array and pick the element at the desired quantile index; compute Expected Shortfall by averaging tail elements. This is simple and exact (modulo floating-point rounding), but it is more expensive for very large arrays.

- **Selection-based:** Use an algorithm that finds the element at a given rank without fully sorting the array, then compute Expected Shortfall from the tail. This can be faster, especially when repeated frequently.

On GPUs, sorting can be surprisingly efficient thanks to highly optimized parallel primitives, and it has the advantage of matching closely what a CPU reference might do. For the purposes of this case study, we assume a sorting-based approach on both CPU and GPU, while taking care to use stable, well-tested library implementations.

This allows us to focus on whether the GPU's parallelism reduces the latency of this final aggregation step, and whether the resulting VaR and Expected Shortfall are numerically consistent with the CPU baseline.

Designing the CPU Baseline

To apply the "benchmarking and fair baselines" principles, we now define our CPU reference clearly. For each stage of the VaR workflow:

- **Random numbers:** We use a high-quality pseudo-random generator and a standard procedure for imposing correlations. Seeds and stream management mirror the GPU version as closely as possible.

- **Portfolio revaluation:** We implement vectorized, cache-friendly pricing loops, taking advantage of optimized math libraries where available. We avoid deliberately naive or slow code.

- **Quantile and tail:** We use an efficient selection or sorting routine from a standard library, applying the same definition of VaR and Expected Shortfall as on the GPU.

The CPU code is compiled with optimization flags comparable to those used on the GPU code (for example, enabling vector instructions but not using exotic or unsafe fast-math options that would not pass validation). In short, we aim to represent what a well-engineered CPU-only Monte Carlo VaR engine would look like in practice.

End-to-End GPU VaR Engine

Putting the pieces together, an end-to-end run of the GPU VaR engine looks like this:

1. **Initialization (once per risk run):**
    - Load portfolio and current market data.
    - Build and upload risk factor model parameters and correlation matrix factor to the GPU.
    - Initialize cuRAND states with fixed seeds.
    - Preallocate device arrays for random numbers, shocked risk factors, instrument parameters, and scenario P&L.
2. **Simulation and valuation (main loop):**
    - Generate a large batch of random shocks for all risk factors and all paths.
    - Transform shocks to correlated space.
    - For each instrument type in the portfolio, launch one or more kernels to revalue that type across all paths, accumulating contributions to the scenario P&L array.
3. **Aggregation:**
    - Apply a parallel sort or selection on the P&L array to obtain VaR.
    - Compute Expected Shortfall by averaging the tail.
    - Optionally compute additional risk statistics (for example, distribution moments).
4. **Result handling:**

- Transfer summary risk measures and, if needed, a subsample of the P&L distribution back to the CPU.
- Log configuration, seeds, and performance metrics for reproducibility and governance.

A key design decision is the batch size: how many paths to process per run. Batches that are too small underutilize the GPU and fail to amortize kernel launch overhead; batches that are too large may run into memory limits or leave the CPU waiting too long for intermediate results. In practice, you pick a batch size that fits comfortably in GPU memory and matches the latency targets of your risk process.

Numerical Consistency: How Close is Close Enough?

Risk managers rightly ask: if we move VaR computation to the GPU, will we see different risk numbers? If so, how large can those differences be before they become a concern?

There are two main sources of difference:

- **Monte Carlo sampling noise:** Even with identical mathematical models, finite sampling leads to random variation in estimated quantiles.
- **Floating-point effects:** CPU and GPU may differ in rounding order, use of fused operations, or math library implementations, leading to small discrepancies in P&L values and therefore in estimated VaR.

To reason about these differences, we conduct controlled experiments:

- Run CPU and GPU VaR with the same seeds and model parameters across a range of path counts.
- For each configuration, compare the resulting VaR and Expected Shortfall, and compute the difference in risk units that matter (for example, basis points of portfolio value).

- Observe how these differences shrink as the number of paths increases.

In many realistic cases, once you reach a sufficiently large number of paths, the GPU vs CPU differences become much smaller than the inherent Monte Carlo noise and much smaller than the uncertainty in model calibration. At that point, from a model risk perspective, the two implementations can be considered functionally equivalent, provided the differences are documented and monitored.

Backtesting GPU VaR Against Historical P&L

End-to-end validation requires more than cross-checking CPU and GPU outputs on a single day. We also need to verify that the risk measures behave sensibly over time when compared with realized P&L.

The standard approach is backtesting. Conceptually:

1. Choose a historical period and obtain daily (or relevant horizon) P&L for the portfolio or a representative proxy.
2. For each day in the backtest window, run both the CPU VaR engine and the GPU VaR engine using the information available at that time.
3. Record the VaR estimates and note whether the realized P&L exceeded the predicted VaR threshold (a VaR "exception").
4. Count and analyze exceptions for both engines, and compare them with what you would expect statistically.

We can then perform standard backtesting checks that risk managers recognize, such as:

- Whether the total number of exceptions over the period is in line with the nominal VaR confidence level.
- Whether exceptions cluster in time, which might indicate model misspecification under certain conditions.

The key point for our case study is that if the GPU implementation is truly faithful to the CPU reference, their exception profiles over a sufficiently long backtest should be nearly indistinguishable, with any differences attributable to Monte Carlo noise and floating-point effects rather than systematic bias.

Benchmarking CPU vs GPU VaR

With design and validation in place, we return to performance measurement using the framework from the previous section. We care about two related questions:

- How do runtimes for CPU and GPU VaR scale as we increase the number of Monte Carlo paths?
- Does the GPU-based VaR maintain the same risk accuracy as the CPU-based VaR over time?

To answer these, we:

- Run both engines over a grid of path counts, from modest to very large, on the same hardware setup.
- For each configuration, measure end-to-end latency, including random number generation, portfolio revaluation, and quantile computation.
- For a chosen backtest period, record exception counts for both CPU and GPU VaR and summarize how they compare.

Interpreting the Results and Trade-Offs

Armed with both performance and backtesting evidence, we can have an informed conversation about the trade-offs of moving Monte Carlo VaR to the GPU.

From a business and risk standpoint:

- If the backtesting profiles and day-by-day VaR values are statistically indistinguishable, the GPU engine can be presented as an implementation change rather than a model change, simplifying governance.
- The performance gains free up capacity: more scenarios, more complex models, or faster intraday updates, which can translate into better risk management or faster research cycles.

From an engineering standpoint:

- The GPU engine introduces complexity: device management, random stream handling, and batched pricing infrastructure. This requires investment in tooling and monitoring.
- The benefits are largest at higher path counts. For very small overnight VaR jobs, the CPU may remain sufficient, but as the institution scales up scenario counts or moves towards intraday VaR, the GPU's advantages become more compelling.

The key is that all of these arguments are now grounded in a careful, reproducible comparison, not isolated anecdotes. We know how runtimes scale, how exception counts compare, and what assumptions underlie the measurements.

This case study illustrates how to take a core quant workload—Monte Carlo VaR—and build a GPU-accelerated engine that satisfies both performance ambitions and risk governance requirements. The main lessons are:

- Break the workflow into clear stages (scenario generation, revaluation, aggregation) and map each to the GPU in a way that respects the underlying financial model.
- Use cuRAND and batched pricing patterns to exploit GPU parallelism while keeping random streams and pricing formulas aligned with a strong CPU baseline.
- Compute VaR and Expected Shortfall on the GPU using robust parallel primitives, and verify numerical consistency against the CPU reference.

- Apply the benchmarking framework from the previous section: sweep across problem sizes, measure end-to-end latency, and present results in terms of both performance and risk accuracy.
- Backtest both engines against historical P&L to demonstrate that the GPU implementation behaves as expected over time, not just on synthetic examples.

In the next section, we will move from this relatively "batchy" workflow to a more dynamic one: an event-driven backtester where a hybrid CPU-GPU architecture must react to heterogeneous market events while still reaping the performance benefits of the GPU. The benchmarking and validation habits you have developed here will carry over directly to that more complex setting.

7.3 Case Study: Event-Driven Backtester on GPUs

In the Monte Carlo VaR case study we saw a relatively "batch-oriented" workload: simulate a large number of independent scenarios, revalue the portfolio, and aggregate results. Many research and trading workflows, however, are not batch driven but *event driven*. They react to a stream of market data and orders, update strategy state, and decide when and how to trade.

In this section we design a hybrid CPU-GPU architecture for an event-driven backtester. The goal is to keep the strengths of traditional CPU-based engines—flexible control flow, easy debugging, and rich strategy logic—while offloading the numerically heavy, highly parallel work to the GPU. That work typically includes:

- Cross-sectional feature computation over large universes.
- Portfolio and risk revaluation across many instruments or scenarios.
- Scenario "fan-outs" where we explore multiple what-if paths in parallel from the same event stream.

We will proceed in stages:

- Start from a canonical CPU-only event-driven backtester and identify computational hotspots.
- Introduce a hybrid CPU-GPU architecture that preserves the event-driven nature of the system.
- Discuss batching and scheduling strategies that make GPU use efficient without distorting the event timeline.
- Address state synchronization and strategy plugin design.
- Close with performance and correctness evaluation, using the benchmarking discipline from earlier sections.

From CPU-Only to Hybrid: The High-Level Architecture

A traditional event-driven backtester is organized around an *event loop*. Conceptually, it does the following:

- Pull the next event from an event queue. Events can be market data updates, order fills, strategy timers, and so on.
- Update internal state based on the event: order books, positions, indicators, and risk metrics.
- Invoke strategy logic to decide whether to generate new orders or adjust existing ones.
- Push any resulting orders or internal triggers back into the event queue.

This model is simple and powerful, but when we extend it from a single instrument to, say, 2,000 equities with multiple strategies and risk overlays, the numerical work in step 2 can become very heavy. If we want to simulate years of tick or book-level data, the runtime quickly becomes a bottleneck.

The core idea of the hybrid design is:

- Leave the *event loop and strategy logic* on the CPU, where branching, complex control flow, and debugging are easier.
- Offload *data-parallel numerical kernels* to the GPU: calculations that apply similar operations across many instruments, time buckets, or scenarios.

Shortly after introducing this idea, it is helpful to anchor it visually with an architecture diagram of the data and control flow.

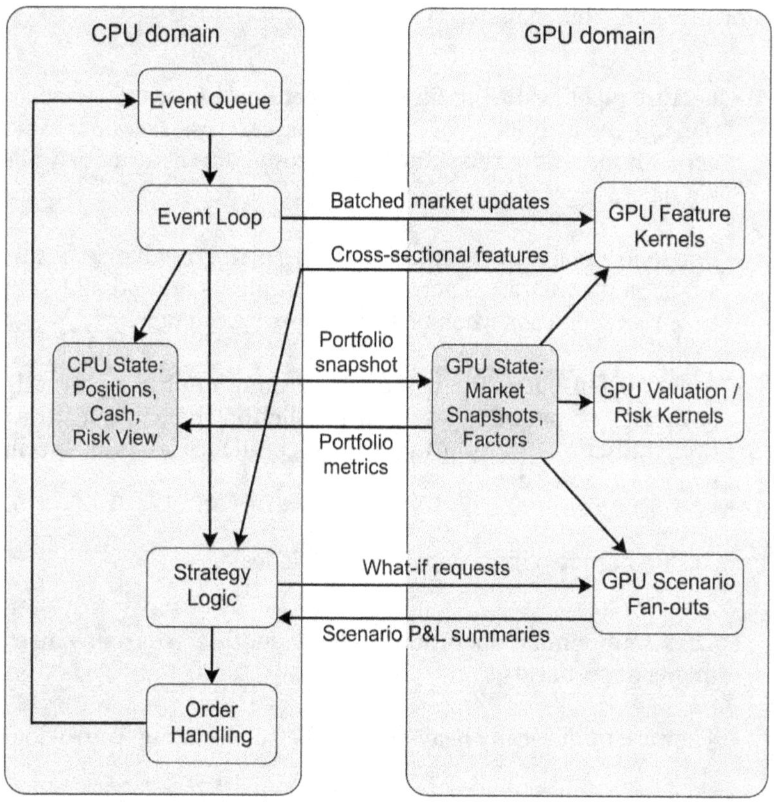

On the left, the CPU domain processes events and runs the strategy. On the right, the GPU domain holds the large, structured data arrays and executes heavy kernels. The arrows illustrate batched data exchanges: rather than sending single ticks or orders back and forth, the CPU sends small, well-defined work packages to the GPU and receives summarized results.

Identifying GPU-Friendly Hotspots

To design a useful hybrid system, we first need to know where the CPU-only backtester spends its time. Typical hotspots in a multi-asset, event-driven engine include:

- Feature pipelines: Updating cross-sectional indicators (for example, moving averages, volatility estimates, cross-sectional ranks) across hundreds or thousands of instruments whenever new market data arrives.
- Portfolio revaluation: Recomputing portfolio value, risk measures, and constraints across all instruments and possibly multiple risk scenarios when positions or prices change.
- Scenario fan-outs: For research, running multiple alternative strategies or parameter sets in parallel on the same historical event stream, or exploring what-if branches around specific events.

These tasks share two important characteristics:

- They apply similar operations independently across many instruments or scenarios.
- They are numerically heavier than the surrounding control logic.

This makes them excellent candidates for GPU acceleration. In contrast, tasks like event routing, order matching, and intricate strategy state machines involve complex branching, small amounts of data, and intricate control. Those are better left on the CPU.

Designing the Hybrid Event Loop

The challenge is to keep the event-driven semantics intact while batching work for the GPU. In a purely CPU-based engine, the event loop might process one event at a time, fully updating state before fetching the next. If we naively did the same with a GPU launching kernels per event—we would drown in overhead.

Instead, we adopt a *micro-batching* approach:

- The CPU continues to pull events one by one from the queue.
- For each event, it classifies whether GPU work is needed:
  - A market data event might require feature updates.
  - A position change might trigger a portfolio revaluation.
  - A strategy request might trigger scenario fan-outs.
- Rather than sending work to the GPU immediately, the CPU collects similar tasks into small batches—such as "update features for all names touched over the last millisecond" or "revalue the portfolio after these N small position changes."
- Once a batch reaches a threshold (in time or count), the CPU dispatches it as a GPU work unit and continues processing other events while the GPU runs.

This design balances two concerns:

- We want to *amortize* GPU overhead by feeding it reasonably large batches.
- We must respect the event ordering and not distort the simulated timeline beyond acceptable tolerances.

In practice, you introduce a controlled lag: instead of updating every indicator on every individual tick, you allow updates in small time buckets or event-count windows that are much smaller than the strategy's decision timescale. For many daily or intraday strategies, this compromise is acceptable and does not change the trading logic meaningfully.

Feature Computation on the GPU

Feature pipelines are a natural first target for this approach. Suppose your strategy consumes a set of features per instrument and per time step: moving averages, realized volatility, order book imbalance, sector-relative ranks, and so on.

On the CPU, you might maintain these in arrays indexed by instrument and time and update them incrementally as new data arrives. On the GPU, we mirror these structures in device memory:

- A large array holds the latest prices, volumes, and other raw inputs for each instrument.
- Additional arrays store intermediate feature states, such as rolling sums or variances.

A feature update batch then looks like this:

- The CPU collects a set of market updates (for example, price ticks or bars) affecting a subset of instruments.
- It prepares a compact description of the updates: instrument indices, new prices, and timestamps.
- It sends this batch to the GPU, which:
  - Writes the new raw values into the main data arrays.
  - Launches kernels that update all dependent features for the affected instruments, possibly in parallel across instruments and features.
  - Produces an output buffer containing just the features needed by the strategy at this point in the simulation.

Back on the CPU, the event loop consumes this summarized feature buffer and passes it to the strategy logic. Importantly, the strategy does not need to know that the features came from the GPU; it just receives a consistent view of the world at each decision point.

Portfolio Revaluation and Cross-Sectional Risk on the GPU

Whenever the strategy trades, the portfolio changes. Many strategies include real-time or end-of-period checks on:

- Total exposure by asset, sector, or factor.
- Concentration limits.
- Simple risk metrics, such as delta or notional sensitivities.

These checks involve aggregating over all positions, instruments, or risk factors—another ideal match for GPU parallelism. The hybrid design mirrors the Monte Carlo VaR case study, but at a finer time granularity and potentially with simpler models:

- The CPU maintains a "truth" representation of the current portfolio: a list of positions with sizes and identifiers.
- Whenever positions change materially, the CPU sends a compact snapshot of the portfolio to the GPU. This can be incremental (deltas from the last snapshot) to reduce bandwidth.
- The GPU holds up-to-date market data and risk factor states in device memory; combined with the position snapshot, it runs valuation and aggregation kernels:
  - Compute instrument values and greeks across the portfolio.
  - Aggregate exposures by chosen buckets.
  - Optionally run small sets of stress scenarios or shocks.
- The GPU returns only the summarized metrics required for constraint checks and risk overlays.

Because these valuations are structurally similar to the Monte Carlo VaR revaluation stage, you can often reuse kernels or library routines, simply with smaller scenario counts and more frequent invocations.

Scenario Fan-Outs for Research

One of the most powerful uses of GPUs in an event-driven setting is *scenario fan-out* for research. Rather than running a single strategy with a single parameter set over a historical event stream, you may wish to:

- Test many parameter variations simultaneously.
- Compare alternative execution or risk overlays.
- Explore counterfactuals around key events ("what if we had used a tighter stop?").

In a CPU-only engine, this usually means rerunning the backtest multiple times. In the hybrid design, we can instead:

- Keep the event loop and base strategy logic on the CPU.
- When reaching a branching point—such as a potential entry or exit—the CPU defines a set of alternative choices or parameter tweaks.
- Package the current state and these alternatives as a scenario batch and send it to the GPU.
- On the GPU, clone the relevant parts of the strategy and portfolio state across scenarios and run forward simulations for a short horizon in parallel, using preloaded market data.
- Return summarized scenario outcomes, such as distribution of P&L or drawdown under each branch.

This pattern reuses ideas from both Monte Carlo and event-driven simulation. It can be expensive if done too often, so it is usually reserved for focused research experiments rather than routine daily backtesting. But when used well, it allows quants to explore the "space of possible strategies" much more aggressively than would be feasible on CPUs alone.

State Synchronization Between Host and Device

A subtle but crucial aspect of the hybrid design is keeping CPU and GPU views of the world synchronized. We have at least three different but related states:

- **Event state:** The sequence of market and internal events being processed.
- **Strategy state:** Positions, cash, internal indicators, and flags maintained on the CPU.
- **Data and risk state on GPU:** Latest market data arrays, feature states, and any mirrored portfolio or factor information.

To avoid inconsistencies, we adopt the following principles:

- The CPU's event and strategy state is the "source of truth." The GPU mirrors only what it needs for numerical work.
- Updates flow in one direction at a time for each interaction:
  - When features are updated, the CPU sends raw market updates to the GPU and receives feature outputs.
  - When valuations are updated, the CPU sends position snapshots and receives risk metrics.
- Each GPU work unit is explicitly tagged with the event time or sequence index it corresponds to, so that late or out-of-order results can be detected and discarded if necessary.
- Data transfers are minimized and structured: large, infrequent updates (such as initial instrument parameters) are sent once, while small, frequent updates (such as prices or position deltas) are packed into compact buffers.

By thinking carefully about these data flows, you reduce the cognitive load on both developers and validators. They can reason about which parts of the state live where and how they are kept in sync.

Strategy Plugin Interfaces

From a usability standpoint, the hybrid system succeeds only if strategy developers can plug into it without becoming GPU experts. We therefore design the backtester with a clear separation between:

- A *strategy API* that exposes features, risk metrics, and order submission functions in a simple way.
- An *engine core* that maps strategy requests into CPU and GPU work.

A strategy author might write code that, for each event:

- Reads current features and risk metrics for instruments of interest.
- Updates internal state.
- Optionally requests a scenario fan-out evaluation.
- Submits orders via a standard interface.

Behind the scenes, the engine ensures that:

- The features exposed to the strategy come from the GPU-accelerated computations when enabled, or from CPU implementations otherwise.
- Portfolio and risk metrics are computed consistently on either CPU or GPU, based on configuration.
- Benchmarking hooks record performance information (latencies, batch sizes, GPU utilization) for later analysis.

This design allows the same strategy to run in different modes—for example, a pure CPU mode for debugging and a hybrid mode for performance benchmarking—without changing strategy code. It also supports gradual adoption: new GPU-accelerated components can be introduced behind the existing interfaces.

Performance and Correctness Evaluation

As with the VaR engine, the hybrid backtester must be assessed on both speed and correctness. We rely on the benchmarking principles laid out at the beginning of the chapter.

For correctness:

- Run the same strategy over the same event stream in both CPU-only and hybrid modes.
- Record detailed traces of key quantities: positions, orders, fills, P&L, and risk metrics at each decision point.
- Compare traces end-to-end. For many strategies, you can expect exact or near-exact agreement; small differences can occur if floating-point rounding or batching slightly change update ordering.
- Where differences exist, quantify their impact on trading decisions and performance statistics, and ensure they are acceptable given the batching and numerical approximations introduced.

For performance:

- Vary problem dimensions: number of instruments, length of backtest, complexity of feature sets, and number of concurrent strategies.
- Measure total wall-clock time for full backtest runs in both modes, as well as breakdowns for feature computation, valuation, and scenario fan-outs.
- Examine how latency per event and effective throughput (events or days simulated per second) scale with these dimensions.
- Pay particular attention to stress scenarios, such as market opens or volatility spikes, where event rates and complexity are higher.

In many realistic setups, you will see that:

- For small universes or simple strategies, CPU-only and hybrid modes perform similarly, because GPU overhead dominates.
- For large universes, rich feature sets, or many simultaneous strategies, the GPU-accelerated components substantially reduce total runtime.
- Scenario fan-outs can provide orders-of-magnitude speedups for research explorations that would be prohibitively slow on CPUs alone.

The exact numbers depend on your hardware, data, and strategy characteristics, but the methodology for measuring and interpreting them is now well established.

In this case study we moved from batch-style Monte Carlo to a more complex, event-driven world. We designed a hybrid CPU-GPU backtesting engine that:

- Keeps the event queue, event loop, and strategy logic on the CPU for flexibility and clarity.
- Offloads numerically intensive, data-parallel workloads—feature computation, portfolio revaluation, and scenario fan-outs—to the GPU.
- Uses micro-batching and careful state synchronization to make GPU use efficient without distorting the simulated event timeline.
- Presents a stable, strategy-friendly interface that hides GPU complexity while still allowing rigorous benchmarking and validation.

This architecture illustrates a broader pattern: you do not need to rewrite your entire quant stack in CUDA to benefit from GPUs. By identifying and accelerating the right numerical kernels, and by integrating them thoughtfully into existing event-driven engines, you can achieve substantial speedups while preserving the transparency and control that quants and risk managers require.

In the next section, we will step back from full applications to extract the common building blocks—such as reductions, random streams, and specialized solvers—into a reusable CUDA finance toolkit, making it easier to apply these ideas across many different models and backtesting workflows.

7.4 Reusable CUDA Finance Toolkit

The previous case studies focused on complete applications: a Monte Carlo VaR engine and an event-driven backtester. In both, we kept encountering the same computational patterns: generate many random numbers, aggregate large arrays into summary statistics, and solve structured linear systems. These patterns are not unique to a single model; they appear across option pricing, risk, portfolio analytics, backtesting, and stress testing.

This section takes a step back from full systems and distills those recurring patterns into a *reusable CUDA finance toolkit*. The idea is simple but powerful:

- Identify a small set of core numerical building blocks that appear everywhere.
- Implement them once, carefully and well, in CUDA.
- Expose them through clean, safe Python bindings so quants can use them from research notebooks without needing to write GPU code.

By investing in such a toolkit, every future model or backtest can benefit from GPU acceleration with far less effort and far fewer chances to introduce bugs. We will focus on three foundational components:

- Parallel reductions for aggregations and risk statistics.
- Random number streams for Monte Carlo and scenario generation.
- Tridiagonal solvers for finite-difference schemes and term-structure models.

We will look at what each pattern does conceptually, how it maps to the GPU, common pitfalls, and how to wrap it into a high-level interface suitable for day-to-day quant work.

Why Factor Out Numerical Patterns?

Before diving into specific components, it is helpful to understand why factoring out patterns is so important in GPU-accelerated finance.

In a typical quant library, there may be dozens of models: different option pricing formulas, term-structure dynamics, risk engines, and backtesting tools. Naively, each model might implement its own random number generation, its own array aggregations, and its own numerical solvers. On CPUs this duplication is already undesirable; on GPUs it becomes dangerous:

- Each hand-rolled kernel introduces risk of subtle race conditions or performance issues.
- Changes to low-level details (such as random generator choice or numerical tolerances) must be propagated manually.
- Validation and governance teams must review many very similar pieces of code, which is inefficient and error-prone.

By contrast, a small, common toolkit:

- Centralizes delicate logic in one place that can be heavily tested and optimized.
- Provides a uniform behaviour and configuration surface across many higher-level models.
- Makes validation easier: you validate the primitives thoroughly, then reuse them confidently.

The following subsections show how to build such primitives in a way that respects both computational and governance requirements.

Parallel Reductions: Summaries from Large Arrays

A *reduction* is any operation that takes many values and combines them into a smaller set of summaries. Examples in quant finance include:

- Summing scenario P&L to compute expected value.
- Computing portfolio exposures by aggregating sensitivities across positions.
- Calculating moments of a distribution, such as variance or skewness.
- Finding minima or maxima, for example the worst loss over scenarios.

On the CPU, you might write a simple loop that adds up numbers one by one. On the GPU, you want to exploit thousands of threads working together. The pattern is:

- Split the input array into chunks.
- Let each block or group of threads compute a partial result for its chunk.
- Combine the partial results into a final answer.

Conceptually, you can think of it as a tree: many leaves (individual elements) are combined pairwise up the branches until you reach the root (the final sum, minimum, and so on).

Design principles for GPU reductions

For our toolkit, a reduction primitive should:

- Support common operators such as sum, minimum, maximum, and possibly more sophisticated ones (like sum of squares for variance).

- Be numerically stable enough for financial use; for summations this often means using techniques that reduce rounding error compared with naive accumulation.
- Work efficiently for different array sizes and data types (for example, single and double precision).

Because these primitives are shared across many models, you should be conservative in their design:

- Avoid overly aggressive "fast math" approximations unless clearly justified and documented.
- Provide explicit control over precision; for example, allow the user to choose between speed-oriented and accuracy-oriented modes.

High-level Python interface for reductions

From a quant's perspective, the goal is to avoid thinking about tree structures and block sizes. A Python-facing interface might look conceptually like:

- A function that takes a device array and an operation name (for example, "sum" or "max") and returns the result as a Python scalar or small array.
- Optional flags to select precision mode or to compute multiple statistics at once (for example, mean and variance).

Internally, these calls map to CUDA kernels or GPU library functions, but to the quant they feel like calling familiar array operations—just much faster for large data sets.

Random Streams: Controlling Monte Carlo on the GPU

Monte Carlo simulation is ubiquitous in quant finance: option pricing, VaR, expected shortfall, XVA, and scenario-based stress testing all rely on it. On the GPU, we typically need:

- Many random numbers in parallel.
- Good statistical properties (for example, absence of obvious correlations).
- Reproducibility: the ability to rerun an experiment with the same seeds and obtain consistent results.

The toolkit's random stream component brings order to this complexity.

Conceptual model of random streams

Think of a random stream as a virtual dice that each thread can roll independently. We want:

- Multiple dice (streams) that do not interfere with each other.
- The ability to assign streams to different parts of the computation (for example, to different paths, instruments, or time steps).
- A clear mapping from user-level seed choices to GPU-level generator states.

In practice, GPU random libraries like cuRAND provide various generators and ways to initialize them. Our job in the toolkit is to:

- Choose a small set of generators with good quality and performance.
- Wrap their configuration into a simple, documented interface.
- Enforce consistent usage patterns to avoid subtle mistakes such as stream overlap.

Toolkit responsibilities for random streams

A reusable random stream module should handle:

- **Seeding:** Turning a user-provided seed and stream index into deterministic generator states on the GPU. For example, if a user requests 10,000 independent paths, the toolkit assigns them 10,000 non-overlapping subsequences.
- **Distribution transforms:** Providing generators for standard distributions (uniform, normal, lognormal, Poisson, and so on), including any correlation-imposing steps if needed.
- **State management:** Allowing users to advance streams in a controlled way, for instance when simulations are resumed or extended.

From a governance standpoint, the key is transparency:

- The type of random generator, its period, and its known properties are documented.
- The mapping from user-level seeds to GPU streams is fixed and versioned, so results can be reproduced later.

Python bindings for Monte Carlo workflows

To make this easy to use, the toolkit can expose higher-level constructs such as:

- A Monte Carlo "engine" object that, given a number of paths and a seed, returns a device array of random draws with a specified shape and distribution.
- Utility functions that take these device arrays and immediately apply transformations common in finance, such as constructing correlated factors or applying simple stochastic differential equation steps.

In Python, a quant can then write code that looks conceptually like generating an array of random shocks and transforming it, while all the heavy lifting is done on the GPU in a controlled, validated way.

Tridiagonal Solvers: Structured Linear Systems in Finance

Many pricing and risk problems in finance lead to linear systems with a special structure. In particular, finite-difference methods for partial differential equations and some term-structure models produce *tridiagonal* matrices: matrices where only the main diagonal and the two adjacent diagonals are non-zero.

These systems arise, for example, when:

- Solving backward for option prices under diffusion models using finite differences.
- Propagating term-structure dynamics along a discretized maturity grid.
- Computing certain smoothing or regularization operations along a time or maturity axis.

On a CPU, solving a single tridiagonal system is straightforward and efficient. On a GPU, performance comes from solving *many* such systems in parallel, for example:

- Multiple option strikes or maturities.
- Multiple scenarios or parameter sets.
- Different points on a calibration grid.

Why specialize tridiagonal solvers?

A general-purpose linear solver is overkill and slower for tridiagonal systems. Specialized tridiagonal algorithms exploit the structure to achieve:

- Lower computational cost.
- Less memory access.
- Simpler control flow.

On GPUs, this specialization is even more valuable, because it allows better use of memory bandwidth and thread synchronization. A well-designed toolkit primitive can batch thousands of small tridiagonal solves into a single or a few kernel launches, achieving high throughput.

Design considerations on the GPU

For our toolkit, a tridiagonal solver component should:

- Support both single and double precision, with clear documentation of expected accuracy.
- Handle large batches of systems efficiently—think thousands of systems, each of moderate size.
- Be robust to edge cases often seen in financial grids, such as very small or very large coefficients at boundaries.

Because different models may need slightly different boundary handling or variations, it is useful to distinguish between:

- A *core solver* that takes clean tridiagonal coefficient arrays and right-hand sides.
- Thin adapters in higher-level libraries that map finite-difference schemes or model-specific setups into the core solver format.

This boundary keeps the core primitive simple and reusable, while still allowing flexibility in model construction.

Python-facing interface for tridiagonal problems

For quants working in Python, the interface might present:

- Functions that take batches of tridiagonal coefficients and right-hand sides as device arrays and return solution arrays.

- Optional utilities to construct these coefficient arrays from common finite-difference schemes or term-structure discretizations.

Quants then think in terms of "I have this grid and these coefficients; please solve the system," without worrying about block sizes or synchronization.

From CUDA to Python: Safe and Simple Bindings

So far we have focused on what the primitives do on the GPU. To make them truly reusable in a quant environment dominated by Python, we need clean bindings. The goals of the binding layer are:

- Hide low-level CUDA details such as device pointers, streams, and synchronization from most users.
- Integrate with existing array libraries (for example, Numpy-like interfaces or GPU array types) where possible.
- Provide clear error handling and input validation.

Separation of concerns

A useful mental model is a three-layer stack:

- **Core CUDA layer:** Implements reductions, random streams, and tridiagonal solvers in C++/CUDA, with minimal external dependencies and clear interfaces.
- **Binding layer:** Uses a tool such as pybind11 or a foreign function interface to expose core functions to Python, taking care of data type conversions and resource lifetime management.
- **Helper APIs:** Provide higher-level, Pythonic functions tailored to quant use cases (for example, "compute VaR from this device P&L array" or "solve this batch of finite-difference grids").

This structure keeps the performance-sensitive parts in C++/CUDA, while allowing most users to interact with simple, documented Python functions.

Designing Python APIs with quants in mind

When designing Python interfaces, think about how quants naturally express problems:

- They think in terms of arrays and data frames, not device pointers.
- They expect broadcasting and slicing semantics similar to familiar numerical libraries.
- They like composability: being able to chain operations in a clear, readable way.

Therefore, the toolkit's Python layer should:

- Accept and return array-like objects, ideally compatible with the rest of the quant stack.
- Avoid exposing technical CUDA concepts unless absolutely necessary; for example, provide reasonable default streams and synchronization, with advanced options available for power users.
- Include docstrings and examples that connect each primitive to typical quant tasks.

Testing and Numerical Validation

Because these toolkit components sit at the bottom of many models, their correctness is critical. A bug or subtle numerical instability in a reduction or solver can contaminate many downstream outputs. Therefore, you should invest heavily in:

- **Unit tests:** Small, targeted tests that compare GPU outputs against trusted CPU implementations across a wide range of inputs, including edge cases.
- **Property-based tests:** Checks that enforce general properties, such as "sum of positive numbers should be positive" or "solving a system and then applying the matrix should recover the original right-hand side."

- **Stress tests:** Large, randomly generated problems that push memory, precision, and performance limits to expose rare issues.

For random streams, validation also includes statistical tests:

- Comparing sample moments of generated numbers to theoretical values.
- Checking correlations between streams and across dimensions.

From a governance perspective, you should:

- Version the toolkit primitives and record which version each model or backtest uses.
- Document known limitations or approximations, such as reduced precision modes or bounds on matrix conditioning for which the solvers have been validated.

This makes it easier to respond to questions like "what changed between last year's VaR implementation and this year's?" or "why did these stress test results shift when we upgraded the GPU library?"

Composing Toolkit Pieces into New Workflows

Once you have reliable primitives for reductions, random streams, and tridiagonal solves, you can accelerate entirely new workflows with modest incremental effort. Two illustrative examples are:

Calibration loops

Model calibration often involves:

- Proposing a set of model parameters.
- Running a pricing or risk engine under those parameters to generate model outputs.

- Comparing those outputs with market observations and computing an error measure.
- Adjusting parameters to minimize the error.

With the toolkit:

- Random streams can generate common shocks or scenarios shared across parameter guesses, reducing variance in comparisons.
- Tridiagonal solvers and reductions can accelerate pricing and aggregation inside each calibration step.
- Reductions can aggregate error measures across instruments efficiently on the GPU.

By pushing the heavy inner loop onto the GPU using these primitives, you can explore much richer parameter spaces in the same wall-clock time.

Stress-testing engines

Stress testing involves evaluating portfolios under many extreme but plausible scenarios. Conceptually:

- Generate a grid or set of stress scenarios for risk factors, possibly using Monte Carlo or structured shocks.
- Revalue the portfolio under each scenario.
- Aggregate results into distributions of losses and identify worst cases.

Here, the toolkit contributes:

- Random streams or deterministic scenario generators to create wide stress sets.

- Reductions to compute loss distributions and risk measures (such as tail averages) from large scenario arrays.
- Tridiagonal solvers if any pricing models used in stress revaluation rely on finite-difference methods.

Because the same primitives underlie both routine risk calculations and stress testing, validation work carries over.

The reusable CUDA finance toolkit is the "infrastructure layer" beneath the case studies in this chapter. By focusing on three core numerical patterns—parallel reductions, random streams, and tridiagonal solvers—and wrapping them in safe, simple Python interfaces, you gain:

- Consistency: the same well-tested building blocks support VaR, backtesting, calibration, and stress testing.
- Efficiency: developers avoid reimplementing complex low-level logic for each new model.
- Governance: validators can focus on a small set of primitives whose behaviour is well documented and broadly reused.

In practice, building such a toolkit is an iterative process. You will likely start with a few primitives needed for a specific project and gradually generalize them as more use cases emerge. The guiding principle is always the same: whenever you find yourself writing similar GPU code for the third time, stop and consider whether it should become part of the shared toolkit.

In the final section of this chapter, we will connect these technical ideas with the broader themes of experiment tracking and model risk governance, showing how to wrap GPU-accelerated research in processes that make it auditable, reproducible, and ready for production.

7.5 Experiment Tracking & Model Risk Governance

Up to this point in the chapter we have focused on building fast things: fair benchmarks, a GPU-accelerated Monte Carlo VaR engine, an event-driven backtester, and a reusable CUDA toolkit. Speed and elegance, however, are not the end of the story in a real institution. A model that cannot be reproduced, explained, or audited will not make it into production, no matter how impressive the performance charts look.

This section is about wrapping all that technical work in a framework that satisfies model risk governance. The central idea is straightforward:

> Every important GPU-accelerated run should be an *experiment* with a clear identity, traceable inputs, and verifiable outputs.

We will:

- Define what information needs to be captured to make an experiment reproducible.
- Show how experiment tracking integrates with the benchmarking discipline you have already developed.
- Connect these practices to the expectations of model risk management and regulators.
- Outline a practical workflow and checklist for taking a GPU prototype into a governed production model.

The goal is not to turn you into a compliance officer, but to give you habits and structures that make your fast code *trustworthy code*.

Why Experiment Tracking Matters More with GPUs

On the surface, running a Monte Carlo VaR on a GPU or a CPU is the same from a risk perspective: the same model is being evaluated. In practice, GPUs bring new dimensions of variability:

- Different devices, drivers, and library versions.
- Greater sensitivity to thread scheduling and memory layout.
- Explicit management of random streams across thousands of threads.

Small changes to any of these can nudge numerical results. Most of the time these differences are harmless, but you must be able to answer questions like:

- "Can you reproduce the VaR run we used for last quarter's capital report?"
- "Why does the new GPU cluster give slightly different numbers than the old one?"
- "What exactly changed between Version 1 and Version 2 of the backtester?"

Without systematic experiment tracking, answering these questions becomes painful and imprecise. With tracking in place, you can respond calmly with concrete evidence.

What to Capture: The Anatomy of an Experiment

An *experiment* in this context is a single, well-defined run of a model or backtest: for example, "Monte Carlo VaR with 5 million paths on 31 March," or "Backtest of Strategy X over 2018-2022 with parameters Y, Z."

To make an experiment reproducible and auditable, you should capture at least the following categories of information.

Code and configuration

- **Code version:** A commit hash from your version control system, or an equivalent unique identifier. This ties the run to a specific source tree.

- **Model configuration:** A structured description (often a file) covering:
  - Model type and version (for example, "Hull-White 1-factor, v2.1").
  - Parameter values (volatilities, correlations, spreads, and so on).
  - Numerical settings (number of paths, grid sizes, tolerances).
- **GPU configuration:** Flags and settings that affect GPU behaviour, such as precision choices, fast-math toggles, or kernel sclcction.

Together, these define "what program was run and how it was configured."

Data and environment

- **Data snapshot:** A clear reference to the market and portfolio data used:
  - As-of date and time.
  - Identifiers for data feeds or database snapshots.
  - Any transformations or filters applied (for example, outlier cleanup).
- **Hardware details:** The GPU and CPU models, memory sizes, and, ideally, driver versions.
- **Library stack:** Versions of key libraries: CUDA toolkit, cuRAND, math libraries, Python packages, and the toolkit components from the previous section.

This information explains "what world the code saw when it ran."

Randomness and seeding

- **Global seed(s):** The high-level seeds provided to the Monte Carlo or scenario engine.

- **Stream mapping scheme:** A versioned description of how seeds are turned into GPU streams and sequences.

Because random streams can be delicate on GPUs, this is essential for reproducing Monte Carlo runs and diagnosing changes in numerical results.

Outputs and performance

- **Primary outputs:** Risk measures (VaR, Expected Shortfall), backtest P&L curves, exposure reports—whatever the business cares about.
- **Diagnostics:** Secondary quantities, such as summary statistics of Monte Carlo samples, or calibration error measures.
- **Performance metrics:** Latencies, throughput, GPU utilization, and any breakdowns (for example, time in random generation vs valuation vs aggregation).

Capturing performance alongside results is important because governance discussions often weigh both: "we gain this much speed at the cost of these small numerical differences."

A Lightweight Experiment Tracking Workflow

Experiment tracking does not require heavy infrastructure to be useful. A simple, disciplined workflow is enough for many teams and can later be plugged into more formal tools.

Structured run descriptors

For each substantial run, create a small, structured descriptor file. Conceptually, this file contains the items listed above: code version, configuration, data references, seeds, environment, and so on. It can be:

- Generated automatically by the model at startup.

- Stored alongside the run outputs in a directory or database.

The key is that it is machine-readable and human-inspectable. If an auditor asks, "What exactly was run here?" you open the descriptor rather than chasing through emails and notebooks.

Centralized logging of experiments

Next, ensure that each run:

- Logs its start and end times and a unique experiment ID.
- Writes its descriptor and key results to a known location: a shared filesystem, a version-controlled repository, or an experiment tracking system.

Even a simple table—experiment ID, model name, date, commit hash, status, performance summary—goes a long way. It allows you to answer "have we run this before?" and "when did we change that parameter?" reliably.

Tying experiments to benchmarks

From earlier sections, you already have a benchmark harness: scripts that sweep over problem sizes and configurations and generate performance plots. Integrate this harness with your experiment tracking so that:

- Each benchmark run leaves an experiment record, not just a figure.
- Performance comparisons between CPU and GPU baselines are reproducible months later, even after hardware changes.

This becomes crucial when you need to justify, for example, a migration from one GPU model to another or to show that a seemingly small code change did not materially alter performance or risk characteristics.

From Experiments to Model Documentation

Model risk governance requires more than well-structured metadata; it requires explanations that non-developers can understand. Fortunately, your tracked experiments form the empirical backbone of that documentation.

A robust model document for a GPU-accelerated system usually includes:

Plain-language description of the role of GPUs

Explain:

- Which parts of the model run on GPUs and why (for example, Monte Carlo paths, feature computations).
- What is unchanged in moving from CPU to GPU (the mathematics and model assumptions).
- What is potentially changed (numerical precision, parallel aggregation order).

The goal is to reassure readers that adopting GPUs is an *implementation change*, not a stealth model change, unless you explicitly state otherwise.

Numerical validation summary

Here, you summarize the experiments that compare CPU and GPU outputs:

- Cross-sectional comparisons of key outputs (for example, VaR levels, greeks, P&L paths).
- Backtesting comparisons, such as exception counts for CPU vs GPU VaR.
- Sensitivity of differences to the number of Monte Carlo paths or grid resolutions.

This is where you might show, for instance, that GPU and CPU VaR are within a few basis points for practical path counts and that their backtest exception patterns are statistically equivalent.

Performance envelope

Governance stakeholders care about promises you make implicitly when you claim speedups. A "performance envelope" describes:

- The range of problem sizes and configurations for which you have benchmark data.
- The observed speedups and latencies in those regimes.
- Any conditions under which performance degrades (for example, very small jobs or extreme concurrent loads).

Importantly, you distinguish between:

- *Measured* performance results for specific configurations.
- *Expected* performance for similar, but not identical, configurations, with appropriate caveats.

This avoids overpromising, which can create governance friction later.

Fallbacks and contingency plans

Finally, documentation should explain what happens when:

- GPUs are unavailable or fail mid-run.
- New hardware or drivers are introduced.
- The model must run in a "degraded mode" under stress conditions.

Often, this means having a CPU path that can be switched on, possibly with fewer scenarios or simplified models, and having clear rules for when that happens and how results are flagged.

Validation and Independent Review

Most institutions require an independent model validation team to review significant models. GPU acceleration does not remove that requirement; if anything, it introduces new validation questions. A cooperative approach between model developers and validators is essential.

What validators typically care about

From the GPU perspective, validation questions often include:

- Are the GPU-based results materially consistent with the established CPU reference?
- Are numerical differences well understood and bounded?
- Is the use of randomness (seeds, streams, generators) controlled and documented?
- Are there stress tests that probe extreme but plausible scenarios and numerical edge cases?
- Is there a clear, tested fallback path if the GPU environment changes or fails?

Your experiment tracking and documentation directly support these questions. For example, you can provide validators with curated sets of experiment records and cross-check plots.

Validation test suites

In addition to ad-hoc comparisons, it is good practice to define a stable validation test suite for each major model. Conceptually, such a suite includes:

- **Unit-level tests:** For example, checking that the tridiagonal solver in the CUDA toolkit matches a high-precision CPU solver across a variety of matrices.

- **Scenario-level tests:** Fixed, representative configurations of the full model (small portfolios, small path counts) for which expected results are known or precomputed.
- **Regression tests:** A collection of experiments that must not change materially when you upgrade hardware or libraries. For each, you define acceptable tolerances on key outputs.

You then integrate these tests into your development cycle: when you change GPU code, you rerun the suite, compare against historical baselines (stored via your experiment tracker), and only proceed if differences are within agreed bounds.

Managing Change: Hardware, Libraries, and Models

One distinctive feature of GPU-based systems is that the environment evolves quickly: new GPU generations, driver updates, and library upgrades can all affect numerical behaviour or performance. Model risk governance must explicitly address this.

Change classification

Not all changes are equal. It helps to classify them into buckets:

- Pure environment changes: New GPU hardware, updated drivers, or updated CUDA libraries, with no intentional code changes.
- Implementation changes: Modifications to CUDA kernels or toolkit components that *should not* alter the financial model, only performance or numerical detail.
- Model changes: Adjustments to financial assumptions, payoffs, or calibration methods that change the meaning of the outputs.

Each category can then have a prescribed testing and approval pathway:

- Environment and implementation changes often require rerunning validation suites and selected production experiments to demonstrate stability.
- Model changes usually require a fuller validation and governance cycle, including updated documentation and, potentially, new backtests.

Using experiments as a safety net

Well-tracked experiments serve as anchors during change:

- When you introduce a new GPU generation, you can re-execute a standard set of experiments (for example, representative VaR runs and backtests) and compare to the stored results.
- When a CUDA toolkit update is rolled out, you can immediately see whether differences arise and whether they are within acceptable tolerances.

This greatly reduces the risk of silently introducing errors due to environmental changes.

A Practical Checklist for Promotion to Production

To make the discussion concrete, consider a GPU-accelerated Monte Carlo VaR engine that you wish to promote from research into a production risk system. A practical checklist might look like this:

1. Technical readiness

- The implementation is based on the shared CUDA toolkit (reductions, random streams, solvers) rather than ad-hoc kernels.
- Benchmarks against a strong CPU baseline have been run across meaningful problem sizes, with results stored as experiments.
- Latency and throughput in the intended production regime meet business requirements, with headroom for growth.

2. Numerical validation

- Cross-sectional comparisons of CPU and GPU VaR outputs for fixed seeds and configurations show differences within pre-agreed tolerances.
- Backtest comparisons (exception counts, P&L profiles) between CPU and GPU engines over a representative historical period show no material divergence.
- Stress tests and edge-case experiments (extreme volatilities, stressed correlations, boundary parameter regimes) have been run and analysed.

3. Experiment tracking and reproducibility

- The engine automatically creates experiment descriptors for each run, capturing code, configuration, data, seeds, and environment.
- There is a searchable index of past experiments, including those used for validation and benchmarking.
- Re-execution of historical experiments on the current environment has been tested and differences documented.

4. Governance artefacts

- Model documentation clearly explains the role of GPUs, the numerical methods used, and the validation evidence.
- A performance envelope is documented, specifying the regimes in which benchmarked performance applies.
- Fallback and contingency processes are defined, including how and when to switch to CPU-based runs and how to flag such events.

5. Ongoing monitoring

- Production runs log not only financial outputs but also key performance and environment metrics (for example, GPU type, driver version, runtime).
- Automated checks look for drifts in performance or numerical behaviour, prompting review if thresholds are exceeded.
- Change management procedures specify which validation experiments to rerun whenever hardware, libraries, or code are updated.

Once you can honestly tick off items like these, a GPU-accelerated model is much closer to being a first-class citizen in your firm's risk infrastructure.

Experiment tracking and model risk governance may feel far removed from CUDA kernels and performance plots, but they are the bridge between research and real-world impact. In this section we have:

- Motivated why GPUs increase the need for careful experiment tracking, not decrease it.
- Described the essential elements of a reproducible experiment: code, configuration, data, environment, randomness, and outputs.
- Shown how to connect tracked experiments to model documentation, validation, and performance envelopes.
- Outlined practices for dealing with environmental and implementation changes in a controlled way.
- Provided a practical checklist for promoting GPU-accelerated prototypes into governed production models.

By adopting these habits early, you ensure that the GPU-accelerated VaR engines, backtesters, and toolkits developed in this chapter not only run fast on your machine today, but also stand up to scrutiny in front of risk committees and regulators tomorrow.

www.ingramcontent.com/pod-product-compliance
Lightning Source LLC
LaVergne TN
LVHW052017200926
848481LV00005B/1517